Luminos is the Open Access monograph publishing program
from UC Press. Luminos provides a framework for preserving and
reinvigorating monograph publishing for the future and increases
the reach and visibility of important scholarly work. Titles published
in the UC Press Luminos model are published with the same high
standards for selection, peer review, production, and marketing as
those in our traditional program. www.luminosoa.org

The Prison of Democracy

# The Prison of Democracy

*Race, Leavenworth, and the Culture of Law*

———

Sara M. Benson

UNIVERSITY OF CALIFORNIA PRESS

University of California Press, one of the most distinguished university presses in the United States, enriches lives around the world by advancing scholarship in the humanities, social sciences, and natural sciences. Its activities are supported by the UC Press Foundation and by philanthropic contributions from individuals and institutions. For more information, visit www.ucpress.edu.

University of California Press
Oakland, California

Suggested citation: Benson, S. M. *The Prison of Democracy: Race, Leavenworth, and the Culture of Law*. Oakland: University of California Press, 2019. DOI: https://doi.org/10.1525/luminos.66

Cataloging-in-Publication Data is on file at the Library of Congress.

ISBN 978–0–520–29696–1 (paperback)
ISBN 978–0–520–96949–0 (e-edition)

27   26   25   24   23   22   21   20   19
10   9   8   7   6   5   4   3   2   1

# CONTENTS

ILLUSTRATIONS

# Introduction

*The Idea of Leavenworth and the Prison of Democracy*

The grid lines of the nation's capital city stretch out like a fan from the front of the White House and the back of the US Capitol Building. The streets form radial axes that extend from these centers of federal power, creating places where things come together in central nodes and then radiate out again on the other side of those meeting places. The radial shape is a map of federal power that extends to the center of the nation, to a place that looks like the Capitol Building but is actually a prison. The prison that mimics the capitol was also built on the radial design and was also one of those meeting places. The US Penitentiary at Leavenworth, Kansas, was built in the 1890s as the nation's first prison and the beginning of a federal prison system that radiates from the center of the nation. It was the flagship institution of a carceral state always grounded in a politics of mass incarceration, one that reorganized understandings of the prison's relationship to democracy. It was always a place at the borders.

The building itself was a map of federal power that emerged when federal control over crime and punishment was supposed to be weak. Yet the nation's largest prison construction project, which spanned nearly thirty years, used the front facade of the prison to replicate the image of the Capitol Building as it existed just a short time before in 1850. The prison's argument about federal power was articulated in a front facade made of limestone columns and a massive dome that hovered above two seven-story wings. This facade echoed the architecture of a bicameral legislature, with separate "chambers" for House and Senate.[1] The prison extended over five city blocks and was anchored in walls built forty feet high and buried forty feet below the surface. Those walls were decorated by barred windows and forty-three stairs flanked by stone lions, and were interrupted only by two sally ports, "great bolt-studded portals," that once allowed for the entrance of the

FIGURE 1. John Plumbe, East Front of the Capitol Building, Washington, D.C., 1846. Copyprint from glass negative. Prints and Photographs Division, Library of Congress.

prison train.[2] The train moved symbolically from east to west, introducing ideas about national geography and regionalism into the context of federal punishment. The prison turned "the people's house" into the Big House by radiating a claim to federalization from the nation's capital to the nation's center. In imitating the capitol, Leavenworth created an icon that recalled for the spectator one of the ultimate monuments of American democracy, yet contained freedom's inverse on its inside.

Leavenworth was an idea about the carceral state set down in brick and mortar in the 1890s, but it was part of a much longer story of the federalization of punishment. The emergence of a national apparatus for dealing with crime occurred long before the 1930s, when the establishment of the Federal Bureau of Prisons supposedly turned federal attention to the matter of punishment, and long before the 1890s, when the prison was built at a very particular set of regional borders. The idea of Leavenworth was born in Indian Territory, survived slavery and abolition in Bleeding Kansas, and finally stood as a post-Reconstruction monument to a certain kind of racial state.[3] It represented in architecture a state that was carceral in its origins, even as state and local jurisdictions assumed, in theory, the burden of crime and punishment. The federal law-and-order project that preceded Leavenworth operated in the shadows of administrative law, increasing in power and capacity through structures and institutions of territory, slavery, and political culture. In the study of mass incarceration, this other shadow carceral state offers lessons not just in the history of state building but in the cultural history of democracy.[4]

Placed at the edges of the city map, Leavenworth was a "city within a city" where the prison became part of a way of life.[5] This was reflected in how the prison was built into the local visual economy. The architects, William Eames and Thomas Young, required in the construction specifications that the prison's lines be coordinated with the already existing grid lines of the town.[6] The meaning of these radial lines was transmitted through the local newspaper, which followed the prison's progress from 1896 until the dome's completion in 1927. The *Leavenworth Times* explained that when "viewed from a distance the building will carry almost identical lines of the central structure of the nation's capital. Flights of broad stone steps will further carry out the similitude of architectural design."[7]

The divergence between the idea of Leavenworth and the prison it became grew from disagreements over the meaning of its architecture. Eames and Young proposed to "let the prison face the city" on Metropolitan Boulevard, a landscaped and "beautiful" road that would "open up that section of the town and make it a perpetual and growing thing."[8] The attorney general's preference, however, for "plainness and severity" led the architects to abandon these plans for "monumental gateways" connecting the nation to its prison town.[9] Eames and Young wanted a building "as impressive as other national institutions" that would generate praise as a "marvel of custodial architecture."[10] The final design was praised by the government for its "somewhat Federal appearance."[11] Eames and Young later cowrote in the *American Architect* only that they were instructed to "ignore all precedent in prison architecture" and to "give to their design . . . the character of the usual Departmental building . . . , consistent with the purposes of the building, and expressive of the dignity of the Federal Government."[12]

The prison required an audience who would understand its message of democracy and terror. The curious language of Leavenworth's architecture had cultural and political power as a familiar symbol and as a terrifying inversion. According to Native American political prisoner Leonard Peltier, "The overwhelming size of the place is frightening, made even more bizarre by its silver-painted dome, mockingly reminiscent of the Capitol Building in Washington, D.C.—along with its phalanxes of stone walls and cyclone fences and coils of razor wire, and its empty-eyed stone lions guarding its front steps beneath a looming gun tower—all of it seemingly the work of some demented and sadistic architect, every detail arranged, no doubt, for the sheer nauseating terror of it."[13]

The prison's relationship to terror and democracy relied on a connection between the prison's inside and outside. Letters from the warden describe the tradition of prison tourism and the custom of admitting citizens to Leavenworth in "excursion parties" of fifty to five hundred at a time.[14] In 1910, the Kansas City Railway Company chartered four railroad cars for two hundred "excursionists" who "poured out to the prison."[15] "The desire to see the New Prison," the warden wrote, was part of a tradition as old as the 1830s, when Gustave de Beaumont and Alexis de Tocqueville documented how "the people" waited in lines and paid fees to see buildings "considered [as] belonging to all. . . . The prisons are open to every one who chooses to inspect them."[16] As crowds "poured out" to Leavenworth, the warden sought to restrict tourism to the "lowest limit compatible with affording the public a reasonable knowledge of what is going on inside."[17] When public visits were limited to Thursdays by 1907, "crowds" of five hundred to eight hundred people still "besieged the entrance,"[18] and the practice "interfere[d] seriously with the running of the institution."[19]

When the prison was closed to the public in 1910, the direct relationship between the prison and the citizen was severed and replaced by the more mundane but no less important sound of the prison siren, which extended a full ten miles in each direction to warn of escapes. Local citizens were given printed cards with patterns of blasts as a kind of code. The escape signal was five blasts, fifteen seconds long with five seconds in between, a pattern that was repeated every ten minutes during an escape. The choreographed aurality of the ritual was explained in an accompanying pamphlet that reminded the citizenry that escaped convicts could be "legally arrested by any citizen" and that the $60 reward remained the same "should the convict be killed in endeavoring to escape or in resisting arrest."[20] The participatory ritual of hunting fugitives brought Leavenworth into the everyday life of those living in its shadows. Denied access to the institution but written into its script as part of the prison's security, the citizen was part of a cultural politics of federalized power.

Today, in the nation's prison town, highway signs along the region's main road point the way not just to Leavenworth but to a matrix of penal institutions that dot the landscape. In a town with four federal prisons, two military prisons, a state prison, and a county jail, one in four residents is institutionalized. The Kansas State Penitentiary stands unmissable along the main highway. It is a large gothic castle, built during the Civil War of deep red brick, and stands in a residential neighborhood with its own museum on the front lawn.[21] Further down the road, a quick turn to the right reveals the Leavenworth Detention Center, a federal prison operated by Core Civic (formerly known as Corrections Corporation of America) on behalf of the US Marshals Service. The building itself is barely visible because it is wrapped so deeply in barbed wire. The city also has a minimum-security federal prison camp (FPC) and a county jail on Third Street. At the end of the road on the edge of town is the Fort Leavenworth Military Base, the home of the US Disciplinary Barracks, the only maximum-security prison operated by the Department of Defense inside the United States, and the Midwest Joint Regional Correctional Facility, built in 2010. The military reservation shares a perimeter with Leavenworth Federal Penitentiary, which served as the nation's maximum-security institution from 1896 until 2005, when the facility was downgraded to "medium security" as a federal "correctional institution." In back of the town, on a stretch of road that seems to crown a community shaped like a cross, the prison stands as a monument, in Peltier's words, with "every detail arranged for the sheer, nauseating terror of it."

In a town where the thoroughfares of daily life became roads to the prison, the social life of the community became so intertwined with the institution that even today the history of the town is narrated through the history of the prison. Leavenworth, Kansas, self-identifies as the nation's original "Prison Town, U.S.A.,"[22] and the president of the local guard labor union boasts that "nobody's been doing it longer or doing it better."[23] Billboards along various local highways invite travelers to "do time" in the city or to drink Hard Time Vodka. Brochures for heritage tourism beckon travelers with "How 'bout Doin' Some Time in Leavenworth?" At the local antique mall, T-shirts represent Leavenworth as the nation's expert on punishment, as the "University of Hard Time," and while executions are no longer carried out at the prison, other shirts with symbols of the electric chair offer "Warm Regards" from Leavenworth. The local airport once sold bright orange T-shirts printed with "Property of Leavenworth Penitentiary" and children's shirts that read "Future Guard." It is an identity always on display in the exhibitions of two prison museums and in a town tourist circuit called "The Great Escape."[24] A third museum, proposed but never built, was a $3 million Regional Prison Museum, to be erected on state prison grounds with federal funding. The museum was to feature a mock prison "complete with fake watchtowers and 12- to 14-foot-tall stone walls" and a gate that "clang[s] behind them." It was described as a "tribute to a major cultural and economic force in northeast Kansas, and its construction would produce major economic dividends for the Leavenworth and Lansing area." Its purpose was to "preserve the culture and memorialize the people that have given their lives" for punishment in Leavenworth.[25]

When Leavenworth's architecture embedded itself in the very shape of the town, it aligned the region with federal control and symbolized the expanded power of the federal government in matters of crime and punishment. The prison's place on the Kansas prairie was significant architecturally because it amplified that power. The view from a distance produced the effect of minimizing the viewer—the dome interrupts the sky, refocusing the audience's eye on the prison's massive reach across the landscape. This reach of the institution across the horizon normalizes the sense of terror that is produced in the building's first encounter, one that recedes into the familiar upon a second look. This shift in perception makes the institution seem smaller, less threatening, more familiar, even benign. This work examines the double function of Leavenworth's architecture—to produce terror and then to normalize that terror—as the key to understanding the dispersed and fragmented sources of the prison's power in the American political imagination.

## RETHINKING THE POLITICAL GEOGRAPHY OF THE RACIAL CARCERAL STATE

Because prisons are embedded in popular culture and in the everyday visual environment of the regions where they are placed, the nation is continually learning about and learning to forget about them through the production of "experiential knowledge." This is why Angela Y. Davis's *Are Prisons Obsolete?* asks a set of questions about the curious circumstances of the prison's simultaneous absence and presence in US culture.[26] The penal spectator is subject to what Thomas Dumm has called penal "techniques of pedagogy."[27] Penal spectatorship references simultaneously the normalizing influence of prison architecture and a method of creating political distance between the prison and the citizen. This distance shields prison spectators from what Michelle Brown describes as "the most fundamental feature of punishment—its infliction of pain."[28] Because the prison is part of a "series of scripts and roles" through which the spectator learns to naturalize the prison's place in American political life, the citizen is asked simultaneously to recognize the prison's authority in the arc of justice and to accept the prison as a settled part of democratic life.[29] Leavenworth, as the foundation of the federal prison system and a building with a national audience, is a site where ideas about state violence and the nationalization of justice were introduced and challenged. It represents an opportunity to read for what came before it, with the hope of understanding how the prison became part of a taken-for-granted political landscape that warrants no attention, even when the building's architecture makes it impossible not to look.

*The Prison of Democracy* begins with the assumption that the prison has always been one of the central institutions of American democracy. It draws from the work of critical prison studies in questioning the place of the prison in theories of the state and recharts the course of the prison's historiography, which has been built around disparate fields that focus exclusively on prisons of different scales, times, and regions. Because most accounts of punishment isolate federal and state prisons from their shared histories, scholars have often assumed that national power over punishment remained weak until the formation of the Bureau of Prisons in 1930. To expand the study of state punitive power, this project grounds the placement of the first federal prison in terms of its political geography: the prison's strategic placement in a specific site of legal instability in order to federalize power over the region. The book begins in the state prisons where federal power over punishment first emerged and traces that power's origins in the military institution at Fort Leavenworth and in the federal projects of Indian Territory and Bleeding Kansas as ideas about mass incarceration.

The book therefore works against the presumption in much of the literature that mass incarceration is a moment in time rather than a legal status that has always been embedded in the law. Mass incarceration is a political problem not only because it disappears mass numbers of people from society but because the prison is an idea about unfreedom that masquerades as an idea about democracy. This book suggests that to locate the roots of the carceral state in the late twentieth century is to misunderstand the power of the state as a force that regulates, condemns, and assigns status to the body.

With the exponential growth of prisons in the United States, scholars have worked to challenge the emergence of a carceral state and the buildup of a prison-industrial complex that has resulted in the mass incarceration of nearly three million people.[30] Some have pointed to the War on Drugs in the 1980s and 1990s as the primary cause of a prison-building boom,[31] while others have designated the period of the 1970s and the emergence of a carceral Keynesianism as the root of a recent crisis in punishment.[32] Still others have argued that the problem dates back to the 1950s and 1960s, when the state waged a retributive war against the successes of the civil rights movement and built a "civil rights carceral state" in which the prison became the solution to a problem of individualized racial violence.[33] More recent work has developed a language for thinking about incarceration in the broader context of policing and surveillance, not just in matters of crime, but in the racialized systems of welfare, immigration, and education.[34] American political development and law-and-society scholars have examined how this shadow carceral state operates through administrative detention and other modes of punishment beyond criminal law.[35] A related field of study examines the political consequences of mass incarceration by focusing on felon disenfranchisement and other civic costs of "governing through crime."[36] Others have historicized mass incarceration in terms of public culture, so that penal culture itself plays a hidden but state-sponsored role in the proliferation of prisons.[37]

This book suggests that each of these critical moments in the history of the twentieth-century prison accelerated the development of state and federal power over matters of punishment. As nodes in the history of an old institution, these new iterations of carceral capacity were developed in fits and starts, guided by a theory of the state with a prison at its center.[38] This assertion repatterns the relationship between mass incarceration as a recent moment in time and the carceral state, which is sometimes understood as having "sprouted in the shadows of mass imprisonment."[39] This way of reconceptualizing mass incarceration as a legal status perhaps first emerged in the work of Georg Rusche and Otto Kirchheimer, who analyzed the prison as a function of economic conditions and as a site that siphons citizens from labor markets en masse.[40] David Garland has also analyzed the way in which mass imprisonment might be endemic to the state, not just in terms of dramatic increases in the number of people in prison, but also in terms of the way new forms of law target whole communities for punishment.[41] Because mass incarceration is not a period of disproportionate punishment but a theory that constitutes the American state, the history of the US prison system needs to be reperiodized to reflect the entrenched nature of the carceral state. The book takes the long route to a theory of carceral democracy to explore the "historical and social conditions" of the prison's foundation as a state-building project.[42]

As a study of institutional capacity and change in a state that has always been carceral, this work is part of a larger challenge to the study of state power. It is most concerned with how institutions take on lives of their own as self-reinforcing structures that create new forms of power. To assume that the state has only recently become deeply carceral or that imprisonment has only recently come to define the state's relationship to the masses is to oversimplify the form of the American state. Scholars of state building and American political development have traditionally described the United States as a weak state form. As Megan Ming Francis has suggested, the "statelessness presumption" of much of the early literature on the American state has been grounded in ideas about state powerlessness.[43] As William J. Novak has suggested, "An enduring and exceptional tendency to view the American state throughout its history as distinctively 'weak' continues to frustrate a reckoning with American power in the twenty-first century."[44] The US state, particularly with regard to matters of punishment, is said to have lacked the institutional capacity to build and direct punitive policy. Even in studies that "bring the state back in," carceral capacity is largely understood in terms of institutional resources.[45]

The analysis of mass incarceration, when restricted to a recent moment in time, relies on the idea that the acceleration of punishment in the postwar era marked a radical departure from the norm. After half a century of "stable" prison populations (the rate of punishment hovered around 110 per 100,000 for most of the twentieth century), a punishment system unique to its time is said to have emerged, breaking with established traditions and fundamentally changing the American political system.[46] This shift has been registered in the way that social science represents the prison in statistical terms, through percentages, rates, and regressions that make mass incarceration visible.[47] Just as social scientific knowledge has produced the terms for describing the increases in the state's carceral capacity, it has also produced the very "crime problems" that have justified a continuing process of reform and retrenchment in "data" that has historically been racialized in its production, organization, and arrangement.[48] Instead of understanding the deeply harmful system of racialized mass incarceration as a departure from a norm, the most recent instantiation of the project of the racial carceral state has to be grounded in an analysis of the racialization of the US prison system over time. The assumption that federal power was absent in the creation of carceral democracy is possible only through a story that begins too late and that obscures what it means to take the prison for granted as a form of justice.

Although the prison population may have been "stable" in the years before the dramatic expansion of the prison population, the "normal" use of cages and walls in a democratic society still created a mass of people who were ensnared in the state's carceral matrix. Almost every state in the union built a prison in the nineteenth century, and the one hundred thousand people they collectively held each year between 1880 and 1930 are not marginal to the history of the carceral state. Nor are the federal prisoners housed in those state institutions for nearly one hundred years before the creation of Leavenworth. This is the key moment of institutional development when the prison was consolidated as a "democratic" institution in politics and culture. The federal and state prison systems are rarely studied as interrelated architectures or parts of a whole, and because the federal system constitutes a smaller proportion of the overall system, most studies use state prisons to stand in synecdochically as representations of "American punishment." New York and Pennsylvania are often situated as the origins of American punishment, leaving institutions in other regions on the margins. By focusing on the federal prison system in relation to state-level institutions, this study works against the idea that federal prisons were merely symbolic institutions. In the prison's relationship to the long arc of American state building, federal authorities directed the course of punishment for the nation through politics and culture, finally creating a flagship institution of the carceral state in 1896.[49] What came before that system was significant because federal power was already imprinted with the forms of capacity that made mass incarceration possible. When examined through this lens, Leavenworth becomes a prism for understanding key moments in the acceleration of federal power over crime and punishment in the context of race, slavery, and settler colonial state building. These legal arrangements were always ideas about punishment.

In addition to reconceptualizing the history of the state, *The Prison of Democracy* draws from the fields of institutional ethnography and political geography to turn the gaze from the prisoner to the institution.[50] The purpose of this book is not to represent what prisoners or prisons are like but to contribute to different ways of understanding the work that prisons do in society. As part of this project, the book spatializes the penitentiary form, building on research in the field of carceral geography, which attends to the "geographical distribution of sites of incarceration across space" and the "affectual and emotional geographies of prison buildings."[51] Such research—Ruth Gilmore's *Golden Gulag* analyzing the prison as a "chain of islands" across California, Mona Lynch's *Sunbelt Justice* discovering a cluster of prisons that stretched from Virginia to Arizona, Robert Perkinson's *Texas Tough* mapping a "prison belt" that overlays the cotton plantations of an earlier time, and Mishuana Goeman's "From Place to Territories and Back Again" challenging scholars to understand why prisons like New York's Auburn are built on sites of colonial conquest—reconceptualizes not only geography but law by showing how the legal regimes of earlier times continue into the present, underlying newer understandings and modes of control.[52] I draw on this work by centering my analysis on what I call "legal time"—the palimpsest of competing legal arrangements in operation during any particular era. And I locate Leavenworth at a series of political borders where North meets South and East meets West, and where the prison was a symbol of law and order set down in the nation's heartland.

In working to denaturalize through a study of legal culture the connections between prisons and democracy, this book offers a theory of the carceral state that is grounded in the idea of political inversion. The legal subjectivity that the prison produces is the negation of democracy's subject, while the political status of the prisoner exists in "a dialectical relationship with freedom, as its necessary negation."[53] The negation of citizenship's subject and the presence of fractured subjectivities in a democracy was not exceptional or excessive; it was rather the fundamental basis of liberal governmentality.[54] Because it was always a carceral state, the prison marked the tyranny of liberalism's inversion: it was the "epistemo-logical project of the Enlightenment" and the betrayal of its subject.[55] It incorporated a form of antidemocratic punishment into democracy, and it did so in the name of the people's punishment. As political philosopher and activist Angela Y. Davis has asked, "What if the prison is so . . . tied to democracy, that we cannot undo it much less unthink it without also rethinking the fundamental basis of democracy?"[56] This book asks how the prison, as an institution of state violence, became the quintessentially "democratic" institution on which the whole house of democracy was built.

## LOCATING LEAVENWORTH

Each chapter in this book addresses a different moment in the history of mass incarceration and in the prison's emergence as an idea about justice. Taken together, these moments demonstrate that there was nothing natural about the prison's asso-ciation with democracy; it was an idea that had to be fashioned over time in culture and politics. Because the history of Leavenworth is almost always told in terms of sensationalized escapes and violent prisoners, this book tries to widen the frame as a study of the state.[57] In telling a story about the carceral state that reconceptualizes mass incarceration, the book reads the prison's official record against the grain in order to study the system as an artifact of power rather than merely to register the state's narrative. This is a methodology that subjectivizes the state, working to find power in gothic architecture, federal Indian law, state and territorial laws, slave records, congressional reports, local newspapers, and moments when things could have been otherwise.[58] The idea of Leavenworth is scattered, like federal prisoners before its time, across an array of institutions. This work therefore relies on an archive culled together from the state's paper trail. This idea of Leavenworth is con-tained in original blueprints, fabric samples, prison siren cards, and photographs. It is also in letters, memoirs, oral histories, and acts of resistance.

The first chapter examines how a federal system of punishment first emerged in state institutions designed like gothic castles. Focusing on an intergovernmen-tal project that put federal prisoners in state institutions in the years before the building of federal institutions, the chapter historicizes the kind of shift that Leav-enworth represented in prison architecture when it abandoned the gothic and asserted its connection to democracy through architecture. The chapter argues that despite Leavenworth's visual frame, the nineteenth-century gothic prison was already wedded to democracy through narratives of freedom, equality, and economy in literature, popular culture, and political thought. The prison was a symbol of the state's relationship, not just to the body of the citizen, but to a form of legal personhood enfolded in a dialectical organization of freedom. Because the prison was always an idea about mass incarceration, the chapter grounds the emergence of a federal prison system in already existing ideas about the prison house door as a symbol of civil death. It traces how castles and fortresses came to "look like" prisons in the American imagination and outlines a theory of the carceral state that normalized state violence through the meaning of the carceral gothic.

The intergovernmental structure of power that existed before Leavenworth was eventually replaced by a militarized regime of federal punishment. When Congress authorized the building of a federal prison in 1891, it provided no supporting appropriation, and the Department of Justice borrowed the US military prison at Fort Leavenworth, Kansas, for the prison's first decade. The Secretary of War told a House committee that the Department of Justice could operate the military prison, which consisted of "two cell-houses, with kitchens, shops, laundry, electric plant, boiler houses, chapel and school room, etc., surrounded by a stone wall, twenty feet high."[59] The three-story institution was built in 1840 as a quartermaster's depot and was converted into a prison by placing "on each floor a row of steel cages about eight feet high."[60] In 1896, Congress "set apart from the contiguous military reservation" a plot of land for "United States Penitentiary purposes" and began one of the largest prison construction projects in US history.[61] While the new Leavenworth was being built, the prisoners remained at the old Fort Leavenworth military prison until 1903, with several hundred marched "in columns of four . . . across the field and through the woods to labor in the quarries and on the new prison site."[62] From 1903 until 1906, "the prison" was a joint operation; some prisoners were housed in the new federal prison, and others remained confined on the military reservation. When the final transfer occurred and a new federal records system was developed, its 418 prisoners were living, not in "the prison" as it existed even a short time later, but in the prison's laundry room, which had finally been enclosed by the prisoners themselves. When the federal institution was finally built, the majority of its prisoners were from a place called the Indian Territory.

The second chapter focuses on the political significance of the Fort Leavenworth military prison in the history of the settler colonial state and the legacies of Native punishment that were carried forward into Leavenworth. It begins with the trial of John Grindstone, a Shawnee man from the Quapaw Agency of Indian Territory, who was prosecuted in federal court for killing a Peoria man named Joe Sky on Quapaw land. When Grindstone became Leavenworth's first prisoner, it was because of a legal architecture that federalized "Indian crime" and "Indian punishment" in the 1880s and led Native people to Leavenworth as a mass. Because of its relationship to Fort Leavenworth, when Congress fully federalized all "Indian crime" with the Major Crimes Act of 1885, Leavenworth was already imagined as a place for punishing Indians. Locating the idea of Leavenworth in the Indian Territory as a bound space of control, the chapter examines how punishability became a legal relation, creating forms of subjectivity rooted in the concepts of group guilt, substitution punishments, and "enemy nations." Because the nation's first prison was designed to punish Native people, the chapter historicizes what it meant to choose Fort Leavenworth as the site for the nation's first prison.

As part of the history of the carceral state, Indian Territory and the federal prison that followed are forms of settler colonial justice that require shifts in the conceptualization of American statelessness. Because the settler colonial state is also a carceral state, it relies simultaneously on a "logic of elimination" and on modes of punishment that discipline targeted populations and administrate and imagine colonial spaces "like prisons."[63] The settler colonial state relies on a politics of forced recognition to claim criminal jurisdiction over sovereign nations; to assume that the American state has only recently been carceral is to overlook the legacies of carceral capacity that began in the Indian Territory.

Chapter 3 focuses on another legal arrangement that brought federal power to Kansas. In the aftermath of Indian Territory, the legal doctrines of squatter and popular sovereignty led to Bleeding Kansas, a period of civil war over slavery at the Kansas-Missouri border. The chapter looks for the idea of Leavenworth in the legacy of a legal arrangement defined by competing claims to the right to govern the territory by proslavery Missourians and antislavery Kansans. The people of abolition Kansas rejected slavery and refused to abide by federal or territorial law, leading to the development of a local justice tradition in which law was practiced by the people rather than by the state. Federal law was seen as an invading force that protected the interests of slavery and punished abolition Kansas in makeshift prisons, in Missouri jails, and in Fort Leavenworth's military guardhouse. As an assertion of federal power over local practice, Leavenworth disrupted the interrelated and customary practices of squatter and popular sovereignty, which imagined the work of punishment as the work of "the people." In these legal borderlands, Leavenworth disrupted local ideas about democracy in a moment when abolition justice might have ended the congenital institutions of slavery and prisons. The prisonization of Kansas drew on those older traditions but rerouted collective power into state power, separating the memory of the prison from the memory of Bleeding Kansas. This chapter puts the prison back into the story of Bleeding Kansas, returning to a landscape without law to explain the cultural upheavals required to bring the nation's first federal prison to Kansas. In this context, Leavenworth was a monument to the carceral state.

Chapter 4 turns to the most gothic of borders between slavery and freedom in order to explain the racialization of the penitentiary form. Locating Leavenworth at the end of a line, the chapter examines how the federal prison crowned a regional constellation of penal institutions that traced the North-South border, stretching from Maryland to Virginia to Kentucky and Missouri. The chapter uses the framework of the border prison to understand how Leavenworth carried forward the carceral capacities of slavery into a postemancipation legal time. As border states became "northern" and "southern" institutions after slavery's end, the presence of slaves in prisons in the border states was overshadowed, along with the carceral matrix of "slave jails" that existed throughout the South. This was a system overlaid by "federal slave law," which created a carceral apparatus to regulate the course of fugitive hunts and slave punishments. Within this carceral state, slavery was imagined as a form of mass incarceration.[64] As part of the history of federal punishment, it was connected to the prison as an institution not only in terms of the bodies targeted and the unfree labor extorted from them but in terms of the status assigned to those bodies.[65] These were also connections forged in the landscape.[66]

This chapter traces how an already existing network of punitive institutions for slaves made it possible to imagine the prison as a "Black institution." On this basis, some southern states refused the penitentiary in the legal time of slavery but became leaders and innovators in a new generation of postwar prison building. The chapter begins with a map of these two institutional frameworks—the embrace of the prison as part of slavery in the border states and its rejection in key southern states—and reorients Leavenworth at the border between slavery and freedom. The chapter argues that the racialization of the penitentiary form is part of the legacy of the nationalization of the border prison as an idea about managing Black freedom.

Building on the analysis of the prison as a racial script in the previous chapters, chapter 5 offers a cultural history of mass incarceration and mass resistance. The chapter begins by examining how federal authorities developed a structure of segregation beginning in 1914 and used the social spaces of prison leisure to draw lines around racialized groups and maximize federal control. The chapter details the mass incarceration of political prisoners in 1917, including prisoners who came to Leavenworth as political activists in the Industrial Workers of the World, the Black Twenty-Fourth Infantry, and the Partido Liberal Mexicano. These activists built movements that worked across the prison's walls to force the contradictions of group guilt, criminalized speech, and federal violence into the public eye and into the courts. The chapter examines this work in relation to that of a later generation of activists at Leavenworth in the early 1970s who used federal law to try to dismantle the carceral state. As a history of social movements at Leavenworth, the chapter focuses on the analysis of mass incarceration that comes from political prisoners and on ways of working across difference that undermine the power of the carceral state.

The book's postscript begins in the 1970s, when the carceral state is said to have emerged in the wake of mass incarceration. It was instead another moment in the history of the prison's consolidation in American politics and in its legal enclosure from public regulation. In a time that was supposed to mark the beginning of mass incarceration, Leavenworth was already at the end of its institutional life but was reborn in the rebuilding of the federal prison system as a place for immigrants and a place where violence necessitated a regime of securitization so severe that the courts turned a blind eye. In ending with another moment of institutional buildup, the analysis returns to the question of the prison's relationship to democracy and imagines what it would mean to redesign a theory of the state that would not be bound to the project of the prison. It urges political scientists and prison abolitionists to reimagine a theory of justice that refuses to take the prison for granted as a "democratic" institution. In the space between the prison's rejection and its revivification, the book ends by imagining new terrains of democracy and belonging in the prison's aftermath.

Each chapter traces a moment in the history of mass incarceration in order to denaturalize the prison and acknowledge its status as a contested institution. Taken together, *The Prison of Democracy* tries to locate moments when justice might have meant something else. Each chapter historicizes the prison's status and staying power as a democratic institution and puts the prison at the center of American political history, a place where it has always resided, even as the prison's normalization as a taken-for-granted aspect of political life has depoliticized its status as an institution. In locating Leavenworth at the intersections of political geography and legal time, the book works to subjectivize prisons, not to give them a rational life, but to show how the prison is an idea about civil death that haunts the political landscape. In the service of seeing prisons differently, as cages with cultural and political consequences for the meaning of democracy, this book historicizes punishment in order to imagine a more radical future.

# 1

# The Architecture of Liberalism and the Origins of Carceral Democracy

*A throng of bearded men, in sad-colored garments and gray, steeple-crowned hats, intermixed with women, some wearing hoods, and others bareheaded, was assembled in front of a wooden edifice, the door of which was heavily timbered with oak, and studded with iron spikes. The founders of a new colony, whatever Utopia of human virtue and happiness they might originally project, have invariably recognized it among their earliest practical necessities to allot a portion of the virgin soil as a cemetery, and another portion as the site of a prison. In accordance with this rule, it may safely be assumed that the forefathers of Boston had built the first prison-house. . . . Certain it is, that, some fifteen or twenty years after the settlement of the town, the wooden jail was already marked with weather-stains and other indications of age, which gave a yet darker aspect to its beetle-browed and gloomy front. The rust on the ponderous iron-work of its oaken door looked more antique than any thing else in the new world. Like all that pertains to crime, it seemed never to have known a youthful era. Before this ugly edifice, and between it and the wheel-track of the street, was a grass-plot . . . which evidently found something congenial in the soil that had so early borne the black flower of civilized society, a prison.*

—NATHANIEL HAWTHORNE, "THE PRISON DOOR,"
*THE SCARLET LETTER*

*"Buried how long?"*
*The answer was always the same: "Almost eighteen years."*
*"You had abandoned all hope of being dug out?"*
*"Long ago."*
*"You know that you are recalled to life?"*
*"They tell me so."*
*"I hope you care to live?"*
*"I can't say."*

—CHARLES DICKENS, *TALE OF TWO CITIES*

The prison house door was an icon in nineteenth-century political life. "Heavily timbered with oak," the door was "studded with iron spikes" because it represented passage from the world of the free to a place beyond civic status. It was a place shrouded in mystery beyond the public eye, and its door looked "more antique than anything else in the new world." The prisons of Hawthorne's time were designed to resemble medieval castles, and they symbolically reached back from the time of "modern" democracy and rationality in the nineteenth century and drew the language of tyranny and despotism into the framework of American governance. As part of an iconography of civil death, the door was the state's representation of a transformative departure to a place without political status. In recording freedom's inversion in the prison house door, the state left open, in the power of the doorway, the possibility of a return—of being "recalled to life" from the space beyond. Because the door and the building behind it were imagined as a kind of legal border, the prison became, as a matter of law, a crossing into a particular kind of space.[1]

When Hawthorne wrote about colonial prisons with "iron rivets," he used them as a site for exploring the gothic institutions of his own time. When he wrote *The Scarlet Letter* in 1850, the colonial prisons it depicted had been condemned as antiquated and antirepublican institutions and had been replaced by the first generation of American prisons, which had already failed and been replaced by another set of gothic penal architectures in the late 1820s and early 1830s. Nearly every state penal institution built between 1829 and 1890 drew on the idea of the carceral gothic, including Pennsylvania, New York, New Jersey, Tennessee, Kentucky, Ohio, West Virginia, Kansas, Arkansas, Maryland, Louisiana, Illinois, Indiana, South Carolina, North Carolina, Michigan, and Missouri. When the federal government created a class of federal prisoners beginning in 1787, gradually increasing the number of federal crimes and therefore federal prisoners over the course of the nineteenth century, it housed federal prisoners in gothic state institutions. In the time before Leavenworth, a federal prison system existed without a building, as the nation's earliest prisoners were sent to gothic institutions in Pennsylvania, New York, New Jersey, Illinois, Ohio, West Virginia, Missouri, and Kansas.

What was gothic about the legal architecture of civil death was the possibility of eternal enclosure—a horror from which there was no return. One of the central problems with these prisons, according to the earliest reports of federal prison administrators, was that they relied on the idea of state violence against the body of the prisoner. The gothic prisons were symbols of that violence and the forms of infamy they assigned to the body. As a kind of degraded status bestowed on that body when the state defiled the prisoner through physical violence, infamy was inherited in the common-law tradition and defined the status of the prisoner in the United States. William Blackstone's *Commentaries on the Laws of England* recorded the way in which infamous punishments were connected to "ignominy" and included the shame of "public labor, in the house of correction or otherwise, as well as whipping, the pillory, or the stocks."[2] When it marked that body with degradation, the state attached "infamation" to the body for life, creating a kind of gothic script and a source of state terror beyond escape.[3] This form of state violence, which assigned the status of *infamia juris* (infamy of law), was distinct from the legal mark left behind when crimes were considered infamous in fact (*infamia facto*).

The federal prison system had its origins in the state institutions that assigned *infamia juris* to the body. The earliest government reports on federal prisoners housed in state institutions index the violence of gothic prisons and present the formation of a federal system as the answer to that structure of violence. As detailed in the 1885 reports, New Jersey was built in an Egyptian gothic style, and punishment was "by the dungeon, chaining down, and tying up."[4] In Missouri's stone castle, which held hundreds of federal prisoners over the years, the standard practice was "flogging with the raw-hide."[5] Large numbers of federal prisoners were also sent to Indiana, where the dark cell was used with the cat, "a rubber whip handle with five strands of raw hide attached to it."[6] Illinois practiced forced standing with "the hands put through the grated door and handcuffed on the outside."[7] Federal prisoners in Ohio's state prison experienced "ducking," which involved a "stream of water directed from a hose with some force upon the naked person," and "the slide," an "arrangement by which the convict is drawn up by the wrists, handcuffed till he stands on tip toe."[8] In West Virginia, where substantial numbers of federal prisoners were held, discipline was governed by the lash, the shoo fly (a "frame work made of wood with slots for the prisoner's legs, hands and wrists") and the bull ring (a "ring fastened in the wall considerably above the floor to which the prisoner is drawn by his wrists").[9] Although much of the federal report is critical of this violence, it is acknowledged as a routine part of the prison's design—there are dungeons, chains, and medieval devices of torture in an architecture that is repeatedly described as antique. In these shared jurisdictions of state and federal power, gothic prisons were ideas about mass incarceration in the way that they assigned civil death to a mass of bodies in buildings that stood for a century.

As part of a larger theory of the carceral state, the gothic prisons that dotted the landscape by the time of Hawthorne's writing used the revival idiom of the medieval castle to build an argument about a form of state that was beyond and without time. The timelessness of prison architecture normalized gothic citizenship in political memory, as the castle was a symbol of *that which remained* despite decaying grounds and the end of monarchy. The prison in Hawthorne's tale, the "black flower of civilized society," was "never to have known a youthful era" because the prison was part of a memory of justice that appeared to be endless. It was the gothic prison's appearance of timelessness that gave it a sense of permanence and common sense, since timeless institutions can be taken for granted as naturalized features of the landscape. When Hawthorne drew the reader's attention to prison architecture and the prison house door, he challenged the naturalization of iron rivets as symbols of the state's right to deprive the citizen of the body in the gothic prison and suggested that prison reform was an attempt to redesign an institution that could not be repaired.

Despite the gothic prison's relationship to the masses and its place in the history of a nationalized prison system, the written history of US punishment has largely depoliticized the nineteenth-century carceral gothic and obscured the arguments at the heart of its design. The study of prison architecture has generally focused on the internal organization of time and space rather than on the buildings' outward appearance.[10] The prison's meaning as a cultural artifact has escaped cultural inquiry in part because of architecture's turn away from the "fortress school" and its subsequent recasting as a mistaken and expensive period in the prison's history.[11] This echoed the state's narrative. By 1949, the director of the Federal Bureau of Prisons described the gothic generation of American prisons as "outmoded, obsolete shells and cages."[12] The Bureau of Prisons Advance Planning Unit recommended that these gothic relics of another era be replaced by highly securitized institutions whose outward appearances were designed to draw less attention.[13] What is obscured in the depoliticization of the gothic is how the American prison came to be shrouded in intrigue, superstition, and terror because it drew on the power of the democratic imagination.

This chapter traces the history of the federal prison system to the gothic institutions of the nineteenth century in order to make visible the form of gothic governance that Leavenworth would eventually conceal. As the brick-and-mortar manifestation of the American penal state, Leavenworth abandoned the gothic but entrenched and concealed the legal architecture of civil death in American political culture. By the time the federal prison looked like democracy in 1896, the state's carceral capacity was already in place as an intergovernmental form of power. Both state and federal regimes of punishment coexisted in prison towns that dotted the landscape, and they relied on local ideas about carceral democracy long before Leavenworth emerged as the flagship institution of a federal prison system. This chapter examines how these castles and fortresses came to "look like" prisons in the American imagination and historicizes the carceral gothic as a form of common sense. The chapter begins with John de Haviland's original vision of the carceral gothic and the changing meanings of "the gothic" in narratives of freedom, equality, democracy, and status. In moving from the carceral gothic to the carceral state, the chapter offers a study of mass incarceration as an idea inscribed on the building. It works to denaturalize the prison's relationship to freedom in a state that has always been carceral and to contextualize the prison as an icon at the center of a complex legal and cultural relationship that was enshrined in the prison house door.

## THE FORTRESS SCHOOL AND THE GOTHIC
## IMAGINARY

The gothic prisons of Hawthorne's century were built between the 1790s and the 1880s as monuments to a certain kind of state. The carceral gothic was expressed in the thick and arched iron doorways that were entrances to a lost civic status and in the castellated features of fortified turrets and embattled parapets. The medieval towers that hovered above the walls drew the eye to a door with warnings etched on the surface of the building. The entrance to the Pennsylvania prison at Philadelphia, the original gothic institution in the United States, was decorated by a disproportionately large iron doorway. Kentucky inscribed above its arch Dante's depiction of the entrance to the gates of hell: "Abandon Hope, All Ye That Enter Here."[14] Missouri's prison designers used the image of the clock at the top of the gothic facade to express the importance of time in the meaning of state deprivation. How did these monuments come to define the shape of punishment in the United States?

As the self-described "original architect of the system," the British-born architect John de Haviland inspired a whole generation of American prisons.[15] Beginning with Eastern State in Pennsylvania, Haviland's "heavy and gloomy Gothic" became part of the foundation of state prison systems across the nation. Haviland built prisons in New Jersey, Arkansas, Missouri, and Rhode Island and drew unused plans for a prison in Louisiana.[16] At the local level, he built most of the county jails in Ohio and Pennsylvania and New York, including the infamous Tombs, and he was commissioned to prepare "standard models" for the Prison Discipline Society as part of a nationwide project of jail reform.[17] In his journals, Haviland imagined scaling that project to county governments across the nation, charging $65,000 for a gothic facade, $60,000 for one in the Egyptian style, and $55,000 for something Roman.[18] His style of building jails and prisons established a tradition in prison architecture and a customary way of expressing the political function of the building. Three hundred prisons around the world were eventually built like gothic castles.[19]

The carceral gothic tradition was defined by a certain relationship between the prison's inside and outside. In marking this relationship, the revival of gothic castles as prisons was designed to make an impression on an audience.[20] Haviland came out of a tradition in architecture that used space to create stark contrasts. He "rarely, if ever, took into account compositional figure-ground relationships between a structure and the space surrounding it," which made his buildings appear "removed" from their immediate environment.[21] The idea of the prison as matter out of place gave it a certain visibility so that its message could continually be translated to its audience. Haviland's teacher, the British architect James Elmes, had written in 1817 that a good prison was unmistakable in this act of translation: "No one viewing this edifice can possibly mistake it for anything but a gaol . . . as gloomy and melancholy as possible."[22] By 1826, the gothic tradition

FIGURE 2. Facade of Eastern State Penitentiary, Philadelphia, 1920s. Courtesy of Eastern State Penitentiary Historic Site, Philadelphia, Pennsylvania.

established by Elmes and his students was entered into the *Encyclopedia Londonis* as a matter of "no slight importance":

> It offers an effectual method of exciting the imagination to a most desirable point of abhorrence. Persons, in general, refer their horror of a prison to an instinctive feeling rather than to any accurate knowledge of their privations or inflictions therein endured. And whoever remarks the forcible operations of such antipathies in the vulgar, will not neglect any means however minute, of directing them to a good purpose. The exterior of a prison should, therefore, be formed in the heavy and sombre style, which most forcibly impresses the spectator with gloom and terror. Massive cornices, the absence of windows or other ornaments, small low doors and the whole structure comparatively low, seem to include nearly all the points necessary to produce the desired effect.[23]

When Haviland Americanized the carceral gothic, the impression of the prison that was created through architecture joined the idea of the state to the idea of public terror. Sounding remarkably like the door in Hawthorne's tale, Haviland's prison, with its "massive wrought-iron portcullis and double oaken doors studded with iron rivets," used a familiar image to conceptualize a gothic kind of carceral state.[24] John de Haviland's designs were selected by the building commissioners of Eastern State because they evoked state terror: they wrote that "the exterior of a solitary prison should exhibit as much as possible great strength and convey to the mind a cheerless blank indicative of the misery which awaits the unhappy being who enters within its walls."[25] Haviland's message, described by Benjamin Rush as a program of "successful terror," magnified and created political distance through the "avenue to this house."[26] Rush believed that a prison, as both a mystery and an exhibit, used the space between the building and its surroundings to define the prison's structure of feeling, which meant that "the gothic" was a kind of "emotion about buildings rather than any specific way of building them."[27] This textured surface of the prison was part of a speaking architecture that transcribed the meaning of the building:

> Let the avenue to this house be rendered difficult and gloomy by mountains or morasses. *Let its doors be of iron;* and let the grating, occasioned by opening and shutting them, be increased by an echo from a neighboring mountain, that shall extend and continue a sound that shall deeply pierce the soul. . . . Children will press upon the evening fire in listening to the tales that will spread from this abode of misery. Superstition will add to its horrors, and romance will find in it ample materials for fiction, which cannot fail of increasing the terror of its punishments.[28]

The prison's purpose, in marking out this space of transition, was not just to imprison but to bind a community of prison spectators, in Rush's words, "to the meaning of the penal process."[29] In this context, prisons became "places of real terror, to those the law would terrify."[30]

In Haviland's gothic vision of Eastern State, prisoners would be held in solitary confinement as part of a ritual of legal burial. When Charles Dickens visited Haviland's Eastern State Penitentiary in Philadelphia in 1841, he described "black hoods" drawn over the faces of entering prisoners: "And in this dark shroud, an emblem of the curtain dropped between him and the living world, he is led to the cell from which he never again comes forth, until the whole term of imprisonment has expired. He is a man buried alive."[31] It also banished the prisoner to walls beyond the city's boundaries, and prisoners who resisted total silence were punished with the use of chains and the "iron gag," a device "placed in the prisoners mouth, the iron palet over his tongue, the bit forced in as far as possible, the chains brought round the jaws to the back of the neck; the end of one chain was passing through the ring in the end of the other chain . . . and fastened with a lock."[32] The prisoner was then "strung up" with "the hands forced upward toward the head."[33] The use of stress positions was accompanied by the practice of ducking, which "suspend[ed] the offender from the yard wall by the wrists, and drench[ed] him with water, poured on his head from buckets, in nature of a shower bath."[34]

The violence of Eastern State in Philadelphia is often depicted as exceptional in the sense that most of the other states chose to adopt New York's competing model of factory discipline. But New York was likewise anchored in a theory of carceral state violence. The prison hovered on a hilltop above the city, its dark and crenellated roofline framing a doorway of iron grating topped by a statue of a soldier in a prison governed by the whip.[35] State law allowed prisoners to receive up to thirty-nine lashes with what Gustave de Beaumont and Alexis de Tocqueville described as "an instrument that Americans call 'the cat' and [the French] call the knout."[36]

When prisoners entered the institution, the warden explained the terms of civil death: "While confined here, you can have no intelligence concerning relatives or friends. . . . You are to be literally buried from the world."[37] The whole regime was ratified by a New York court, which agreed that "the convict should feel his degraded situation."[38] In New York, Pennsylvania, New Jersey, Illinois, Ohio, West Virginia, Missouri, and Kansas, federal prisoners were arranged into these structures of civil death as part of an intergovernmental project guided by federal oversight.

These gothic institutions of civil death, as hubs in the development of the federal prison system between 1787 and 1896, had once promised to end the dungeons of the king's justice. The federal system that emerged to challenge the structure of violence in state prisons only reinforced that violence, even as it claimed to build the prison of democracy. In what Angela Y. Davis has called the "two-hundred-year-old drama of prison reform," the carceral state imagined new iterations of an already failed institution because the prison had become central to the process of state making and the forms of loyalty and consent it required.[39] The prison's association with democracy was a contradiction—it functioned as a mechanism for replacing collective power with acquiescence to a burdened citizenship always threatened by the possibility of terror without escape. If prisons were understood as places of state-sanctioned violence against the body, how were they ultimately reconciled with democratic language and thought? What was the theory of the state at the heart of the gothic nightmare?

## IT HAS ALWAYS BEEN A CARCERAL STATE: FROM THE CARCERAL GOTHIC TO THE CARCERAL STATE

Gothic prisons came to make sense as carceral features of political life because they materialized terror in the language of democracy. The contradictions of carceral democracy made sense to American audiences because of the cultural meaning of the castle as a place of terror in gothic literature. The idea of a castle as a prison was familiar to American audiences through the plotlines of nineteenth-century gothic texts, which crossed boundaries, registered ghosts, and used the figure of the castle to explore the terrors of the home, the mind, and the nation through the motifs of entombment, imprisonment, and claustrophobia.[40] It was the literature of contrasts, of "twisted convolutions" played out in labyrinths of winding staircases and mazes of the self.[41] Gothic plotlines unfolded in buildings that decayed but lasted beyond time and inspired sublime feelings of awe through architecture: "When the walls that outlast generations crumble, the powers of time appear even more awesome."[42] Because the gothic castle was a terrifying place, "prisons found their models in the Middle Ages, in the castles that to readers of Gothic fiction meant dark secrets and silent suffering."[43]

As the stage of the gothic tradition, castles that functioned like prisons became literary sites for exploring the contradictions of state power and the terrors of gothic citizenship. The prison brought together the terror and horror genres of gothic literature as distinct forms defined by an escape from terror or the horror of permanent enclosure.[44] While terror gothic explored the soul's potential return from the dead, horror gothic focused on the permanence of confinement. This is part of what was symbolized in the prison house door—both the possibility of imprisonment without end and the citizen's potential return from the dead. In introducing readers to the meaning of the prison house door, the *carceral gothic* was a language recorded in a literary genre that was both a source of critical knowledge about the politics of confinement and a central site for the prison's normalization.

As an artifact already embedded in public culture, the prison relied for its power on the participation of its audience. Penal spectatorship made meaning of the prison, teaching the citizenry to look and then to look away—to feel something in the structure of terror that was signified in the institution's very design and then to normalize that structure as a relation.[45] The purpose of the prison was therefore to produce both terror and political distance: one was "supposed to view [the scene] from close up so that he loses his 'objective distance' toward it and is immediately 'drawn' into it."[46] The whole system worked by "transmuting fear of external power into identification with its strength and thereby stabilizing both self and the social other."[47] Through penal spectatorship, the prison became part of the taken-for-granted terrain of a political culture that, as Thomas Bender has suggested, is "rarely . . . subject to examination" but is "continuously enacted culturally in detail after detail of living."[48] It was in the prison's details, its "images, stories, and legends," that a theory of the gothic state was articulated in the language of democracy, equality, and modern governance.[49]

The gothic prison's staged appearance as a democratic institution was possible because it appealed to the cultural idiom of freedom. The original Goths, who invaded Europe between the fourth and sixth centuries, were associated with self-governance and were celebrated for a practice of self-rule that survived Roman occupation.[50] As an idiom, "the gothic" was part of a memory of white ancestry and the history of self-rule: "Parliaments and the legal system, it was believed, were derived from gothic institutions and peoples who were free and democratic."[51] The association between Gothic governance and its revival in the Western "democratic" legal tradition was also part of a conjoined memory of fit lineage and noble roots. The Goths were celebrated in an 1843 speech by George P. Marsh as "the noblest branch of the Caucasian race," and as an idea about white self-governance the revival of this past in the carceral gothic signaled that the prison was built for dignified bodies.[52]

This memory of the gothic enabled an institution built on state violence to be read by its audience as an emblem of freedom. The gothic prison was imagined as a place where aristocratic bodies could avoid the taint of public violence. In Europe, nobles, clerics, and the wealthy were spared the public degradation of violence against the body and the accompanying status of *infamia juris* (infamy of law).

To avoid the taint of having been touched by the state, aristocratic bodies served time not in prisons but in the towers of castles or in appointed rooms in local inns. The early idea of the prison was also then an idea about the dignified body, as a place where aristocrats avoided state violence. The British idea of prisons as places of dignity was incorporated into the laws of colonial Virginia, so that its legal tradition in 1619 did not punish "persons of quality" who were by virtue of status "not fitt to undergoe corporal punishment."[53] Instead, they would be "imprisoned at the discretione of the commander & for greater offences be subject to a fine."[54]

It was this idea of the prison as a dignified institution that enabled the prison's embrace by the masses despite their status as targets of mass incarceration. Because it put the poor into buildings designed for aristocrats, British prison reformers sometimes lamented the class disjuncture of building elaborate castles for the "dangerous classes."[55] John Howard regretted this contradiction but recognized its utility: "The new gaols," he wrote, "having pompous fronts, appear like palaces to the lower class of people."[56] In his 1892 *History of Prison Architecture*, John Rochester Thomas explained that prisons were easily "mistaken for palaces" by the masses.[57] In the European context, the prison was evidence of a tyranny overcome by freedom: in the memory of the Bastille, the castle-prison was a place where bodies were disappeared in dungeons but where citizens stormed the building to reclaim them in the name of democracy.[58] In the United States, the prison was positioned as a great equalizing institution, and its allure was shrouded in the idea that, in theory, everyone was equally subject to state punishment.

In the design of the carceral state, the people "consented" to the prison precisely because society was rooted in the idea of equal deprivation. As Michel Foucault has suggested, the prison was an institution that *appeared* to equalize the citizenry by taking not always life and limb but certainly time: "How could prison not be the penalty *par excellence* in a society in which liberty is a good that belongs to all . . . ? Its loss has therefore the same value for all; unlike the fine, it is an 'egalitarian' punishment. The prison is the clearest, simplest, most equitable of penalties. Moreover, it makes it possible to quantify the penalty exactly according to the variable of time. There is a wages-form of imprisonment that constitutes, in industrial societies, its economic 'self-evidence'—and enables it to appear as a reparation."[59] In these "equalizing" deprivations of body and labor time, the prison was given its "self-evident character"—its appearance as "hav[ing] no alternative, as if carried along by the very movement of history."[60] The prison, as an idea about a building, drew on this narrative of equality, even as it introduced a form of political membership that could be taken away by the state under the guise of the public.

Although the prison appeared as an equalizing institution, the carceral state was a theory of mass incarceration in the way that it was fundamentally shaped by the principle of less eligibility. By design, the prison was the boundary between status and nonstatus, and it was this line that was engineered to balance utilitarian ideas of the prisoner's pain and the citizen's pleasure. In Bentham's terms, prison life was designed to be fundamentally "less eligible" or less desirable than life out-side of the prison, so that structured suffering would incentivize returns to the free world and the virtuous behavior of citizens. In the United States, this idea devel-oped out of utilitarian and republican ideologies in the 1770s, as carceral architects sought to imagine the prison as a border between less eligible lives and a free world governed by the threat of civil death. In its ordering of the carceral gothic, the principle of less eligibility was materialized through the use of intrigue and super-stition, as part of a structure that drew the eye of the spectator to the prison house door and then normalized that door as part of the cost of freedom.

The prison was paraded as a democratic institution not only through the gothic memories of whiteness, freedom, and equality but also through the normalization of the gothic in everyday life. In the domestication of gothic architecture between 1830 and 1860, "the gothic" was reintroduced as a feature of the "wealthy home" and came to signal an "upward, aspiring, imaginative feeling" that conveyed eco-nomic stability.[61] Prison designers introduced this version of the gothic in the cit-ies, counties, and townships near gothic penal institutions as a counterimage. John de Haviland himself, along with Benjamin Latrobe and Andrew Jackson Downing, designed gothic homes to be "wonderfully captivating" scenes of "otherworldli-ness."[62] The gothic prison and the gothic home were both expressions of sover-eignty. The prison was an emblem of the state's power to punish, and the home was a symbol of the castle doctrine, which authorized self-defense on the grounds that the home was a kind of legal castle. The domestication of gothic architecture during the gothic period of prison reform introduced new and everyday ways of experiencing the power of the carceral state. It also reinforced, as a form of "expe-riential" knowledge of the meaning of the building, the idea of the prison as an institution for bodies with status.

The appeal of the gothic as a democratic image was also sometimes solidified in the architecture of the statehouse. State capitals often reinforced the idea of the prison's relationship to democratic governance by spatially concentrating the meaning of the prison house and the statehouse. In Kansas, the same architect, Erasmus Carr, built the prison and the capital as coequal architectures of the state. Louisiana went so far as to actually build a gothic state capitol, creating between 1852 and 1932 a certain symbiosis between the prison and the state as visual references. Mark Twain in *Life on the Mississippi* blamed the "little sham castle" on the literary influence of Sir Walter Scott's "medieval romances."[63] "It is pathetic enough, that a whitewashed castle, with turrets and things—materials all ungenuine within and without, pretending to be what they are not—should ever have been built in this otherwise honorable place," Twain wrote. Although Loui-siana was exceptional in designing its statehouse to look like a prison, other states connected the prison to democracy in less visible ways. Arkansas built a new state capitol on the former site of its state penitentiary in 1899, burying "bricks salvaged from the original penitentiary" in "the walls located around the outside of the basement of the state capitol."[64] Connecting mass democracy to mass incarceration through architecture, the gothic statehouse was part of the history of the prison's visual tradition.

The "horrific prison facades" and their domestic counterparts reinscribed state power by recalling a memory that had to be made. Recalling "a time and place that never existed," the prison was an inheritance of gothic bricolage, a coming together of "bits and pieces of various traditions, transformed and superimposed upon a new landscape."[65] In the entrance to the prison house door, the state confessed the gothic horror of an unfreedom that lingered in the transition from despotism to democracy. In a political moment in which state power was consolidated in the name of democracy, these sites of legal inversion recalled the gothic design in order to make compatible with democracy a form of punishment that was fundamentally incompatible with democracy. Against this backdrop, Leavenworth became the flagship institution of the carceral state. It was not the origin of the state's carceral capacity—it was the emblem of an already existing federal capacity that had been nurtured in the gothic landscapes of the states. In this shadow carceral state, the long relationship between federal and state prisons was not about federal weakness and state control but about engineering the public embrace of a prison built to look like democracy.

## LEAVENWORTH AND THE GOTHIC CARCERAL STATE

When Leavenworth suggested through architecture that the prison was a democratic institution, it combined Auburn's "five tiers of back-to-back cells . . . flanked by long dark corridors" with Pennsylvania's arrangement of the cell houses in a radial pattern. This meant that Leavenworth's cellblocks were arranged like the spokes of a wheel emerging from a lengthy front wall.[66] In this way, the prison echoed the architecture of the US capital city, which was patterned in 1790 in a mode that later came to look like a prison. Haviland's architecture crossed corridors around a central node in order to form a prison epicenter. With cells emanating from an institutional center, Haviland centralized the prison's power in a theory of rational functionalism that increased its utility in "watching, convenience, economy, and ventilation."[67] Haviland's vision of centralized power matched the vision of the US federal city. When the French architect Pierre L'Enfant arranged the city's gridlines in 1790, he created "radial patterns imposed on orthogonal streets."[68] These gridlines brought travelers organically to designated sites of commemoration, including statues, plazas, and memorials. L'Enfant placed the coequal branches of the legislature and the executive on two hills, creating a topographic map of the separation of powers. Around these "pedestals" he arranged "twelve wide avenues radiating out from the site like a massive sunburst."[69] It was a city that reflected centralization and federalized power, and Haviland drew on this framework in articulating the power of the prison.

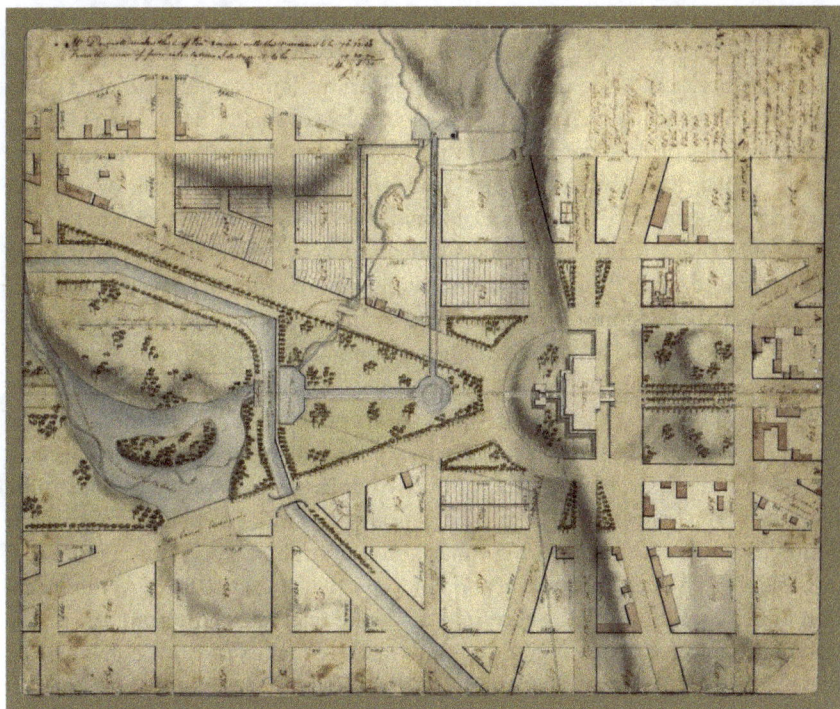

FIGURE 3. Benjamin Henry Latrobe. *Map exhibiting the property of the U.S. in the vicinity of the Capitol: colored red, with the manner in which it is proposed to lay off the same in building lots, as described in the report to the Sup't of the city to which this is annexed.* 1815. Watercolor on paper. Geography and Map Division, Library of Congress.

Because of the prison's central place in the theory of the American state, it was significant that nearly all of the federal architects between 1790 and 1860 were prison designers. Pierre L'Enfant was replaced by Benjamin Henry Latrobe, who, along with Thomas Jefferson, designed the Virginia State Penitentiary. Latrobe's students included John de Haviland, Robert Mills, and William Strickland.[70] Robert Mills, who was appointed federal architect from 1836 until 1852, designed Louisiana's state prison in the 1820s.[71] He later proposed drawings for a jail in Burlington County, New Jersey, and a state prison in South Carolina.[72] William Strickland designed the Western State Penitentiary in Pennsylvania, which John de Haviland abhorred and was later hired to rebuild.[73] These architects used radial patterns to connect the prison to the state in a theory of carceral democracy that was rooted in the centralization of power.

The architects of the carceral state were influenced by liberal and utilitarian frameworks that intersected in the idea that the state is obligated to punish its citizens as part of the social contract. In this tradition, individuals in society were bound by the exchanges of consent and contract to the state's "penal right."[74] When Thomas Hobbes wrote that one "divests himself of his natural liberty" and joins in civic association, he described membership in the language of "artificial chains, called *civil laws*, which they themselves, by mutual covenants, have fastened at one end, to the lips of that man, or assembly, to whom they have given the sovereign power; and at the other end to their own ears. These bonds, in their own nature but weak, may nevertheless be made to hold, by the danger, though not by the difficulty of breaking them."[75] John Locke's theory of government likewise articulated a subject free from the "inconstant, uncertain, unknown, arbitrary will of another" but compared "freedom of men under government" to putting on "the *bonds of civil society*."[76] The social contract tradition was bound to the prisonized terrain of the state, since it took for granted an "agreement" to submit to state violence. Not just physical but legal violence was at the heart of the contract. The prison therefore represented all of the contradictions of a free society with unfree subjects. It existed in a "dialectical relationship with freedom, as its necessary negation."[77] Lisa Lowe has suggested in her "unsettling genealogy of modern liberalism" that the boundary between rights-bearing subjects and nonsubjects was "the condition of possibility for Western liberalism, and not its particular exception."[78] As the "negation of the conditions which allow one to define oneself as a person," the prison was an inversion of political status that was made to make sense through the negative aesthetic of prison architecture.[79] The prison was the "epistemological project of the Enlightenment" and a betrayal of the free individual it produced, and yet it became the quintessentially "democratic" institution on which the whole house of democracy was built.[80]

Perhaps the prison could be taken for granted in the theory of the liberal state because the United States was seen as a place colonized by criminals. After the American "revolution," the presence of between thirty and fifty thousand prisoners who had been "cast for transportation" to the colonies led to concerns about the prisonized nature of the American landscape.[81] The revolution itself was described by the British as the work of a "race of convicts," and this identity remained embedded in the course of the new American state.[82] Even after England turned to Australia to banish its prisoners, Europe's criminals continued to "swarm" the United States under cover of private enterprise. Fearing floods of criminals at the shores, James Cooper of Pennsylvania complained on the Senate floor in 1855 that there was "scarcely an emigrant ship which arrives in our ports that is not, to some extent, freighted with this kind of cargo . . . wearing as the badges of their conviction, chains upon their limbs."[83] He insisted that Europe had no right to "make of the United States a penal colony."[84] In 1866, Charles Sumner stood on the Senate floor holding a German newspaper detailing the practice of transportation to the United States as a substitute for domestic punishment.[85] As a response, the 1875 Page Law banned "persons . . . undergoing sentence for conviction in their own country of felonious crimes other than political."[86] In 1896, a unanimous Senate resolution directed immigration authorities to "inquire whether or not any legislation is necessary to prevent the introduction into the United State of aliens imprisoned in penal colonies of European nations."[87] This idea of criminals at the borders, which lasted for generations, transformed the association between prisons and democracy, federalizing the matter of crime and setting in motion routine increases in carceral capacity because of a nation in need of mass punishment.

In this context of national anxiety about endemic crime, the placement of a flagship institution at the center of the nation was yet another moment in the institutional development of the carceral state rather than the mark of its origins. That institutional development accelerated after 1887, when Congress prohibited states from selling the labor of federal prisoners in state institutions to private entrepreneurs. This led to tensions between federal and state authorities over prison profitability as the number of federal prisoners increased from forty-eight in 1846 to several hundred by 1880 and more than two thousand by 1896.[88] The political push for a new federal prison gained support in the late 1880s when five former presidents, three attorneys general, and countless public interest groups campaigned for the building of a new federal institution to replace the "antiquated and inefficient" system of scattering federal prisoners to the states.[89] This scattering is often interpreted as a sign of federal weakness rather than a function of intergovernmental power guided by federal policy. According to the theory of American statelessness, the federal government went one hundred years without the institutional resources to house its own prisoners.

In moving from the "weak state" framework to a theory of intergovernmental power through the lens of geography and culture, it becomes critically important that it was the Billon Dollar Congress, the first northern/Republican-controlled Congress since the end of Reconstruction, that consolidated federal authority over matters of punishment with the passage of the Three Prisons Act. The Three Prisons Act (1891) required that three prisons be built—one in the West, one in the center, and one in the East—to serve a unifying function in a prison system that differed across regions and local justice cultures. The original legislation called for two prisons on either side of the North-South border to serve as models of penitentiary reform, particularly for southern institutions—those "inhuman, unchristian, if not murderous" institutions in which "some state scandals . . . have shocked the whole public conscience of the country."[90] In response to the North-South orientation of congressional debate, Representative Thomas J. Clunie (D-CA) gave an impassioned plea for law and order in the West. His argument, frequently interrupted by applause, insisted that western states deserved a federal prison in honor of their status as full members of the Union. He argued that this equal distribution of American prisons was a question of democracy:

> We are like the rest of the country; we have our criminal classes, requiring prisons for their confinement. We are a part of this great Republic. . . . We have been treated in the past as if we were not a part . . . of this great nation. . . . We have no public

buildings worthy of note. Our rivers and harbors have been neglected by the General Government.... Now ... we are told that none of our prisoners convicted in the territory west of the Rocky Mountains shall be committed to the prisons ... established under this act.... In all fairness to the people of the great empire west of the Rocky Mountains, ought not their rights be considered in this legislation? ... We are willing to give you a prison north and south, and we claim, as a matter of justice to the entire Pacific Coast, that a prison should also be located west of the Rocky Mountains.... It should be our aim to place all the great States and Territories of this nation on an equal footing.... I appeal to this House for justice.[91]

Clunie's appeal resulted in the rearrangement of the nation's political geography: in addition to Leavenworth at the center, the prison of the East would be built in Atlanta, while the prison of Clunie's dreams was fashioned from a converted territorial prison on McNeil Island in Washington.[92] Because the Three Prisons Act was given no supporting appropriation, federal prisoners remained scattered among the various state, territorial, and military prisons, with over 500 prisoners at Fort Leavenworth and 2,500 in thirty state prisons.[93]

When federal funds were secured in 1896, the government withdrew some of its prisoners from gothic institutions and began the largest prison construction project in US history. The result was a carceral complex that reached radially from Leavenworth to Atlanta and from Leavenworth to McNeil Island. Those lines also extended in theory from the capital, and to the long traditions of penal federalism and carceral citizenship that had originated in the gothic prison towns of the nineteenth century. The reach of intergovernmental power into those places generated a kind of cultural allegiance to the prison as an idea about state governance. In the context of this carceral citizenship, the public clamor for Leavenworth came from grand juries and city councils in St. Louis, Augusta, Huntsville, Chattanooga, and Dallas, where citizens gathered and passed resolutions to locate Leavenworth in their jurisdictions.[94] In letters to the attorney general, federal prisoners and guards in state institutions requested transfers and promises of employment, while judges, reformers, and architects advised that the prison be built in their districts.[95] Others invited themselves into the structure of Leavenworth by offering to build the prison, mostly in places where the boom in prison construction over the course of the nineteenth century had already created a kind of local prison-industrial complex. Railroad companies, merchants, and steel companies specializing in prison architecture wrote to the attorney general to offer presentations on "available models" of steel cages. The Stewart Jail Works Company in Cincinnati notified the federal government of its specialization in "tool proof steel construction, operating devices, and prison locks."[96] These companies were so busy in this early moment in the history of mass incarceration that Adam's Steel and Wireworks Prison and Jail Construction of Joliet, Illinois, wrote that they would be able to show the Department of Justice only a "one-half size working model of two cell fronts designed especially for concrete construction," because the full model was currently on display at the Minnesota State Prison in Stillwater.[97]

FIGURE 4. US Penitentiary, Leavenworth, Kansas. "View of Partially Constructed East Cell Building." Album of Views of United States Penitentiaries at Atlanta, Georgia and Fort Leavenworth, Kansas, circa 1900—circa 1925. Record Group 129, Still Photographs, National Archives II, College Park, Maryland.

Despite the folklore often repeated by the prison's historians that the federal prison system was "weak" before the Bureau of Prisons was established in 1930, the prior strength of the federal carceral state was evidenced in its ability to mark the bodies of its prisoners. In Allison Poe's 1910 book on the reach of the carceral state, he documented the prison's institutional power: "You stand handcuffed to the steel door ten hours a day. . . . Everywhere you look, you are reminded that you are a convict, and that you are in the U.S. Penitentiary. Guards have 'U.S.P.' on the lapels of their coats, 'U.S.P.' is stamped upon the harness, upon the wheelbarrows . . . ; in fact, you cannot look at anything without seeing 'U.S.P.' stamped on it. You are constantly being reminded of the fact that you are a U.S. prisoner."[98] The scale of Leavenworth's operation in the years when federal control was supposed to lack institutional capacity is astounding. In the prison's archive, a 1910 expenditure list appended to a typed appropriations document shows the scale of Leavenworth's economic reach:

For miscellaneous expenditures . . . for fuel, forage, hay, light, water, stationery . . . hay and straw for bedding; blank books, blank forms, type-writing supplies, pencils and memorandum books for guards, books for use in chapel, paper, envelopes, and postage stamps for issue to prisoners; for labor and materials for repairing steam-heating plant, electric plant and water circulation, and drainage; for labor and materials for construction and repair of buildings; for general supplies, machinery, and tools for use on farm and in shops, brickyards, quarry, limekiln, laundry, bathrooms, printing office photograph gallery, stables, policing buildings and grounds; for the purchase of cows, horses, mules, wagons, harness, veterinary supplies, lubricating oils, office furniture, stoves, blankets, bedding, iron bunks, paints and oils, library books, newspapers, and periodicals, electrical supplies; for payment of water supply, telegrams, telephone service, notarial and veterinary services, for advertising in newspapers; for fees to consulting physicians called to determine mental condition of supposed insane prisoners, and for other services in cases of emergency; for pay of extra guards when deemed necessary by the Attorney General, and for expense of care and medical treatment of guards who may be injured by prisoners while said guards are endeavoring to prevent escapes, or suppressing mutiny, forty thousand dollars.[99]

In the blank and preprinted forms of a state that anticipated mutiny, injury, and insanity, the state's carceral capacity was in fact already iconic by the early 1900s. It circulated as an idea in popular culture, in postcard images like the one featured on the book's cover, and in the threat of getting sent "up river" to the Big House.

Leavenworth was an intervention in earlier prison archetypes, and it departed radically from the long tradition of building prisons as obvious illustrations of deprivation. Its facade nevertheless concealed an important gothic subtext: the limestone that gave the building its "federal" look was in fact layered on top of an already existing brick wall, which made it functionally unnecessary except in the presentation of its argument. What the reader of this building could not see was Leavenworth's dungeon—the six unlit, triangular solitary cells detached from the main administrative building. They were designed this way to prevent comfort in sitting or standing. In addition to the dark cells, Building 63 housed the isolation cells, where prisoners either broke rock or were chained in stress positions. The deprivations of infamy included a ball and chain, sometimes called the Oregon Boot, a fifteen-pound shackle bolted around the leg that over time caused the loss of muscle control. Prisoners from this period in the prison's history report brutal physical violence, prolonged sensory deprivation, starvation, the application of shocks through electrical batteries, and even the pumping of ammonia gas into the cells.[100] After Thomas Kating smuggled a twenty-page letter to President Woodrow Wilson in 1913, the socialist newspaper *Appeal to Reason* began a series of investigations into the use of sexualized violence, electrical shock, and the beating death of Clarence Maitland at the hands of the deputy warden in a prison it described as an "instrument of torture."[101] James Bennett, who later became director of the Bureau of Prisons, confirmed the violence, recalling that on his first visit to the institution he saw "men . . . routinely strung up by the thumbs, handcuffed to high bars, kept for weeks in solitary confinement on bread and water . . . whipped, paddled, and spanked, spread-eagled in the hot sun, locked up in sweatboxes, confined in tiny spaces where they can neither sit nor stand."[102] The subsequent reports of federal investigators entering federal prisons read like the earlier generation of state reports that indexed the violence of the carceral gothic. Leavenworth had already become an epicenter of carceral violence.

Against the backdrop of routinized brutality, Public Law 71–218 established the Federal Bureau of Prisons not because federal prisons were perceived as "weak" institutions with little power but because Congress wanted to reign in the power of the wardens. There were already fourteen federal prisons and thirteen thousand prisoners by 1930, and Public Law 71–218 appointed a director of the bureau to improve the "safe-keeping, care, protection, instruction, and discipline" of federal prisoners.[103] It required that federal prisoners be employed and that escaping fugitives be punished with an additional five-year sentence. It criminalized bringing drugs and weapons into a federal prison, which now carried a sentence of "not more than ten years." Systematizing the carceral state brought about another

boom in federal prison construction, and by the end of 1940 the federal apparatus had grown to twenty-four prisons and nearly twenty-five thousand prisoners.
As part of New Deal state building, an "Advance Planning Unit" was created within
the Bureau of Prisons in 1949, which significantly accelerated prison growth in the
United States by developing a "reservoir of blueprints and details for the construction of penal and correctional institutions."[104] These plans "were to be held in
reserve and ready for immediate use in the event economic conditions were such
as to require a nationwide public works program."[105] As a catalog of the prison's
future, the unit's *Handbook of Correctional Institution Design and Construction*,
which was printed by Leavenworth's prisoners, offered a blueprint for mass incarceration that was imaginable only because of the long arc of federal power.

Leavenworth was a critical moment in the centralization of state power, one that
redefined the course of the federal prison system and nationalized the meaning of
punishment. It stands today as a largely unread text. Its radial reach across the
landscape nevertheless signifies a moment between gothic and minimalist trends
in prison architecture and a moment when the prison system was defined by intergovernmental power and a shared commitment to law and order. Because Leavenworth promised to depart from the violence of the carceral gothic but ultimately
returned to state terror as its founding project, it now crowns the very gothic institutions it was designed to end. Some of these institutions, like the Kansas prison,
remain in operation in its shadows, while others, like Pennsylvania, have become
crumbling, timeless artifacts of another era. Haviland's Eastern State leaves today's
visitors "both awestruck and confused by the incomprehensible architecture."[106]
Despite these problems with translation, the meaning of carceral democracy, in
all of its cultural details, remains etched on the surface of the buildings. In the
shape of the prison house door, architects recorded a theory of a carceral state that
was grounded in violence and relied on the institution of civil death.

# 2

# Territorial Politics

## Mass Incarceration and the Punitive Legacies of the
## Indian Territory

*We are reminded that Indian Country had no prisons.*
—LUANA ROSS, *INVENTING THE SAVAGE*

When John Grindstone was convicted of murder in a federal courtroom in Wichita, Kansas, in 1888, he was a prisoner without a prison. As part of a biannual ritual of prosecuting prisoners from the Indian Territory, the courtroom was packed with "murderers, horse thieves, and whiskey prisoners."[1] The "Indian murderer," as he was labeled in the local papers, had taken the stand in his own defense, and when it appeared he might be convicted, his mother slipped him a poisonous root. The *Wichita Star* reported that when officers confiscated the poison, the prisoner was "like a child in the powerful hands of the officers."[2] When the judge handed down a ten-year sentence for murder, he lectured Grindstone with a speech reprinted in the local paper, about "a class of men" in the Indian Territory "who think that to be a man of bravado or desperate character was necessary" and stated that "this class of people have been dealt with very leniently. . . . Hereafter it will be the duty of this court to deal in a most emphatic manner with this class of criminals."[3]

When the judge ordered the US marshal to "deliver or cause to be delivered the body of the said John Grindstone" into federal custody, Grindstone became part of a class of federal prisoners without federal prisons. He was routed to the Kansas State Penitentiary because of the intergovernmental structure of power that existed before Leavenworth. Although states could no longer profit from holding federal prisoners, Kansas agreed to take Grindstone into its gothic castle, where he worked in the prison's coalmine.[4] He remained in state prison until 1895, when Fort Leavenworth's military prison became the temporary home of the federal institution.[5] He was photographed in the military prison as Prisoner No. 12, where he was kept in a "cage," with "iron rods and cross-pieces, with sheet steel partitions, the door of each cell having an ordinary padlock."[6] When hundreds of prisoners

FIGURE 5. John Grindstone. Inmate File No. 3760, Record Group 129, Records of the Bureau of Prisons, US Penitentiary, Leavenworth, National Archives at Kansas City.

were transferred from the military reservation to the newly built federal prison, John Grindstone was catalogued as Prisoner No. 1, the nation's first prisoner.[7] He was released on February 6, 1896, but returned on a seven-year sentence in 1903 as Prisoner No. 3760, when "Leavenworth" was still a pile of rocks encircled by razor wire. The record of his time in the earliest rudimentary structure of the place that became Leavenworth is a forty-two-page inventory of the body that came in and the body that went out—an archive of the marks, scars, and inherited allotments of land in the Indian Territory, and of his death and burial in the prison's graveyard.[8]

The political significance of *United States v. John Grindstone* was that it accelerated the reach of US law into previously unreachable places and laid the groundwork for the emergence of the federal prison system. In Grindstone's trial and punishment, the United States claimed jurisdiction over a Shawnee man accused of killing a Peoria man named Joe Sky on Quapaw land. Crimes between Indians on reservations had been untriable from the 1817 General Crimes Act until 1885, when the Major Crimes Act expanded the reach of US criminal law to all Native peoples on and off the reservations. In federalizing Native crime, the government required federal prison time for "major crimes" against anyone "within or without an Indian reservation."[9] Grindstone's confinement marked a critical juncture in a long attempt to bring indigenous people inside US law.[10] As a Shawnee man from the Quapaw Agency of a place called Indian Territory, Grindstone could have arrived at Leavenworth's gates only through the very specific legal architecture that was used to claim jurisdiction over "Indian crime" in Indian Territory. As the seat of governance for the region, Fort Leavenworth implemented a federal project of "Law for the Indian" as part of a set of disciplinary institutions that included reservations, boarding schools, "Indian asylums," and military guardhouses.[11] The history of Fort Leavenworth, as part of the mass incarceration of Native people, made it a strategic site for the beginning of the nation's first prison. The Three Prisons Act and subsequent legislation brought the prison to Kansas to borrow a military prison with an already existing relationship to the settler colonial carceral state.

Against the backdrop of legal incorporation, Grindstone was the first of a whole cohort of "criminal Indians" sent to Leavenworth from the Indian Territory. Indian Territory prisoners were convicted of a separate class of federalized crimes, including misdemeanor offenses, that could be committed only in Indian Territory. Because this history of the carceral state has largely been forgotten, photographs of Black and Native women from the Indian Territory were not discovered in Leavenworth's papers until 1996, when the Bureau of Prisons transferred the files to the National Archives.[12] In the investigations that followed, their presence was explained away as though they were "just passing through."[13] Nannie Perkins, the first woman ever sentenced to federal time at Fort Leavenworth, arrived on January 19, 1896, after a conviction for "manslaughter in the Indian Territory."[14] Minnie Jones joined her in April of 1896 for the misdemeanor offense of "introduction [of liquor] in the Indian country."[15] Eliza Grayson arrived on May 15, 1896, after a conviction for "assault with intent to kill in the Indian Territory."[16] The prison's first warden, J. W. French, wrote to the attorney general that he had these women "in a building, apart from the men . . . making convict clothing."[17] The second floor of the military prison was "furnished with larger grated cells or cages, in one of which these women were placed together."[18] Nellie Thomas was the last woman to spend the duration of her two-year sentence at Leavenworth; she was kept "locked in her cell" to keep her from the view of male prisoners and was later moved to the back of the prison hospital.[19]

When federal prisoners were transferred from the military site to the construction site beginning in 1895, women prisoners from the Indian Territory were rerouted to the Kansas State Penitentiary, beginning with twenty-one-year-old Mary Snowden, who was marked in the prison files as "Colored (partly Ind)" and was convicted of "assault with intent to kill in Muscogee, North District, Indian Territory."[20] Snowden and other women prisoners from the Indian Territory have federal prison files, but they contain mostly blank intake cards and letters about the continuing coordination between federal and state prisons. Buried in one of these blank sets of files is the story of Lizzie Cardish, who was sent to Leavenworth at the age of fifteen from the Menominee Reservation after a conviction in federal court in the Eastern District of Wisconsin for setting fire to the reservation school. Her "crime" was attributed to her "Indian hatred" and a desire to escape from the reservation and the school.[21] Cardish was never legally transferred from federal to state jurisdiction and was therefore "carried on [the] books as a prisoner belonging to [Leavenworth]."[22] As one of the youngest federal prisoners, Cardish was joined by Dan Tso-Se of the Dine (Navajo) nation, who was convicted of murder at the age of twelve.[23] He was described during a sensationalized trial as "nature boy" because he spoke no English. Because his story was carried in the white newspapers, he received dozens of Christmas cards in the mail. According to the warden, "I tried to explain the meaning of them to him. I also called in two Indians of the Flathead Tribe, but we have no one who can speak his language he being a Navajo. Among *all our Indians* he is the only one of that tribe here."[24]

This targeted "class" from the Indian Territory soon constituted the majority of federal prisoners at Leavenworth. In 1906, when Cardish came to Leavenworth, fully 70 percent of Leavenworth's prisoners were from the Indian Territory and Oklahoma.[25] In 1908, when Tso-Se went on trial, 517 of the 833 prisoners were from the Indian Territory, even though the region no longer legally existed.[26] This class of prisoners was continually described in prison administrative reports and other federal communications as a "very low class of Indians and negroes."[27] Letters from the warden reported a "sorry lot of human beings. . . . Some could give no home and others knew nothing of their parentage. They were composed of negroes, Indians, half-breeds, white men and 'what-nots.'"[28] Making up the majority of federal prisoners, their presence as a mass in the earliest formations of the federal prison system points to a much deeper historical relationship between military and domestic punishments at Fort Leavenworth. Fort Leavenworth was always an idea about punishing Indians.

This chapter historicizes the mass incarceration of prisoners from the Indian Territory by focusing on the relationship between Leavenworth and Fort Leavenworth. It begins by examining the legal history of Indian Territory as a place that was arranged like a prison in order to show that when John Grindstone arrived at Leavenworth he came from the already prisonized space of the Indian Territory. In tracking the narrative production of the "criminal Indian" in Indian Territory, the chapter works to historicize the prison of Indian Territory as a form of settler colonial justice that used space to reorganize land into structures of confinement. When the reservation system failed to "bring in" resistant Indians, federal authorities built a framework of forced legal incorporation as part of the larger project of Law for the Indian.[29] This political architecture produced a subject that was recognized in law only for the purpose of punishment, turning sovereign nations into prisoners said to be guilty at the level of the group.[30] The carceral complex that emerged in this distinction between sovereignty and jurisdiction has continuing consequences. There are currently over four thousand Native people in federal custody, mostly from Oklahoma, the Dakotas, Nebraska, Montana, and Alaska, where Native people make up one-fourth to one-third of people living in state prisons.[31] As a history of the present, this chapter argues that the mass incarceration of Native people is central to the history of the carceral state. The chapter therefore maps how Fort Leavenworth and Leavenworth came into being as ideas about punishing Indians.

ESTABLISHING THE BORDERS OF INDIAN TERRITORY:
THE JURISDICTION OF IMAGINARY RIGHTS

Indian Territory was a region that existed on the land that became Kansas between 1825 and 1854. That land is the ancestral home of the Kansa and Osage peoples, and the Arapaho, Cheyenne, Jicarilla Apache, Kiowa, Kiowa-Apache, Pawnee, and Quapaw also have relationships to the land.[32] In creating the Indian Territory, the US government forcibly relocated the Otoes, Missourias, Iowas, Sacs and Foxes, Kickapoos, Delawares, Shawnees, Chipewas, Ottowas, Peorias, Weas, Kaskaskias, Piankeshaws, Potawatomis, Miamis, Cherokee, Osages, and Quapas from the places that had already become Ohio, Pennsylvania, New York, Indiana, Michigan, Illinois, Georgia, and Missouri. As a site of detention for nearly ten thousand Native people, the Territory was built around Fort Leavenworth, which served as the seat of the region's settler governance after 1827. Fort Leavenworth brought Indian Territory into being and consolidated its status as a region of punishment. It later dissolved and relocated that space to what is now Oklahoma between 1854 and 1890.

Indian Territory was arranged as an unstable and appurtenanced place with an ambiguous but strategic relationship to US law.[33] The idea of Indian Territory as both a jurisdiction and a border emerged as early as 1805, when the United States declared its intention to create peace through control in the region.[34] By 1825, US treaties referred to a "general controlling power," mapping the landscape as a bound legal space.[35] As part of the region's constitution, Fort Leavenworth mapped the Territory into nineteen lateral reservations that restricted movement and thereby increased the power of surveillance. The internal arrangement of the Indian Territory into a kind of panoptic spatial form meant that individuals and groups could be quickly transported to the Fort's military guardhouse for resisting the economic, sociopolitical, and spatial regulation of the region. The political geography of Indian Territory relied on a matrix of punitive institutions, including the military jailhouse, to increase the power of the reservation system. Although the territory was administered by military authorities, its power was derived from its legal position as a kind of borderlands.[36] Federal law, backed by the military, created this kind of appurtenanced structure by way of reference to Native sovereignty, since US law recognized Native people as having legal standing only to the extent that Indians came "by choice" to "occupy" reservations in the Indian Territory. This manipulated relationship between sovereignty as jurisdiction positioned Native people between the status of domestic prisoner and foreign detainee—as subject to the force of law in matters of punishment but as strangers to status and standing.

As a punitive architecture, the political geography of Indian Territory was also imprinted with the radial design of nineteenth-century prison architecture.

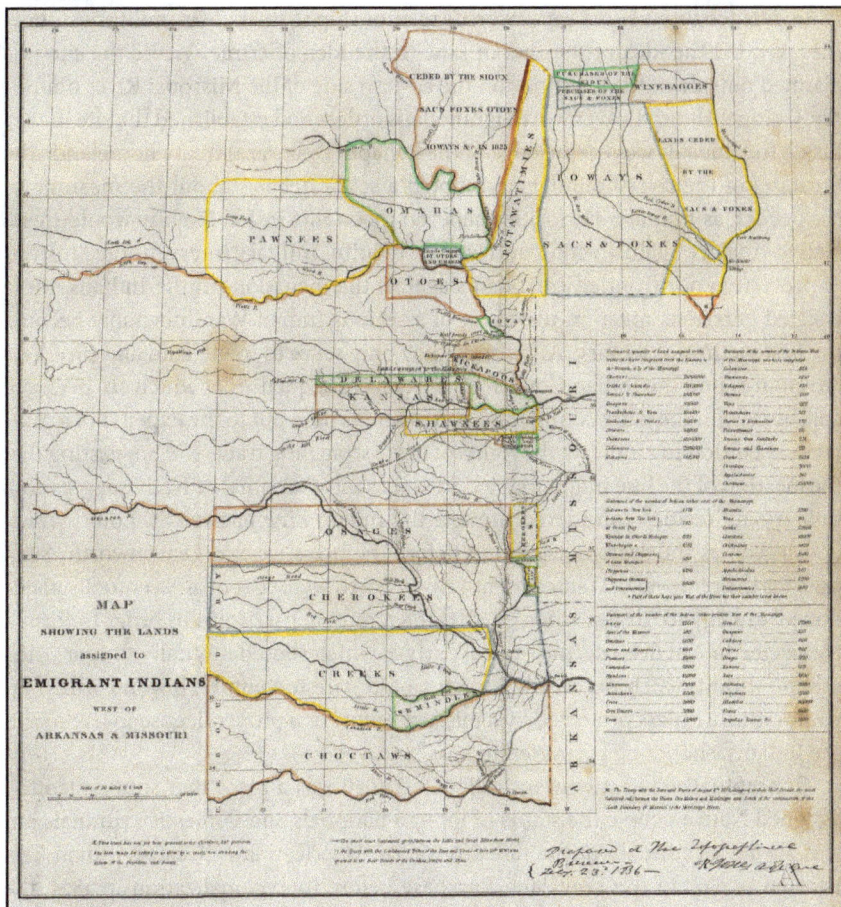

FIGURE 6. *Map Showing the Lands Assigned to Emigrant Indians West of Arkansas and Missouri,* 1836. Courtesy of the Library of Congress, US Topographical Bureau.

Established on the eastern edge of the Territory, Fort Leavenworth marked the radial point of all roads leading west from the center of the US border. It was the central node of the whole apparatus (the guard tower in Jeremy Bentham's formulation) and "opened four or five great military roads, diverging from this point like the ribs of a fan, and traversing the Territory in every direction—to the Rocky Mountains, Santa Fe, Salt Lake, California and Oregon."[37] Standing in the place normally reserved for the prison's administration, Fort Leavenworth governed the region's economic and political structure, instituting by force the separation of Indian Territory from the United States. This separation was part of an idea about an "Indian Line" that would "protect" US citizens from lawless Indians.

In debates about Fort Leavenworth's relationship to the border, military authorities wedded the idea of the Indian Line to the idea of crime. While the site was
planned outside of the Territory on the eastern side of the Missouri River boundary, Colonel Henry Leavenworth ignored his orders and established the site in 1827
inside the line.[38] It was on the edge of the Lenape (Delaware) treaty homeland. The
breaking of the river boundary prompted a set of debates about the meaning of
the border, as military authorities believed that a fort inside the line would incite
Native violence against whites and would "require" military intervention: "Instead
of protecting our frontier inhabitants against the incursions of the Indians, these
isolated garrisons must, in the event of a serious Indian War, inevitably become
the first victims of its fury. At present, they only serve to invite wild and profitless
adventures into the Indian Country, the usual consequences of which are personal
collisions with the natives, and the government is then put to the expense of a military expedition to vindicate the rights of these straggling traders."[39] Suggesting that
the location of the line might make US citizens into "victims" of Native aggression,
military authorities considered moving the Indian Line back to St. Louis, which
had served as the region's legal hub before the press west to Leavenworth. Such
calls for the removal of Cantonment Leavenworth were part of an eventually abandoned strategy to "draw . . . in . . . [the] most remote garrisons, in order to form a
connected line of defense, the several parts of which should mutually support each
other—within which no hostile Indian would dare to venture, beyond which no
white citizen, unless protected by a military escort or a proper license to trade with
the Indians, should be permitted to pass."[40]

Conceptualized as a border, Indian Territory was a place that simultaneously
assigned Native people the status of foreign nationals and domestic criminals but
was always an idea about the failed reach of American law. Because Indian Territory was part of the Louisiana Purchase before its regionalization in 1825, the
region's first major murder trial in 1808 was held in St. Louis, and it generated a
narrative of lawless criminal Indians and the law's failure to punish them. In Louisiana Territory's courts, White Cloud and Mira Natutais (both Ioway) and Little
Crow (Sac and Fox) were convicted and sentenced to death for the murder of a
white man.[41] The Superior Court of the Louisiana Territory ruled that both Ioway
men were unpunishable according to the terms of the 1802 Intercourse Act. This
ruling by Judge John B. C. Lucas meant that Ioway Indians who injured whites in
the Indian Territory were not subject to US jurisdiction. Acknowledging the creation of an untriable class of Indians, the court reversed the convictions of the two
Ioway men but affirmed the death sentence of the Sac and Fox Little Crow on the
grounds that his crime had taken place on land already ceded to the United States
in 1804.[42] Despite the court's affirmation of Little Crow's death sentence, President
Jefferson commuted his sentence.

Against the backdrop of jurisdictional ambiguity, the "Ioway Fugitives" came to
symbolize the contested status of US law in the Indian Territory. Not only did the

men escape from punishment according to the terms of settler justice, but Native people had come to St. Louis in support of the prisoners. According to St. Louis newspapers, the streets of the city during the trial "teemed" with "Indian warriors who remittently beseeched and harassed Lewis and General Clark to pardon their tribesmen."[43] In an open challenge to the right of US law to punish Indians and to the state's attempt to take three Indian lives for the death of one white man, the men asserted sovereignty in the face of jurisdiction and escaped from the St. Louis jailhouse unpursued by territorial officials.[44] Their escape became a symbol of the law's failure to reach an "untriable" class of "criminal Indians" just beyond the nation's boundaries and was a catalyst for the eventual rearrangement of Indian Territory.

The legal architecture of the Indian Territory was designed to capture this unpunishable class by creating a framework of group guilt in a legal system designed to punish individuals.[45] Indian Territory became a punitive landscape that functioned to assign group criminality after 1828, when Fort Leavenworth enforced substitution punishments as a matter of federal policy. When an Ioway named Big Neck (also known as Great Walker and Moanahonga) could not be located by military authorities who were investigating the killing of three whites, the Ioway Chief White Cloud was arrested in his place and was taken to Fort Leavenworth with nineteen other men to await Big Neck's capture or surrender. After his eventual surrender, Big Neck's friend Walking Cloud or Pompakin later testified from Fort Leavenworth that he and Big Neck had in fact prevented more deaths—that he had "stayed in jail all winter" to "save my young men."[46] Five years later, in 1833, when the US military punished the Ioway for retaliating against the Omaha during a period of conflict, White Cloud was again forced to submit the guilty parties, and the US military "marched eight Ioways to Fort Leavenworth."[47] White Cloud was later killed by one of the men he surrendered. This practice of substitution punishment was confirmed as a matter of federal policy in President Jackson's 1830 message: "We will march into your country . . . seize your chiefs and principal men and hold them until those who shed blood shall be surrendered to me."[48] Jackson's policy held the nation responsible for the acts of individuals, so that "criminal Indians" could no longer "hide behind the tribe."[49]

The legal composition of Indian Territory was rooted in this idea of group guilt not just because of the escape of the Ioway Fugitives or the use of substitution punishments in the Fort Leavenworth jailhouse. The people of the Indian Territory were also seen as criminally disloyal because of their status as "enemy nations" during the US War of 1812. These nations were considered enemies because the Sac, Delaware, Otoe, Omaha, Shawnee, and Kickapoo fought the United States in alliance with the British, who partially destroyed the US Capitol and White House. Because the nations of the Indian Territory were configured by law as foreign prisoners of war despite declarations of peace, they were detained in the Indian Territory according to the terms of the 1825 Treaty of Prairie du Chien, which formally ended the war in "peace and friendship" but gave the United States a "controlling power" over "disloyal" Indians.[50]

The power of this settler colonial regime was maintained by irons and chains. When the Sac and Fox fought in Black Hawk's War in 1831, Black Hawk was captured and paraded in irons in front of the famed Pennsylvania prison, where he was, according to white newspapers, "shown the manner in which white men punish."[51] Relying on the logic of substitution punishments, the US military marched twenty-two Missouri Sac and Fox to Fort Leavenworth in irons to punish Black Hawk's Illinois Sac and Fox. The exchange of the "murderous savages" who fought US jurisdiction in 1831 was still being discussed in Bureau of Indian Affairs (BIA) reports as late as 1862, and the memory of punishment among Black's Hawk's people was such that when four Sac and Fox men were later taken to Fort Leavenworth on charges of murder they agreed to walk seventy miles with two unarmed guards in order to avoid the taint of chains.[52] In this economy of interchangeable Indians, the fort had become a symbol of conquest—an "unmerciful dungeon" within an already prisonized landscape.[53]

The idea of Leavenworth as an idea about the fungibility of criminal Indians was formalized in federal law with the 1834 Intercourse Act, which served as Indian Territory's first governing charter and put law "in force in the Indian country."[54] Establishing a form of administrative rule over ten thousand people in the Territory, the act classified the region as "part of the United States west of the Mississippi and not within the states of Missouri and Louisiana, or the territory of Arkansas."[55] Carving out a landscape that was both part of and separate from the United States, the act claimed "sole and exclusive jurisdiction" over "assigned" and "occupied" lands in a moment when whiteness was being settled into law as a propertied expectation.[56] The act gave officers at Fort Leavenworth the power to monitor transactions at the region's boundaries, where authorities searched steamboats for the introduction of liquor, distributed fines for trade license violations, arrested criminal Indians and white trespassers fleeing to the Indian Territory, and regulated the "character" of residents, visitors, and "persons merely traveling in the Indian country."[57] This closed political economy established a system of credit and debt in order to create an incentive structure that, as Thomas Jefferson described it, produced debt "beyond what the individuals can pay" so that only "a cession of lands" could level the balance.[58] This "factory system" of law subverted Native sovereignty into US jurisdiction by using debt to create punishable Indians.

Mapping administrative authority onto economic regulation, the 1834 Act also assigned white "Indian agents" to the reservations, who regulated matters of justice and governed reservations like prison wardens. On the Great Nemaha Reserve, where the Ioway and Sac and Fox nations were concentrated, the agent routinely "laid on the stripes for waywardness" and threatened the use of iron chains.[59] When the Ioway left the reservation without permission in 1849 to join a traveling exhibition, local newspapers reported that the Ioway would be punished with physical violence.[60] The act distributed among the reservation agents the power to "procure the arrest and trial of *all Indians accused of committing any crime, offence, or misdemeanor . . . either by demanding the same of the chiefs of the proper tribe,* or by such other means as the President may authorize."[61] In the process, it distorted and destabilized Native justice traditions by giving selected "chiefs" the authority to transfer criminal Indians to US jurisdiction, even as it subordinated the power of those authorities to US law. By 1836, Indian Territory was inside US law for the purpose of punishment but according to a Senate Committee on Indian Affairs Report was "a place which will ever remain an outside."[62]

In the context of this dual framework, Indian Territory emerged as an idea about a line that Indians were not permitted to cross; Fort Leavenworth was a symbol of economic and penal conquest in a region that functioned, at multiple registers, like a prison. Its founding legal narrative, however, was failure—the 1834 Intercourse Act prevented American law from reaching crimes committed by one Indian person against another Indian person. Because the punitive authority of Indian agents reached only Indians who committed crimes against whites and government agents, an unreachable class of "reservation crimes" turned unlicensed white trespassers into residents who defended themselves against "Indian occupiers" and "Indian criminals." Throughout the 1840s, federal authorities condemned the Delaware, Ioway, Sac and Fox, Kickapoo, and Shawnee as "beggars" who "harassed" soldiers and settlers on the trails. Acts of resistance to white invasion were refashioned as apolitical and criminal acts of theft, assault, and murder. BIA reports confirm that Native people in the Indian Territory were "regarded as intruders" and "criminal Indians."[63]

It was this narrative of "crime on the trails" and the fear of an "Indian crime wave" that ultimately justified the land theft of a territorialized Kansas in 1854.[64] The routine punishment of "property crime" on the trails was anchored in the war that ensued after the Lakota High Forehead ate an ox that was wandering on the trails. Following the established procedures of agency law, Brave Bear acted on behalf of the group to restore the value of the property to the Mormons who had reported it stolen. Lieutenant John Grattan nevertheless demanded that High Forehead be surrendered for punishment, and when Brave Bear refused to turn him over, Grattan attacked the Lakota people. When Grattan and thirty-one US soldiers died in the attack, the US military condemned Grattan's actions but plotted revenge at Fort Leavenworth throughout the winter of 1855. When Brave Bear died of his wounds in the spring, Sinte Gleske (Spotted Tail), Red Leaf, and Long Chin retaliated by attacking a mail train and killing three whites in Nebraska. In the war that followed, the logic of group punishment led to the capture of one hundred Lakota women and children, who were held hostage at Fort Laramie, Wyoming, until Sinte Gleske, Red Leaf, and Long Chin presented their own bodies for punishment.[65] When the men "came in," they were marched to Fort Leavenworth, manacled by ball-and-chains "bigger than those for the cannons on their feet, their women going sorrowfully behind them."[66] After a winter in Leavenworth's military guardhouse, where it was rumored they would be hanged, Sinte Gleske was released by President Pierce in January of 1856 and was paraded before the prisons of Washington and New York. During this exhibition of the punishment that awaited resistant Indians, Sinte Gleske inquired whether any of the prisoners in those institutions had ever been convicted of "stealing from Indians."[67] "Crime on the trails" turned the Indian Line that had brought Leavenworth into being into a border now condemned for having "shut in" white citizens, separating them from the westernmost territories.[68] Indian Territory was now a kind of legal island in the nation's center, and the prison had become simultaneously a site of conquest and a site of resistance.

When Indian Territory was recast as a structure that contained whites instead of Indians, it was dissolved in the transition to Kansas Territory. Fort Leavenworth was the center of a military operation that relocated the people of the old Indian Territory to the land that would later become Oklahoma. As trespassers without rights, the nations of the old Indian Territory were caught in a "choice" that was structured to make whiteness a matter of survival—Native people could "choose" to accept citizenship and "become white" or to fight for the right to remain Indian.[69] Despite the threat of military detention at Fort Leavenworth, the Kickapoo, Iowa, Prairie Band Potawatomi, and Sac and Fox nations remain to this day on treaty homelands.[70] The Delaware people have also reclaimed land in the old Indian Territory.[71] In the territorialization of Kansas, one-quarter of the Indian Territory "passed by the treaty process from Indian ownership to individuals, land-speculating companies, and railroads without becoming a part of the public domain or becoming subject to congressional control."[72]

Even after Kansas became a state, the federal government declared its intention to maintain jurisdiction over "Indians in Kansas." State criminal laws focused on "murderous Indians" in *United States v. John Ward* (1863), arguing that "the general punishment of crime including murder is not of the class of subjects on which the federal government has a direct authority to legislate."[73] The state argued that denying Kansas the right to punish criminal Indians deprived it of statehood and a sense of national membership. Kansas reasserted the right of criminal prosecution in *Hunt v. Kansas* (1866), which declared that Indians were "in Kansas," even those who lived "like Indians" on reservations.[74] *Hunt* relied on the idea that Indians were equivalent to foreigners, an idea that emerged in *Dred Scott v. Sandford* (1857) when the court situated Native people as simultaneously foreign and domestic.[75] But federal courts claimed ultimate jurisdiction in *The Kansas Indians* (1867), ruling that "where Indians occupy lands *the ultimate title of which is in the federal government,* it is settled that no State which, subsequently, may be created around those lands has any right over them in the absence of express treaties or congressional legislation to that effect."[76]

Targeting a subject of its own making, the federal project of Law for the Indian created separate categories of "Indian crime" that punished group guilt in a framework built for legal individuals. This was the legal architecture of a system that expanded its reach into "intra-Indian" spaces that, despite state and federal claims to jurisdiction, remained on the edges of law. Indian Territory was a system of reservations designed to institute joint administrative and military rule. Fort Leavenworth anchored that legal regime as a carceral state framework of settler colonial justice. Because Indian Territory was a place defined by the project of legal incorporation, resistance to the prison as a form of justice threw the reservation system into crisis. The response to this crisis was the federal prison system.

## LAW FOR THE INDIAN AND THE CRISIS OF THE RESERVATION SYSTEM

Against the backdrop of a line turned barrier and the end of an Indian Territory, Law for the Indian now recognized two classes of Indians—those who had already "come in" to the prison of the new Indian Territory and those who insisted on the right to "stay out." Over the course of the 1850s, as Leavenworth dissolved the line it had once held in place, it used its radial reach to "bring in" those who refused the reservation system through a series of military expeditions. From Fort Leavenworth, soldiers marched against the Kiowas and Comanches in 1851, the Lakota, Brulé, and Miniconjous in 1855, and the Cheyenne in 1857.[77] Between 1865 and 1891, the army fought a thousand times with the Apache, Modoc, Cheyenne, Ute, Nimiipuu (Nez Perce), Comanche, Kiowa, and Kickapoo. As Law for the Indian was reoriented from the concentrated space of a territory designed like a prison to the "unwieldy" space of the "frontier," it created communities of free and unfree people with different relationships to US law. Fort Leavenworth remained the political center of the new Indian Territory and widened its reach during the "Indian Wars" to all Indians "inside the United States." The twin projects of legal incorporation and mass incarceration anchored the spatial arrangement of the new Indian Territory.

This meant that the struggle over the reservation system was also about the legal framework of mass capture and incarceration. This was evidenced in the Dakota Uprising of 1862, the largest mass escape from the reservation system and the largest mass execution in US history. When the Dakota left the reservation to confront whites claiming title to homelands and to insist that treaty agreements since 1805 be honored, they were punished by the assignment of "enemy" status, the confinement of nearly one thousand people, and the mass trial and conviction of 303 defendants.[78] On the eve of their execution, US president Lincoln divided the condemned into two classes—those who had committed "massacres" and those who had engaged in "battles."[79] The thirty-eight men who had committed "massacres" were found guilty of capital murder *at the level of the group* and were executed as a mass on December 26, 1862. This was a key moment in the history of mass incarceration because it defined the line between acts of war and domestic crimes and consolidated federal power over Indian punishments.

Despite the threat of mass execution and punishment, escapes from the reservation system increased and "unreserved" Indians refused to recognize the right of the United States to establish them. These mass escapes threw the whole system of Law for the Indian into crisis. When a confederation of the Cheyenne, Arapaho, Kiowa, Comanche, and Kiowa-Apache nations refused to "come in" to reservation spaces, they were described in BIA annual reports as "wild and intractable" and "in need of severe punishment."[80] Speaking of these continuing escapes, US Army Lieutenant-General Philip Sheridan insisted that "the whole reservation system of the government—which is the only true policy now left—will be endangered unless every one of these Indians are taken back and made to stay."[81] In the system of legal classification in BIA Reports, the 55,000 Native people entirely "unrelated" to US law were compared to the 150,000 "disciplined" Indians already on reservations. Another 95,000 were "in relation" with an agency but opposed to relocation.[82] The federal government would pursue the "roamers" under the guise of President Grant's Peace Policy, which defined peace as delayed US military attacks until treaties could be "signed" under threat of military violence. Grant's Peace Policy instituted a form of what the BIA described as "legalized reformatory control" through which "marauding bands" would be "relentlessly crushed" by mass "arrest and return to Indian Territory."[83]

The use of the new Indian Territory as a kind of prison was made explicit in the US government's treatment of the Cheyenne nation in the late 1870s. The Cheyenne justice tradition was rooted in banishment, and only sixteen murders were committed in the history of the nation.[84] After an attack on a wagon train passing through Kansas in 1874, Cheyenne justice was represented as so inherently violent that it became the basis of white "captivity" narratives in American literature.[85] In 1990, the German family and the Cheyenne people held a peace ceremony that drew 1,200 people to acknowledge the taking of four white girls and the killing of their parents and to acknowledge the injustice of the punishments that followed.[86] In addition to the fifteen Cheyenne actually accused of violence, eighteen others were marched 165 miles from Fort Sill, Oklahoma, to Fort Leavenworth, Kansas.[87] They were loaded onto trains bound for the old colonial prison at Fort Marion, Florida.[88] Refusing to spend three years at the former Spanish colonial prison in Florida, Grey Beard and Heap of Birds took their own lives; Grey Beard jumped "in chains and shackles" from the moving train, only to be shot in the back by his captors.[89] The military subsequently sent misleading messages to the Colorado Cheyenne in Grey Beard's voice, directing them to "avoid trouble" and "travel in the white man's road."[90] In the use of substitution punishments, the settler state came to rely on the taking of hostages.

US and Cheyenne relations were supposed to be governed by the Fort Laramie Treaty of 1851, but the Fort Wise Treaty of 1861 reduced the Cheyenne land base to a site in eastern Colorado near Sand Creek.[91] Although the United States had previously distinguished the northern Cheyenne from the "peaceful Southern

Cheyenne," it made no distinction between "hostile" and "civilian" Indians in the Sand Creek Massacre, when eight hundred southern Cheyenne were offered "perfect safety" by the US military in exchange for "coming in" and then were killed in a massacre that even the US military acknowledged was a crime of "cold blood."[92] Between Sand Creek in 1864 and the Battle of Washita in 1868, the US military killed every last peace chief of the Southern Cheyenne, capturing fifty-three women and children and holding them in a stockade at Fort Dodge, Kansas.[93] This logic of group guilt meant that by the "Great Sioux War" of 1876, 980 northern Cheyenne fought alongside the Lakota and Arapaho and were condemned for the "crime" of Custer's death at Little Bighorn.[94] After the infamous arrest and murder of the Lakota Crazy Horse in September of 1877, 980 northern Cheyenne were sentenced without trial to a one-year term in the prison of Indian Territory.[95]

When they arrived in the region, they found that their one-year term was a ruse and that their permanent confinement was secured by cannons pointed at the lodges. In a gesture of mass defiance of the reservation-prison, 284 members of the northern Cheyenne walked away from Indian Territory, under cover of night, in the winter of 1878. They ran 1,500 miles pursued by the US military across the former Indian Territory of Kansas, where the Cheyenne were said to have "raided" and "murdered" for food and supplies.[96] While Dull Knife's people "came in" to Red Cloud's agency in South Dakota to claim a place with the Lakota, Little Wolf's band chose to "stay out" for another winter after seeing that Dull Knife's people were treated like prisoners on the Red Cloud reservation. Of those who stayed out, all thirty-four were captured and taken to Fort Keogh for military trial, where they negotiated the terms of a Northern Reservation in Montana.[97] Dull Knife's people, who had laid down arms, were transported from the Red Cloud Agency to Fort Robinson, Nebraska, where they were held by the military in a "prison room" and were denied food and water until they agreed to return to the Indian Territory. On the fifth day of their confinement they ran from the prison, in the dead of winter, and were met by the bullets of the soldiers. The survivors reunited with Little Wolf's people. Their survival was recognized as a crime in BIA reports that criticized a "tribe" still "in need" of punishment.[98]

Kansas also clamored to punish the Cheyenne for the state's "last Indian raid," which had resulted in a failed trial in 1879 and their photograph on the steps of the Dodge City courthouse. They were symbols of the failure of American law and evidence that Indians had "never been controlled."[99] As late as 1885, the Indian agent still complained that the Cheyenne "commit crimes constantly and demand heavy tributes for the privilege of driving through their country. Many of the Indians who commit such crimes are known to me, but I have thus far been powerless to arrest or punish them. . . . A worse class of savages probably never existed . . . up to the present time. . . . They have never been controlled. . . . They complain freely, and force the remedy for their complaints at the mouths of their 'Winchester Rifles'; and they have plenty of them."[100] The prisonization of the new Indian Territory was a process that relied on this narrative of constant crime and federal powerlessness. In the wake of mass capture and punishment, the arrangement of the second Indian Territory recalled the structure of the first but developed its own federal legal architecture.

## MAJOR CRIMES, INDIAN JAILS, AND THE POLITICAL GEOGRAPHY OF THE QUAPAW AGENCY

The second Indian Territory was arranged, like the first, according to the terms of sovereignty and jurisdiction. While the Five Nations were sovereign powers, the rest of the Territory and the Quapaw Agency in particular were part of a jurisdictional matrix that presumed the joint presence of foreign enemies and domestic criminals. The Quapaw Agency was a reservation in the far northeast corner of the Territory that would survive the transition from Indian Territory to Oklahoma Territory to Oklahoma precisely because it came to serve as the region's site of detention. Native people confined in that space were said to have resisted US law by force. Some were considered prisoners of war. Among these were the Modoc and the Nimiipuu (Nez Perce). When John Grindstone was sent to federal prison in 1889, he came from the prison of the Quapaw Agency.

The Cherokee, Choctaw, Chickasaw, Seminole, and Muskogee nations were sovereign peoples in the Indian Territory, but their presence resulted from the Trail of Tears and the logic of dislocation. US claims to jurisdiction over sovereign nations were anchored in the terms of the Reconstruction Treaties, signed between 1865 and 1868, which condemned Five Nations "alliances" with the Confederacy during the Civil War.[101] Establishing the right of the federal government to build and operate courts of justice in the Indian Territory, the Reconstruction Treaties gave the Five Nations jurisdiction over matters of justice when "members of the nation, by nativity or adoption, shall be the only parties."[102] As part of the complicated layers of settler colonial administration, the Five Nations began operating prisons as expressions of qualified self-governance. The Cherokee National Prison at Tahlequah opened in 1875 and operated as the only penitentiary inside Indian Territory until 1901, when Congress "expired" Cherokee law and closed the prison.[103] The Choctaw experiment with imprisonment in 1859, the Chickasaw adaptation of death by hanging, and the Choctaw, Seminole, and Muskogee adoption of the firing squad conformed to US demands regarding the proper form of administering justice.[104] Despite the adoption of US justice practices in instances where Indians committed crimes against other Indians, these methods of punishment were soon condemned as barbarous punishments of "Indian law." Having naturalized the prison in Indian Territory, federal Indian law used the institution to justify a renewed push for total jurisdictional control.

The reach of US law into intra-Indian crime on the reservations in the second Indian Territory originated with federal jurisdictional claims over whites committing crime on the reservations. In 1846, the US Supreme Court in *United States v. Rogers* had ruled that treaty homelands were merely a "domicile for the tribe. . . . They hold and occupy it with the assent of the US." The Court gained jurisdiction over "crimes between Indians" because of the legal groundwork established in a case where a white man had "become Indian" by marriage.[105] In refuting William Rogers's claim that intermarriage placed him outside the bounds of US jurisdiction (he said he was an intermarried Indian who had committed a crime against another intermarried Indian), *United States v. Rogers* (1846) confirmed the reach of US criminal law to American-born white men who had "become Indian" by marrying Cherokee women even when the crime occurred inside Cherokee lines.[106] In asserting that Rogers was "not an Indian" but that *it had legal access to the reservation space* he inhabited, the Court imagined the future intrusions of jurisdiction, first over whites assuming Indian identities, and then over Indians who committed crimes against other Indians. Five Nations governments retained limited control over "internal" matters of punishment, but crimes committed off the reservation were considered federal crimes.

The legal arrangement of the Indian Territory was bound by the federal court at Fort Smith, Arkansas, which regulated a region made famous in "wild west" depictions of a place without the machinery of law. Administered by the "hanging judge" Isaac Parker, the court at Fort Smith condemned more people to death in group executions than any court in US history.[107] Forty-one percent of prisoners executed at Fort Smith were Native American; 11 of them were Cherokee, Choctaw, and Creek.[108] Being "dragged to Fort Smith in irons," as the practice was described in the *Cherokee Advocate,* was part of a powerful ritual of punishment in a region where Native, Black, and white criminals intermingled, sheltered by the absence of law.[109] The fugitive status of the Indian Territory was grounded not just in the mass presence of "criminal Indians" but in the complex status of Black Exodusters, who had fled the South to build new lives in all-Black towns.[110] There was also a class of thirty-five thousand white trespassers in the Territory, whose land claims were eventually authorized by the federal government but who remained criminalized "Sooners" in the national imaginary.[111] Condemned in the Cherokee press as "morally unfit to live anywhere outside of prison walls," this class of lawless whites was sometimes celebrated in American popular culture in the songs of schoolchildren: "Oh, what was your name in the States, Was it Thompson, or Johnson, or Bates? Did you murder your wife, and fly for your life? Say, what was your name in the States?"[112] The inability of the federal court at Fort Smith to fully control lawlessness in the region led to its description in the *Congressional Record* as the "Botany Bay of the United States."[113] In comparing the region to a penal colony, federal authorities called for new methods of containment that rearranged territorial law.

The resultant legal project of bringing Indian Territory inside law led to the formation of the Quapaw Agency as a place for the "mostly remnants" of nations that had refused to lay down arms against the United States. Unlike the other regions of the Indian Territory, which were punished at Fort Smith, the 1,076 people of the Quapaw Agency were sent directly to Fort Leavenworth for punishment.[114] Named after the "least developed" and most "indolent, intemperate, and demoralized" people on the reservation, the Quapaw Agency was designed to "teach" nonresistance by mixing "wild" and "domesticated" Indians in a system of colonial administrative rule driven by violence and profit.[115] The Quapaw people were arranged among the 160 Peorias, Kaskaskias, Weas, and Piankeshaws, 150 Ottawas, 90 Eastern Shawnee and 75 Black Bob Shawnee, 222 Wyandottes, and 214 Senecas so that they might learn the power of American punishment.[116] When they were later joined by the Modoc and Nimiipuu (Nez Perce) peoples, the Quapaw served as a zone of legal ambiguity that created the conditions of Leavenworth's future.

Formally designated as prisoners of war, the Modoc were sent first to Alcatraz and then to the Quapaw Agency in the Indian Territory in 1873 for "war crimes" against the United States. The Modoc had fought the US military in the lava beds of Northern California over treaty agreements and forced relocations. During a "peace council" to which both sides brought arms, a Modoc man named Captain Jack shot US general Canby because it was rumored that the military "had a pile of wood already built up, and were going to burn [him] there."[117] In the Modoc War Crimes Trial that followed, Captain Jack was found guilty along with fifty-five other "Indian outlaws."[118] After the trial, the guilt of the nation was explained in a formal statement read to the prisoners on the gallows: "The history of your tribe is filled with murders of the white race. . . . These acts have placed you and your band outside the rules of civilized warfare. In other words, you have made yourselves outlaws."[119] When Captain Jack, Schonchin John, Black Jim, and Boston Charley were hanged on Alcatraz Island in 1873, army doctors beheaded the Modoc in the name of craniology, displaying their skulls for the next one hundred years at the Army Medical Museum and Smithsonian.[120] Barncho and Sloluck were given a last-second pardon on the gallows and were imprisoned on Alcatraz Island, where Barncho died in 1875 and Sloluck remained until 1878, when he was sent to Fort Leavenworth and then on to the prison of the Indian Territory.[121] Eventually, the entire Modoc nation would follow for "violation of the rules of honorable warfare."[122]

Considered guilty at the level of the group, the Modoc were recognized as a sovereign nation in order to be condemned as foreign criminals of war. This was a departure from the legal status previously assigned to Modoc people, who were considered "civilian Indians" "free" to move about treaty homelands in California and Oregon with passes issued by county courts.[123] When Captain Jack traveled off the reservations in 1868, the court declared that he was "an independent freeman entitled to the protection of life, liberty, and the pursuit of happiness by the laws of civilization."[124] Because the shift from civilian to foreign status removed the possibility of criminal punishment, it created contention over the terms of Modoc punishment. General Davis, for example, in pressing for mass execution, described "a band of Indian outlaws—murderers if you please—wards of the government who had revolted against its authority."[125] The *New York Tribune* suggested that treating "common criminals" as prisoners of war was wrong because the Modoc were "mere outlaws and marauders, no more entitled to belligerent rights than so many ruffians escaped from Sing Sing."[126] When it was decided that the rest of the Modoc nation would be sent to the Quapaw Agency on a sentence of thirty-six years, they were locked in a makeshift stockade as prisoners of war, but their hair was cut like that of domestic prisoners.[127] The placement of the Modoc in the Indian Territory was a structure of mass incarceration defined by the space of the Quapaw Agency.

While the Modoc punishment in the Indian Territory was rooted in the legal distinction between sovereign belligerents and domestic criminals, the US military treated the Nimiipuu (Nez Perce) as "captives" entirely without status at Fort Leavenworth and later in the Indian Territory. The Nimiipuu (Nez Perce) were placed into the structure of the Quapaw Agency after refusing to abide by the terms of treaty deception in 1855; this required them to move to what they called the "dead lands" of the proposed reservation.[128] Chief Joseph, Looking Glass, White Bird, and Toohoolhoolzote, and Palus men named Husus Kute and Hahtalekin, were punished as leaders of the "Non-Treaty Nez Perce," and were pursued by US forces from Oregon across Idaho and Montana to a place forty miles from the Canadian border.[129] General Oliver Otis Howard threatened to send Chief Joseph and his people to the prison of Indian Territory "if it takes years and years."[130] In the Nez Perce "surrender," an agreement that they could return to their homeland was broken, and William Tecumseh Sherman insisted on executions and treating "what are left" just "like the Modocs, sent to some other country."[131] Sherman described their status as that of "prisoners" whose "wishes should not be consulted. When the time comes, they should be located on ground at the convenience of the Government, and not of their choice."[132]

Although the US "campaign" was never formally recognized as war, General Howard directed his soldiers to "treat them as prisoners of war, and provide for them accordingly," but neither Congress nor the military ever made a formal appropriation to support indefinite detention.[133] After they arrived on fourteen river flatboats and eleven old passenger cars of the Great Northern Railroad, Chief Joseph's fame as the defeated "Red Napoleon" brought spectators and military bands to stations along the route.[134] The local newspaper in Leavenworth published daily reports of camp life in the center of the horse-racing track that is now Sherman Army Air Field: "Quite a large number of ladies from the garrison and citizens from 'downtown' were on the ground to see the new arrivals."[135] While the camp was treated as a kind of museum, open latrine trenches, leaking tents, and malarial infections caused twenty-one deaths at Fort Leavenworth.[136] The War Department eventually confessed that Nez Perce imprisonment was "of little importance" to the military and requested that responsibility be transferred to the Office of Indian Affairs.[137] William Tecumseh Sherman, who had once argued for mass execution, conceded that "if the Indian Bureau cannot, or will not, provide for these captives," they should be released from "captivity at Fort Leavenworth, Kansas," and be allowed to "find employment where they can. This is cruel, but it seems the law provides no remedy."[138]

In the transfer of penal authority over Nimiipuu (Nez Perce) detention, they were relocated to federal jurisdiction and what elders called the Eeikish Pah (the hot place). They were located first next to the Modoc on the Quapaw Agency, but after the deaths of eighty-four people they were allowed to "choose" a less punitive reservation in Indian Territory beyond the boundaries of the Quapaw.[139] Joseph gave a series of published interviews that increased public pressure to send the Nimiipuu (Nez Perce) home, but continued detention in the Indian Territory was justified on the grounds that thirty-one of them had been indicted *in absentia* for the murder of settlers in the First District Court of Idaho. After seven years of confinement under joint federal-military jurisdiction, they were finally released in 1884 and sent to the Lapwai and Colville reservations in Idaho and Washington, where Chief Joseph's people were joined to the Confederated Tribes of the Colville Reservation in Washington.[140] The treatment of the Nimiipuu (Nez Perce) people illustrates not only the structure of sovereignty and jurisdiction that anchored the Quapaw's relationship to Indian Territory and to Leavenworth but also how this legal ambiguity enabled forms of erasure that came to define Law for the Indian. Recognized only for the purpose of punishment, the nations of the Indian Territory were located in a carceral state that came to define the course of the federal prison system.

This creation of separate federal crimes for Indians accelerated in the early 1880s, when the secretary of the interior established the Courts of Indian Offenses (1883) and Congress passed the Major Crimes Act (1885) in response to the Supreme Court's decision in *Ex Parte Crow Dog*. As building blocks in the architecture that became Leavenworth, these legal arrangements sought to bring Native people inside US law and therefore inside US prisons. The Courts of Indian Offenses were designed to increase the power of reservation agents over the prosecution of crime. They were panels of state-appointed "mixed-blood" peoples who had the power to withhold rations and to impose fines and sentences of hard labor and incarceration at local agency prisons.[141] They often focused on the punishment of indigenous political and spiritual practices, including the Sun Dance movement. According to the 1891 Board of Indian Commissioners Report, the "so-called courts of Indian offenses" were "more in the nature of courts martial than civil courts, and practically registered the decrees of the Indian agent."[142] They were an alibi for the expansion of federal power onto the reservations and over "criminal Indians" who remained "at large upon the reservation unpunished."[143] The perceived failure of these specialized courts led to the legal reconstruction of Law for the Indian and a BIA test case that validated the architecture that became Leavenworth.

To establish the legality of Law for the Indian, the BIA selected an "unpunished" crime that had occurred on Lakota land and argued that the federal government could prosecute all Indians for all crimes regardless of location. The BIA chose to use Crow Dog's killing of Spotted Tail (Sinte Gleske) on August 5, 1881, which had resulted from conflict over the legal authority of the US-backed "Indian Police." Spotted Tail had been appointed as the head of the Indian Police after he "came in" to the Spotted Tail Agency. Finding none of the food he was promised, he threatened to "burn and destroy every building" on the reservation.[144] Spotted Tail used the violence of this incentive structure to turn US justice back on itself by reinstituting Lakota justice practices. Because his status as Indian police chief allowed him to appoint members to the force, he selected only policemen who were not "full-blooded" members of the nation, since, according to Lakota tradition, "full-blooded" people could never be subject to the authority of "mixed-bloods."[145] Against this backdrop, when the Indian policeman Crow Dog refused Spotted Tail's orders to make a particular arrest he was dismissed from the Indian Police. Crow Dog later killed Spotted Tail just outside Dakota Territory. Because Crow Dog practiced Lakota justice, he saw that his actions would burden his family for four generations, and he "purifi[ed] himself in a sweat lodge, shooting his rifle into sacred rocks four times to assuage the spirit of Spotted Tail."[146] Despite Crow Dog's reparation, he was detained at Fort Niobrara, Nebraska, convicted of murder by the territorial court in Deadwood, Dakota Territory, and was sentenced to execution by hanging.

When the BIA brought *Ex Parte Crow Dog* in 1883 to confirm the legality of Law for the Indian, the Supreme Court ruled on the question of whether Congress had repealed a certain section of the Revised Statutes that excluded from jurisdiction all crimes "committed in the Indian country by one Indian against the person or property of another Indian."[147] The ruling in *Ex Parte Crow Dog* referred to Indians as "aliens and strangers" who were foreign to US law because of an "inability to understand" the laws of a "superior" race. The Court maintained that Native justice was rooted in revenge and suggested that to apply US justice to the Lakota would be to "measure the red man's revenge by the maxims of the white man's morality." Using the narrative of Indian difference, the Court ruled against the BIA and reversed Crow Dog's conviction.

Congress responded to the perceived failure of US jurisdiction in *Ex Parte Crow Dog* with the Major Crimes Act of 1885, which federalized Native punishment and relied on the very logic that had constituted the Indian Territory as a *prisonscape*. The act made federal crimes of murder, manslaughter, rape, assault, arson, burglary, and larceny when committed by Native people. Excepting the Five Nations, the legislation brought criminalized Indians inside US law to punish crimes against "another Indian or other person" whether "within or without an Indian reservation."[148] The Major Crimes Act therefore reached the remaining site of Native jurisdiction—the regulation of justice on the reservations in instances where Native people committed crimes against other Native people. The law claimed to equalize criminal Indians and domestic criminals, subjecting both to "the same courts and in the same manner . . . to the same penalties as . . . all other persons charged with the commission of said crimes."[149] But the legislation drew on a long history of legal colonialism to disguise "equality before the law" with the continuation of specialized crimes that only Indians in Indian Territory could commit. These two legal structures—the federalization of all Native crime and the distinction of special Indian Territory crimes—created a mass of federal prisoners in a nation without federal prisons.

As part of the history of the carceral state, the creation of specialized courts and specialized crimes led gradually to the removal of "Indian punishment" from legal regulation. Alongside the trend toward federalization, the Supreme Court decision in *United States v. Clapox* removed reservation jails from the realm of penal institutions altogether. In the legal ratification of the reservation jailhouse as an extralegal institution, the Court created a form of unregulated punishment through the Umatilla Reservation in Oregon, where the Indian agent had jailed a woman named Minnie for adultery. Because adultery was not a crime in the Umatilla nation or according to US law as it applied on the reservation, Minnie was imprisoned for violating an administrative "rule" established by the local agent. When a group of Umatillas, including Clapox, "broke open the jail" to free her, they argued in the federal case that followed that the whole legal apparatus of "Indian Offenses" was unconstitutional on the grounds that courts could be established only by acts of Congress. Because the Courts of Indian Offenses were created by the Department of the Interior to govern local reservation spaces, they were not authentic sources of justice according to the terms of American law. The federal courts in Oregon responded by referring to the Indian Courts as *educational* rather than punitive institutions, as "mere educational and disciplinary instrumentalities by which the government of the US endeavor[s] to improve and elevate the condition of these dependent tribes to whom it sustains the relation of guardian."[150] This legal reclassification of the Indian Courts from sites of punishment to institutions of education was affirmed by the US Supreme Court in 1888, which ruled in *United States v. Clapox* that the reservation jail was "analogous to a school" where Native people received training in the force of law and in the "habits, ideas, and aspirations that distinguish the civilized."[151] In removing Indian punishments from the possibility of legal scrutiny, US law concealed Native punishment within the rubric of education, embedding and then disappearing its violence in a structure of mass incarceration.

The joint localization and federalization of Indian punishment in the 1880s created a carceral matrix. The federal government divided the region into districts, with crimes in the central district punished at Fort Smith, Arkansas, and crimes in the southern region prosecuted in the District Court of Northern Texas. The provisional territorial government of Oklahoma later "placed all the reservations occupied by the so-called 'non-Civilized' Indians, except the Quapaw Agency, within its boundaries and therefore under the jurisdiction of the newly established

Territorial and US district courts for Oklahoma."[152] Quapaw Agency prisoners remained subject to federal jurisdiction and were prosecuted in the federal court at Wichita, Kansas. It was because of this legal arrangement that John Grindstone ended up under federal jurisdiction in a state-level prison for a crime in the Quapaw Agency.

Those outside the Quapaw Agency and in an Indian Territory that no longer legally existed were now subject to a new regime of federal jails. The government built and rented a total of eleven jails in a region with only 120,000 people. These institutions were almost immediately condemned as antiquated institutions not worthy of the federal government. By 1897, the attorney general reported that he was still trying to establish "at least one good jail in each of the three . . . districts" of McAlester, Ardmore, and Muskogee.[153] The Muskogee jail on the corner of Denison and Third Street consisted of a "number of wooden buildings surrounded by a twelve-foot stockade" that held as many as 350 prisoners at a time.[154] During an investigation, authorities found two hundred Black, white, Cherokee, and Creek prisoners in the space of forty square feet and declared the "character of the buildings" a "disgrace to the Government" and "destructive of morals, minds, and bodies."[155] To develop standards for jailhouse construction in the old Indian Territory, the US government hired Eames and Young, the architects who were already building Leavenworth, to design four new federal jails in Vinita, Muscogee, South McAlester and Ardmore, Oklahoma.[156] Prisoners in these jails were routed into a federal prison system without prisons and then into a military prison that was already a long-standing symbol of the carceral state.

Mass incarceration was an idea built into the space of the Indian Territory as a joint federal-military enterprise and was organized according to a regime of administrative law that functioned like a prison. In this way, the nation's first prisoner came from a space already designed radially to make "Indian criminals" subject to federal punishment. Fort Leavenworth's place in the history of the settler colonial state is important because it served as the military arm of a carceral matrix that stretched to the federal courts in Wichita, Kansas, and Fort Smith, Arkansas, and to the Quapaw Agency as a different kind of prison. This entire matrix had been developed to make Indians subject to law, but this form of legal recognition was refused and always in crisis.[157] In the reservation escapes, jailhouse breaks, and the poisonous roots almost in John Grindstone's hand, the history of the federal prison system is anchored in resistance. Lizzie Cardish may have been sent up to Leavenworth, but she also burned down the reservation school house, creating a crisis for "Indian Affairs." The commissioner worried in 1906 that "despite the fact that this office has emphasized the necessity of . . . watchfulness at various Indian schools, fires still occur. Most of these are due to incendiary origin . . . so that stern measures became imperative, and however distasteful such action may have been it was found necessary to make an example of those concerned."[158] Leavenworth was mapped into the larger structure of Native punishment that emerged in the nineteenth century and created forms of mass punishment that remain central to the history of mass incarceration. The federal prison system was an idea about the mass incarceration of Native people.

Because the carceral state is a settler colonial state, the origins of the federal prison system are connected to the project of an Indian Territory that was designed radially as though it were a nineteenth-century prison. Fort Leavenworth's selection as the site of the nation's first prison was part of a longer history of legal colonialism that was mapped onto the formation of Kansas Territory and entrenched into a carceral Kansas state. In the context of this multilayered legal architecture and the transition to the legal time of Bleeding Kansas, the idea of mass incarceration that began in the Indian Territory took on new life in the mass punishments of slavery's borderlands.

# 3

## Federal Punishment and the Legal Time of Bleeding Kansas

During a March 2009 college basketball game between the Kansas Jayhawks and the Missouri Tigers, Kansas University students unfurled a large banner—a reprint of the mural painted by John Steuart Curry on the walls of the Kansas state capitol between 1937 and 1942. The banner of the Kansas students taunts the Missouri Tigers by merging Jayhawk Nation's victory in the game with their triumph in the war over slavery during Bleeding Kansas. In this version, John Brown's Bible has been replaced with a trophy representing the 2008 NCAA National Championship win of the Kansas Jayhawks. This use of the banner represents the proslavery loss in the war at the Kansas-Missouri border, which began in 1854 and marked the beginning of the national Civil War. Brown was at the center of this war, coming to Kansas in 1854 to join his five sons, who were already imagining the illegality of slavery in Kansas. By posing as a land surveyor, Brown passed through proslavery blockades at the territory's borders. He refused to recognize the laws of slavery in a moment when two territorial governments claimed jurisdiction in Kansas Territory and when federal law conspired with the proslavery government to establish the institution of slavery in Kansas. As part of *abolition Kansas*, Brown disobeyed federal and territorial law to imagine new terrains of freedom. His stance in the mural, with his arms outstretched like Moses parting the Red Sea, reflected the way he came to stand in for the realization of the impossible. Jayhawk Nation's commemoration of Bleeding Kansas is part of a larger cultural remembrance that takes place in sports and politics, in classrooms and field trips, in state memorials and museum exhibits, and during stories over family dinners. What is forgotten in these moments of recollection is that Bleeding Kansas was fundamentally about slavery's relationship to law and order.

FIGURE 7. John Steuart Curry, *Tragic Prelude*, 1940.

Brown's position in the mural, between proslavery and union forces, reflected this claim to an alternative practice of law, a legal tradition that emerged in an environment where federal control was a symbol of slavery. Bleeding Kansas was therefore a different kind of legal moment, one in which John Brown and many others created the idea of abolition Kansas, a place in which "the people" refused to recognize the foreign law of slavery. After the 1854 territorial election, when crowds of Missourians crossed the border and voted slavery into existence, abolition Kansas refused to recognize the authority of the elected Bogus Legislature as a proslavery government backed by the force of federal law. A particular legal time of Bleeding Kansas emerged, as military, federal, territorial, and state legal rituals existed alongside the people's procedures of arrest, imprisonment, and execution. This chaotic legal arrangement was the result of the region's transition from Indian Territory to Kansas Territory, when the law of popular sovereignty (the people's right to vote slavery in or out of existence) was mapped onto the colonial structure of squatter sovereignty, a prior legal arrangement that gave certain self-enforced rights to "illegal" white residents in the Indian Territory. In the context of these multiple and overlapping legal arrangements, the idea of *abolition justice* as the work of the people was condemned and then forgotten by the time Curry painted the mural at the Kansas capitol.

When Curry created the mural between 1937 and 1942 as part of a New Deal project to remember the fading rural landscapes of the heartland, his work was being shaped by memories of a war that was seen no longer as an irrepressible struggle but as a needlessly provoked and fratricidal tragedy. The war that was depicted in *Tragic Prelude* was part of a changing historical narrative that recast and even condemned abolitionists for having taken the law into their own hands. Curry attempted to resurrect the memory of John Brown's justice in order to show that the Civil War was the fault of extremists on both sides, but his middle-ground vision and his massive tribute on the capitol walls embarrassed the citizens of Kansas. Preferring to forget John Brown, Kansans in the 1930s and 1940s criticized Curry for focusing only on "the worst" of Kansas. The Kansas Women's Council publicly condemned Curry's display of the "freaks" who "did not follow legal procedure" and the mural's erasure of law-abiding Kansas.[1] Curry's representation of the extralegal forms of justice that haunted the landscape was condemned in a moment of forgetting, as Kansas refashioned its reputation for fanaticism into a reputation for modern governance that made it worthy of the first national prison.[2]

The idea of Leavenworth Penitentiary arrived in what is now called Kansas thirty years into the afterlife of a civil war over slavery at the Kansas-Missouri border. The idea of Leavenworth was a response to the legal time of Bleeding Kansas, where competing claims to state authority by abolitionist, free labor, and proslavery political imaginaries were already ideas about punishment. Leavenworth was a claim to federal jurisdiction in a place that had already developed local customary traditions of law as the work of the people. Leavenworth tried to mark the end of popular sovereignty, the specific form of white political participation crafted by Congress in order to expand slavery into Kansas Territory, as it replaced the earlier regime of squatter sovereignty, which governed trespassing white settlers who made soon-to-be-legalized claims to the land. It was this strange combination of colonial and domestic law that made it possible for abolition Kansas to turn law against itself and to create an extralegal customary tradition in which the practice of justice was simultaneously the practice of freedom. As a symbol of state power, Leavenworth removed the work of justice from the people and secured it for a state that hunted, captured, and eventually killed John Brown for imagining a different kind of justice.

While the federal prison's insertion into the landscape brought a federal politics of law and order to Kansas, it also intervened in an already existing political culture and custom that was lived as law and that remained a powerful part of daily life long after the centralization of state power. The idea of Leavenworth Penitentiary represented the victory of legal violence over the kinds of "public" justice that the state condemned as the work of the "mob," practices that were used by both abolitionist movements and proslavery forces to institute competing forms of justice. This meant that what became Kansas complemented the already existing legal order (one in which justice was a popular practice) but inverted the promise of abolition by encouraging "the people" to practice justice on behalf of the state. It encouraged community participation in state justice rituals, including collective hunts for fugitives escaped from the prison and gruesome spectacles of execution that made citizens into witnesses. Kansas statehood and the federal law-and-order project that supported it transformed the abolitionist vision of popular sovereignty from the central participatory institution of daily life to a mechanism that encouraged the people to do justice on behalf of the state. In taking justice from the people, Leavenworth both interrupted and continued the racial life of punishment that had brought Bleeding Kansas to war. Because the federal prison inherited already existing justice practices that were lived as a form of custom more powerful than law, Leavenworth marked the end of squatter and popular sovereignty but carried the legal time of Bleeding Kansas into the future of statehood.

This chapter is a study of the legal culture that both preceded and interpenetrated the order of Leavenworth Penitentiary. It examines the prison's deep and abiding connections to slavery in a place that went to war to refuse it and then welcomed the prison as a symbol of statehood, forgetting at once their contradictions as congenital institutions and the meaning of Bleeding Kansas for the nation. The betrayal of abolition Kansas is a story about the meaning of justice and about how memories of the legal time of Bleeding Kansas might return abolition to its most important question: What does it mean to be free? How did the prison become wedded to peculiar forms of personhood that are now taken for granted as "citizenship," and how might the story of Bleeding Kansas and the particular moment of abolition it represents be used to recall a memory of freedom not defined by the prison? This chapter examines both how a place on the edges of law was brought "in line" with state control through the prison's racial project and how the disarticulation of law from justice in abolition Kansas could have created a future without mass incarceration. Telling the story of Bleeding Kansas as a story about the complex relationship between slavery, justice, and punishment, the chapter begins with an account of the colonial and territorial laws that legalized and regulated slavery in the region and then analyzes the competing sets of justice rituals that began with squatter and popular sovereignty and that remain embedded in the political and social life of a place like Leavenworth.

## THE WORK OF LAW AT THE KANSAS-MISSOURI BORDER

The story of Bleeding Kansas as a particular moment in the history of law begins with the origins of slavery and the system of regulation that developed in Missouri and then spilled over into Kansas as a remnant of overlapping colonial legal formations. Slavery was embedded in the legal framework of the region long before Kansas would adopt the Missouri Code. In the early 1700s, French colonial law, alongside Spanish claims to the land, instituted both Black and Native slavery in Upper Louisiana with the 1724 Black Code. The Code Noir established punishments for both enslaved and manumitted persons who violated colonial laws, and it criminalized speaking out against slavery.[3] When the Spanish assumed control of the region again in 1763, they prohibited Native slavery in Upper Louisiana by 1769 but did not repeal the Black Codes. The Spanish legal framework simply translated the French Code Noir into Spanish, overlaying the future of law in the region with the status of enslavement. When Spain sold the Louisiana Territory to France and then to the United States as the Louisiana Purchase in 1803, the new Missouri Territory was slow to implement its own legal structure and remained a part of the legal culture of colonial Louisiana. When Missouri became a state in 1820, it incorporated the laws of slavery from the state of Virginia as its legal foundation.[4]

As a descendant of Louisiana's Black Code and Virginia state law, Missouri Territory became a US state through the Compromise of 1820, which gave Missouri to the South and Maine to the free states. Missouri's location disrupted the original idea of the Mason-Dixon Line because it permitted no slavery north of Missouri's southern border. When the Compromise of 1820 produced Missouri as a southern state *above the line*, Missouri was a slave state that intruded into the North.[5] Missouri's jurisprudence of slavery was rooted in its relationship to prisons and criminal law. The prison was built to regulate slavery and criminalize abolition, which it did through a series of provisions for the punishment of "larceny."[6] Like other states with relatively large Black populations, Missouri used the relationship between prisons and slavery to develop racialized mechanisms of control for both free and enslaved Black people that included licensure, spatial regulation, and criminal law.

In the context of its peculiar political geography, larceny law in Missouri was institutionalized as an antiabolitionist practice, and the Missouri State Penitentiary routinely punished abolitionists. Missouri prisoners included slaves who ran away and "stole" their own bodies, white abolitionists who accompanied the enslaved into freedom, and white slave hunters who kidnapped slaves to sell in the Deep South markets, thereby depriving other white people of their "property." The Missouri Penitentiary, built at Jefferson City in 1830 as the largest state prison west of the Mississippi, was often referred to as "the slaveholder's prison" because it housed forty-two Black and white abolitionists from the 1830s until the 1860s and because it was used by private slaveholders to preemptively detain slaves who might escape. When the white abolitionist George Thompson was imprisoned in 1841, he documented the status of an unnamed Black prisoner who was brought to the penitentiary because of a "suspicion on the part of the master that he would run away."[7] In 1835, a new criminal code set a minimum prison sentence of two years for stealing slaves and required Black people to register in local precincts to receive freedom licenses.[8] Unlicensed freedom was a criminal offense for Black residents in the state of Missouri.

Missouri consolidated the power of its proslavery legal architecture with the successful prosecution of the white abolitionists Alanson Work, James Burr, and George Thompson in a case that illustrated the legal contradictions of slave law and its relationship to punishment. The three Illinois missionaries had crossed into Missouri for a "tour of mercy." When they enticed a group of slaves to run away, the group they approached assumed they were slave traders and alerted authorities, who arrested, tried, and incarcerated Work, Burr, and Thompson.[9]

Although Missouri's initial strategy was to try the abolitionists for larceny, the defense successfully argued that abolition could not constitute larceny because larceny required an intention to convert stolen property into personal property. When the state reduced the charges to stealing, attempting to steal, and intending to attempt to steal, the men were convicted and given twelve-year sentences in the penitentiary.

The criminal case of Work, Burr, and Thompson exposed the complicated relationship between law and custom as it emerged in Missouri, a state with two competing and complementary justice rituals—one being the set of state practices that relied on the county jail and the state prison (which was monitored and occasionally taken over by vigilante mobs) and the other being the customary and binding obligation to refuse state involvement in matters of citizen justice. Mark Twain's father served on the jury that convicted Work, Burr, and Thompson, and these competing conceptions of legal authority became the basis of Twain's novel *Pudd'nhead Wilson,* published in 1894.[10] In Missouri, custom often required fighting a duel rather than appealing to the local courts, so "Pistols, dirks, and daggers were everywhere in evidence" and were used in a system of quick justice in which "the trial was held immediately . . . [and] the jury [was] composed of frontiersmen . . . free from legal niceties."[11] The trial of Work, Burr, and Thompson was also therefore a trial for Missouri's emergent system of criminal justice; it was widely known that if the court failed to return a harsh sentence the defendants would be taken from the courthouse by a mob and hanged. According to Thompson's memoir, "The infuriated mob, with their faces all Blackened, had prepared the gallows, and even the ropes."[12] When their sentences were announced, the courtroom erupted with declarations that the citizens had "got clear of mobbing them."[13] The convictions demonstrated the security of the state's claim to punishment, but the culture of extralegal authority still demanded that the state appoint a group of one hundred men to safely transport the prisoners to the state penitentiary.[14] Despite the victory of law, the Missouri legislature passed an 1845 statute requiring a minimum prison sentence of seven years for grand larceny, for "enticing, decoying, or carrying away" a slave and for "*aiding* in enticing, decoying, or carrying away a slave."[15] By 1855, Missouri law prohibited altogether the entry of enslaved people "with the intent to effect freedom."[16]

Against the backdrop of Missouri law as a specific jurisprudence of slavery and prisons, Kansas law developed as a contested and palimpsestic terrain that gradually accumulated ideas about the meaning of law and order as a proslavery practice.[17] These ideas came from the already existing but shifting political geographies of Indian Territory in 1825, Kansas Territory in 1854, and Kansas State in 1861. The legal transitions between territorial and state governance occurred through the claims of squatter sovereignty, a white settler colonial framework of possession that intertwined the law of slavery and punishment in what squatters called a "*region beyant the law.*"[18] In Indian Territory, a space adjacent to but not necessarily subject to Missouri law, customary justice rituals spilled over the border from Missouri into Kansas as illegal squatters made imaginary land claims in the region. These extralegal practices became part of the economic and political landscape of Kansas Territory as settlers claimed the right to govern themselves through the squatter association, the vigilance committee, and the impromptu court in improvised but practiced customary rituals.

In the absence of laws regulating the legal status of whites in Indian Territory, the squatter associations enforced rights in a Kansas Territory that did not yet exist. Acting collectively to establish a set of imagined rights, squatter associations formalized illegal land claims and punished those who failed to recognize the group's authority in disputes. Disagreements over the boundaries of these illegal land claims were routine, in part because the claims were often inscribed in pencil on the trees: "I claim 160 acres, of which this is the center stake."[19] The squatter associations established rules for making claims, required that members build the foundation of a cabin or pitch a tent within thirty days, and expelled "intruders" who violated local customs.[20] The enforcements complicated the relationship between legal and illegal land claims, so that anyone occupying land within a half mile of an already protected claim would be expelled from the region. The associations formed specialized committees to protect illegal settlements on reservation lands if the settler could demonstrate that he was "deterred from commencing his cabin, or otherwise improving his claim, on the ground that it was a violation of the law, but ha[d] in all respects complied with the . . . resolution."[21] Before the actual territorialization of Kansas in 1854, squatter associations claimed the right to police over six hundred illegal land claims, and it was through the power of policing that squatter sovereignty became a legal imaginary.[22]

When Kansas was territorialized, the right to practice these rituals of justice became enfolded into the ideological architecture of abolition Kansas because of the doctrine of popular sovereignty. In Kansas, popular sovereignty was a legal arrangement that enabled abolitionist and proslavery regimes of justice to exercise competing claims to the work of "democratic" law and to create contradictory understandings of justice that would eventually be reunited by the power of the prison. When the Kansas-Nebraska Act of 1854 carved Kansas Territory from Indian Territory and incorporated the region into US law, the law required that "the people" of Kansas Territory would decide whether slavery would be legal within its borders. The doctrine of popular sovereignty established the power of the franchise to determine whether slavery was legal or illegal in the Territory— the people were to "form and regulate their domestic institutions in their own way, subject only to the Constitution of the United States."[23] Popular sovereignty, as a legal idea, rearranged possibilities for the federal regulation of slavery by ending its containment by coordinate boundary, therefore opening the possibility of slavery's legalization everywhere. Because popular sovereignty was to determine the outcome of the first territorial election, proslavery and antislavery groups rushed to Kansas, both self-identified as "the Democracy."²⁴ In the transition from Indian Territory to Kansas Territory in 1854 and up until the first contested territorial election in 1855, "the Democracies" became unseated sources of power that created competing legal imaginaries of slavery and freedom.

Against the backdrop of a territorial civil war over slavery, the various sides developed localized rituals of justice. It was the custom of the proslavery vigilance committees to give "a horse thief, robber, or homicide a fair trial" but to hang "a negro thief or Abolitionist without judge or jury."²⁵ Nearly ten thousand Missourians joined "self-protection" societies in the early 1850s and traveled from Missouri into Kansas to "establish the institution" of slavery.²⁶ In Leavenworth, a squatter association named "the Self-Defensives" criminalized teaching Black people to read and arranged extralegal rituals for those "waited on by a committee and decidedly ordered to leave without any ifs or ands."²⁷ The Self-Defensives criminalized the practice of law by abolitionists in Leavenworth and harassed antislavery lawyers through their Missouri newspaper, the *Platte Argus:* it asked on the front page "whether there was a true friend of 'the goose' in all of Leavenworth" ("the goose question" referred colloquially to a proslavery stance).²⁸ In response to the taunts of the *Platte Argus* editors, the Leavenworth *Herald* demonstrated its firmness on "the goose question" by enticing an antislavery lawyer, William Phillips, across the river into Missouri, where he was stripped, shaved, tarred, and feathered—"carried astride a rail, and mockingly sold . . . on the charge of expressing sentiments so as 'to disturb the domestic relation of the people'—that is, interfere with slavery."²⁹ An unidentified Black man was "brought forward and commanded to sell Phillips at auction: 'How much, gentlemen, for a full-blooded abolitionist, dyed in [the] wool, tar and feathers, and all?'"³⁰

These rituals of justice developed deep roots in the culture of law, as both proslavery and antislavery territorial citizens arranged impromptu performances at the scenes of criminal offenses. Even in antislavery jurisdictions, the absence of state-made law authorized local citizens to stage the roles of judge, jury, and executioner in customs more powerful than law. Because these local justice committees are often subsumed within the study of spontaneous lynch mobs, the works of justice committees have often been described as chaotic and apolitical events rather than staged and rehearsed claims to the work of law. Although the vigilance committees of the squatter associations were sometimes popularly referred to as lynch courts, this practice of justice was also distinct from the practices of lynching that were carried out in campaigns of racial terror throughout the nineteenth and twentieth centuries. Instead of targeting Black citizens, the rule of the lynch courts in Kansas Territory was a form of white self-regulation administered as though it were a fully legal institution.³¹ The cultural force of Black lynching as it developed within and beyond US law was a different instantiation of the practice. The antilynching activist James Weldon Johnson, referring to the 4,015 acts of white mob violence against Black people between 1885 and 1922, distinguished the lynch courts that "accompanied the border troubles . . . especially on the dark and bloody soil of Kansas," from "the recrudescence of lynching, in its present form, [which] dates from the period of Reconstruction."[32]

Although justice committees were distinct from lynching as a postwar regime of terror, the popular rituals that emerged from the doctrines of squatter and popular sovereignty are central rather than marginal to the history of law and legal thinking; they are institutions central to the formation and development of US law. As part of the tradition of US law, "frontier justice" emerged to regulate life on the edges of US jurisdiction, in places where the sentences handed down by justice committees were respected as though they were fully legal institutions. In interviews conducted after statehood, settlers reported that even death sentences from "these committees were seldom considered illegal."[33] In Coffey County, for example, "A mob held trial and asked those in favor of death to pass to the right of [a] building and those against to the left. Nine-tenths went to the right."[34] This "legal work" became such a routine part of the political landscape that the custom, when reported by local newspapers at all, often received the space of a simple sentence: "A gentleman from Franklin County said eleven horses were stolen, six men arrested, two shot, two hung and two dismissed," or "It is rumored that . . . a horse thief had been caught and hung."[35] Invested with the force of custom, justice committees were accompanied by competing legal imaginaries of slavery and freedom that aligned with two competing forms of governance. In creating dueling proslavery and abolitionist governments in the same territory, the border war led to regimes of punishment that shaped the future of Kansas and the nation.

## BLEEDING KANSAS, CIVIL WAR, AND THE FORMATION OF JUSTICE RITUALS

When popular sovereignty put slavery to the vote on March 30, 1855, invading Missourians voted slavery into existence in almost every township on the border, obtaining 6,320 votes in a place with only 831 legal voters. The national newspapers immediately reported that Kansas had proven herself "S.G.Q." ("sound on the goose question") and boasted that Kansas was now "peculiarly fitted for slave labor."[36] The local proslavery newspapers reported that the Missourians, certain of their victory, had come with a live goose displayed—"a pole surmounted by the animal alive and squawking."[37] The national experiment with popular sovereignty in Kansas resulted in the election of the Bogus Legislature, which tried to build a slave state in Kansas.

Despite the election of a territorial government, no formal institutions existed for four months until the fall of 1855, when "justices and sheriffs were appointed under the bogus territorial laws; they were not recognized by the settlers, and did no business."[38] During this time of uncertainty, the legal arm of the proslavery territorial government was often found playing poker at a cabin near the proslavery capital of Lecompton: "Judge Cato was an Alabamian, and always said 'de Cote' for 'the court' and sometimes ordered the sheriff to adjourn 'de Cote' until it could get a drink, which it then proceeded to do from a saloon opposite the court-room."[39] Even after the formal appointment of a territorial governor, he sat, with little authority, at Fort Leavenworth, with only "a few chairs, a writing table, some boxes filled with books and covered with newspapers for seating visitors, a letter press, a stove, [and] other rude contrivances."[40] The region was, according to early settlers, "practically without law and legal machinery, aside from the territorial judges and marshal appointed by the president" between 1854 and 1858.[41] Because the squatter courts were "as much respected and as effective as the government courts," they continued to regulate crime and punishment in the region: "There were but few offenses by resident citizens, and these were promptly and impartially dealt with by the assembled citizens of the neighborhood, without calling upon the bogus officials."[42]

The state-making project of a proslavery Kansas began the following year with the wholesale copying of the Missouri legal code into Kansas law. Incorporating slavery and its system of punishment, the Kansas Black Law was designed to make Kansas an extension of Missouri and to punish Black and white abolitionists beyond what was prescribed in the Fugitive Slave Act of 1850. What federal slave laws punished with one or two years of imprisonment, Kansas now punished with death. It was a capital offense to rebel against slavery (to conduct, aid, advise, or induce rebellion) and to carry away or aid in the carrying away of a slave from Kansas Territory. The Act to Punish Offences against Slave Property banned "statements, arguments, opinions, sentiment, doctrine, advice or innuendo, calculated to produce a disorderly, dangerous disaffection among the slaves."[43] Speaking against slavery was punished by five years of hard labor, and any verbal or written denial of "the right of persons to hold slaves in the Territory" was punished with two years of hard labor. Having secured the right of slavery in the Territory, proslavery citizens and Missourians celebrated the speed with which Kansas joined the South, even as abolition Kansas pledged to live as if the election had not taken place. In refusing to acknowledge the authority of law, the abolition Kansas that John Brown joined developed its own practices of justice, and the state's response led to the prisonization of Kansas.

The Kansas slave laws fashioned a certain relationship between the unfreedom of slavery and the unfreedom of punishment in the absence of a state prison. The government of Kansas, as it was directed by the government of Missouri, drew the practice of imprisoning abolition into its newly formed territorial government. The Black Law built slave ownership into the very fabric of civic participation. Making support for slavery a requirement for participation in governance, the law required Kansas jurors to openly "admit the right to hold slaves in this Territory" as a condition of service. White citizens could vote and practice law only if they had never been convicted of violating the federal fugitive slave laws and if they swore an "oath or affirmation" to pursue fugitive slaves in the territory. Enfolding a belief in the legality of slavery into the very requirements of suffrage and civic duty, proslavery squatter associations declared that the code of Kansas was "more efficient to protect slave property than any state in the Union."[44] By February of 1855, the first official territorial census in Kansas recorded 151 free Black people and 193 enslaved.[45]

These competing claims to legal and cultural authority between 1855 and 1857 meant that slavery simultaneously existed and did not exist. Slaveholders believed that if they brought enough slaves into the territory they could overcome the free-state refusal to recognize their claims of ownership. Because the white proslavery citizenry relied on the presence of black bodies as an indication of slavery's legal status, the bills of sale for Mary Davis, Anne Clarke, Buck Scott, Tom Bourn, Bob Skaggs, Liza, Lizzie, Judy, Nancy, Cely, Patsy, and Martha remain scattered in the records and archives. The bill of sale for Martha, written by Thomas Johnson, namesake of Johnson County, guarantees that she was "sound in body and mind and a slave for life and free from all claims."[46] Despite the complicated presence of slavery in Kansas, the older settlers were shocked by the speed at which the memory of slavery was erased from Kansas's history. In interviews conducted well after statehood, C. E. Cory reported that in the 1890s, he "called upon the venerable Dr. J. N. O. P. Wood at Wichita, a well-known opponent of the free-state movement, and compared notes on . . . personal knowledge of slaves in Kansas, and . . . counted over 400—and quit."[47] Because of the presence of the Underground Railroad in northeastern Kansas, records also indicate that "very few of the small number [of whites] who came from the south dare[d] to bring slaves with them."[48] In 1859, J. Bowles wrote a letter to F. B. Sanborn, John Brown's biographer, detailing "the fact of nearly three hundred fugitives having passed through and received assistance from the abolitionists here at Lawrence."[49] The widespread disappearance of property into people at the Kansas-Missouri border created new terrains of justice that sometimes succeeded in pushing the practice of slavery back across the Missouri border. Slavery always pushed back.

The rebellion against the structure of slavery that began in abolition Kansas as both a place and a legal imaginary began with the self-emancipation of Black abolitionists at the Kansas-Missouri border and with the informal network of civic institutions that emerged to enforce these freedom claims. Operating beyond the course of law, civic associations and vigilance committees worked to enforce the status of Black freedom by imagining new forms of subjectivity and belonging. In antislavery towns along the border, Black freedom claims were rooted in a different kind of legal imaginary, one that authorized the formation of underground depots, escapes from the local jailhouses, and sometimes even the extralegal punishment of proslavery people. Because of the earliest efforts at self-emancipation in Missouri, the routine and yet unrecorded escapes across the border resulted in the exponential growth of the "freed" population in

Kansas. Black abolition crossed the line as early as 1848.[50] In the proslavery town of Leavenworth, the free Black citizenry was limited to 14 people in 1855 but grew from 192 in 1860 to 2,400 by the end of the war.[51] Black Kansas grew from 627 in 1860 to 12,527 in 1865.[52] It was the beginning of a Black Exodus that continued into the 1880s and that Sojourner Truth called the "greatest movement of all time."[53] People like H. C. Bruce "escaped" the prison of Missouri to freedom in Leavenworth in 1855 and recorded his experience in *The New Man: Twenty-Nine Years a Slave, Twenty-Nine Years a Free Man*.[54] Benjamin "Pap" Singleton, Samuel Perry, and Henry Adams established all-Black towns like Nicodemus and Singleton's Colony and prompted a congressional investigation.[55] During the legal time of slavery, the creation of a free Black Kansas was part of an idea about popular sovereignty and the law as a force only as powerful as the people's belief in that law. This meant that slavery could be made illegal if the people believed in its illegality.

Although abolition Kansas disbelieved in the legal fictions of slavery, the federal government actively supported the rights of slave owners. Proslavery federal laws were routinely enforced in Kansas, even though the Missouri courts had established in *Rachel v. Walker* (1836) that transportation to a free space was a willful act of emancipation.[56] The US government not only recognized the right of whites in Kansas to transport, use, and sell slaves within the state's borders but also sent US marshals to intervene in local spaces of freedom. In the abolition newspapers, including the *Kansas Tribune* of Lawrence, the people challenged the right of slave hunters and federal marshals to "come among them" in defiance of local law and in defiance of the home as property protected against illegal search and seizure. Handbills posted in Lawrence warned residents that US marshal Leonard Arms had arrived "into your midst for the avowed purpose of NEGRO HUNTING," and claimed the right to practice justice: "[Arms] is watching your houses, by his piratical minions, night and day, and will enter and search them for victims. KNOW YOUR RIGHTS and STAND TO THEM. He has no right to INVADE your CASTLES."[57]

Because the doctrine of popular sovereignty configured the law of slavery and the federal intrusions that supported it as a kind of foreign invasion, the continuing interventions by an occupying force emboldened an antislavery Kansas, who held a series of nineteen public meetings in 1855 and 1856 to condemn the fraudulent election and pledge to live as if it had not taken place.[58] John Brown's sons were in attendance, and Brown himself participated in the convention at Big Springs in 1855. When the competing proslavery government passed the Kansas Black Laws, the *Kansas Tribune* announced "the day of our enslavement" as speaking out against the institution became a criminal offense. The antislavery newspaper, in a full-page repudiation staged in oversized letters, declared that despite "the law" the people of Kansas "do declare and assert . . . that persons have not the right to hold slaves in this Territory, and we will emblazon it upon our banner in letters so large and in language so plain that the infatuated invaders who elected the Kansas legislature as well as the corrupt and ignorant legislature itself can understand it, so that, if they cannot read, they may spell it out."[59] Interpreting the enforcement of the Black Laws as an act of war that threatened to enslave all of Kansas, antislavery jurisdictions fought to expel federal fugitive slave hunters from the territory and to establish a separate structure of governance.

When the abolition movement elected its own legislature, it gave rise to the formal double governance of Bleeding Kansas—two systems of territorial law at war in the same space. The "free state" government convened under the constant threat of arrest and detention, as charges of treason became central to the territorial government's strategy of using law and punishment to end abolition Kansas. The territorial government sent the military from Fort Leavenworth to disperse the assembled free-state legislature in Topeka in 1856; the military commander followed his orders in disrupting the meeting but refused to dishonor the participants by disarming them. On May 10, 1856, after President Pierce recognized the authority of the Bogus Legislature in a speech before Congress, the proslavery government in Lecompton arrested the free-state government "from the governor down, and clapped them into prison."[60] Governor Robinson spent the next four months at the Lecompton Jail, while one of John Brown's sons was detained in the local judge's house.[61] On May 14, 1856, George W. Brown, editor of the *Herald of Freedom,* was arrested on charges of treason for refusing to recognize the territorial government. He was held by an "armed mob" that "c[a]me in the name of law, clothed with authority of the federal government."[62] Through these displays of federal power in the "local" and contested arena of justice, punishment formed the forgotten background of Bleeding Kansas. The adoption of the prison as a mode of punishing abolition Kansas was rooted in the violence of federal slave law.

With the backing of military soldiers, local judges, county sheriffs, and US senators, the violence of Bleeding Kansas became embedded in territorial law. Alongside the widespread, unpunished murders of abolitionists by public and private authorities, it was the punishment of Lawrence, as a representation of abolition Kansas, that moved John Brown to claim the right to practice law. On the twenty-first of May, as the free-state government sat in the makeshift prisons of the proslavery government, a crowd of proslavery Missourians, backed by US marshals making mass arrests in the township, burned Lawrence, Kansas, to the ground.[63] The "sacking" of Lawrence, which occurred in 1856, preceded the more famous 1863 Lawrence Massacre known as Quantrill's Raid. Enforcing the law against abolitionist speech, proslavery forces stationed a cannon on top of Mount Oread and with a force eight hundred strong destroyed the presses of the *Herald of Freedom* and the *Kansas Free State Tribune.* On the orders of the local judge, Samuel D. Lecompte, the Free State Hotel, an institution central to the work of the New England Emigrant Aid Society, was burned to the ground. The sheriff of Douglas

County, Samuel Jones, who lived across the border in Missouri, reported that the punishment of abolition Kansas had marked the "happiest day" of his life.[64] Jones and others celebrated this first invasion of Lawrence as marking the successful control of the citizenry, particularly since the residents of Lawrence did not resist. John Brown returned to Lawrence, sat among the smoldering remains of the Free State Hotel, and declared open war against slavery and the law.

Before morning, John Brown had committed what W. E. B. Du Bois called a "deed of retaliation from the free state side so bloody, relentless and cruel that it sent a shudder through all Kansas and Missouri, and aroused the nation."[65] In what became known as the Pottawatomie Massacre, John Brown drew attention to the unpunished murders of abolitionists by visiting the enforcers of the Bogus Legislature in the middle of the night, and sentencing them to death in "the flash of an awful stroke."[66] John Brown's rehearsal of the long-standing ritual shocked the nation. It brought public attention to the question of whether war would decide the slavery question, and widespread condemnation of the methods of "John Brown's justice."[67] His claim to the work of law and to self-defense was dismissed as "mob justice" by the proslavery ruffians, by the new free-state officials, and by the agents of the federal government, whose attempts to capture and kill John Brown in the years that followed only added to his mythic stature. What was perhaps most dangerous about Brown was that he reframed slavery not as a right but as a crime. Challenging the unpunished "crimes of this guilty land," Brown's theory of justice was beyond the state and beyond the law.[68] Despite public condemnation of the "immorality" of the hatchet, Kansas knew by now that "something must be done."[69]

Between the Pottawatomie killings and his death by hanging in 1859, John Brown defied the force of law in ways that captured the imagination of the nation. From Kansas, Brown escorted self-emancipating people 2,500 miles in the dead of winter, reaching Canada with twelve people and a child born on the second day. Unscathed by law, Brown's accompaniments were successful in spite of the slave hunters who were always trailing behind, in part because of his ability to move in and out of the territory unseen. According to local newspapers, Brown was dead one day and raiding Missouri plantations the next, "appearing and disappearing here and there—now startling men with the grim decision of his actions, now lost and hidden from public view."[70] Brown and his travel companions outran and outfought their opponents even when outnumbered. Samuel Harper, who escaped slavery in Missouri and traveled with Brown to Canada, recalled that when their hiding place was surrounded by seventy-five slave hunters, "There was only 14 of us altogether, but the captain was a terror to them, and when he stepped out of the house and went for them the whole seventy-five of them started running."[71] During Brown's return from Canada, the Kansas governor wired a federal marshal to "capture John Brown, dead or alive." The marshal responded: "If I try to capture John Brown it'll be dead, and I'll be the one that'll be dead."[72] The failure of the law to punish John Brown's justice became a symbol of the power of abolition Kansas, as an idea that could not be burned, brutalized, or imprisoned out of existence.

The border war became, as Du Bois would later argue, a time when the South "fought to enslave all territory of the Union," and a place where slavery and abolition "met in Kansas, and in Kansas civil war began."[73] Against the backdrop of John Brown's justice, state and federal courts soon changed the methods by which slavery was extended into a territory. Missouri had become the center of the comity question, as *Dred Scott v. Sandford* wound its way through the state's courts and arrived at the Supreme Court in 1857. The Missouri case restructured the legal status of slavery for the nation by overturning the earlier Missouri case of *Rachel v. Walker* (1836), which determined that relocation to a free space was a willful act of emancipation by the owner. The Court ruled that Dred Scott and his wife Harriet were not free by virtue of having been taken from Missouri to Illinois, since Missourians had no duty to recognize Illinois law: "No state is bound to carry into effect enactments [of another state] conceived in a spirit hostile to that which pervades her own laws."[74] The political consequence of this ruling was that slavery was legalized everywhere. It ended the practice of recognizing a political geography of freedom, and it attached slavery as a legal status to the body of the slave.[75] Once hinged to the body, the struggle over slavery and the enforcements of freedom at the Kansas-Missouri border were no longer guaranteed.

As the national legalization of slavery that occurred with *Dred Scott* in 1857 pushed abolition's line toward Canada, the struggle over the power to punish became central to the struggle over slavery. As being Black and being free became a contradiction that was etched onto the body, even those with freedom papers became targets of public and private forces, and attempts at relocation north were now considered crimes. In January of 1859, when "fugitive hunters" targeted people known to be free within the city of Lawrence, thirteen chose to leave the township and head north: "All had their freedom papers, except for two, Wilson Hayes and Charles Smith, who had worked as cooks at the Eldridge House and were known to be free men."[76] Accompanied by the white abolitionist John Doy and his son, the group was apprehended and arrested nearly twenty miles outside of Lawrence near Oskaloosa, Kansas. Thirteen free Black people were sold into slavery under the authority of both public and private jurisdiction, with the exception of an unnamed man, who was sent to the Platte City Jail, where he soon escaped by "burning out the bars from the windows."[77] Letters written by those who aided him, including Ephraim Nute, reveal that in making his escape, he

walked 10 miles to the Missouri River and crossed on the floating cakes of ice; got 1st on to an island or sand-bar in the middle of the river where he spent two days and nights hid in the young cottonwoods; thence again over the running ice to the Kansas side and walked the 35 or 40 miles to [Lawrence] in one night. . . . We have him now hid and are to day making arrangements to have him set forward tomorrow 30 miles to another depot. I think they will not be taken again without bloodshed.[78]

His departure north occurred when, according to those who hid him, he was transported "in a coach from Leavenworth disguised in female attire. We kept him 2 days. I then took him by night and afoot across lots through an 80 acre corn field in which the stalks are standing and to another hiding place from this he has in the same way been moved on from house to house until he is about 8 miles on his way and will be started in the small hours tomorrow morning for Canada."[79] As the peculiar institution became embedded in and enforced through the mechanisms of the jail and the prison, federal law formed the backdrop against which Kansas territorial law consolidated its power over the punishment of abolition.

The contested nature of law in the territory meant that even though the Doys had never left Kansas Territory, they were transported to the state of Missouri and held for trial in Platte City. They were charged under Missouri law for stealing slaves even though they accompanied free people, and were confined in a cell "made of boiler iron, eight feet square by seven feet high, with no ventilation except a small grating in the door."[80] After two months in this "iron box," a change of venue moved the trial to St. Joseph, Missouri, where a heavily armed guard of mounted public citizens prevented their escape.[81] In July, when the Doys were sentenced to five years in the Missouri State Penitentiary, another group of antislavery citizens traveled from Lawrence to refuse to recognize Missouri law. Breaking John Doy from the jailhouse, the "Immortal Ten" returned to Lawrence having refused to recognize the authority of Missouri or its penitentiary.[82] The success of an impossible escape against a proslavery regime of punishment put the prison at the center of the war over freedom in Bleeding Kansas.

## THE PRISON REUNITES THE LEGAL IMAGINARIES OF SLAVERY AND FREEDOM

Over the course of the next several years, "the trouble" in Kansas and the vastly different ideas about statehood, citizenship, and justice that constituted its legal time resulted in four applications for statehood. The federal government denied the first three applications for their ideas about state governance and finally admitted Kansas to the Union in 1861, when its proposed constitution conformed to the federal government's vision—a place that was subject to "law and order."[83] As four state constitutional conventions defined not just what statehood would mean for Kansas but what Kansas would mean for statehood, the project of the prison became part of the commonsense governance of Kansas. Culminating in the Wyandotte Constitution, the process of state making combined a commitment to law and order with a vision of a people's prison.[84] That project required that Kansas abandon its abolitionist visions, and as the free-state people transitioned into the Free State Party and entered the Union in 1861, the idea of a white Kansas betrayed and divided the free-state movement into abolition and "free-soil" factions.[85] This division shifted the focus from the war over slavery toward the right of white Kansans to protect themselves from "foreign" invasions against their ballot boxes, whether by white Missourian invaders or Black fugitive "contraband." Du Bois described the Kansas compromise as resulting from a political coalition in which only "a few . . . hated slavery, more . . . hated Negroes, and many . . . hated slaves."[86]

Having betrayed its abolitionist past, Kansas disenfranchised Black citizens through a series of legislative actions, ballot initiatives, and legal decisions. The Kansas legislature voted in 1863 and 1866 to keep the word *white* in the state's constitution. In 1867, white Kansas voters rejected a ballot initiative on Black suffrage. When the Fifteenth Amendment was ratified in 1870, the state courts immediately defied federal directives, and in 1871 the Kansas Supreme Court in *Anthony v. Halderman* approved the disenfranchisement of 150 Black voters for failing to properly demonstrate their residency in accordance with Leavenworth's city registration laws. Black residents of Leavenworth had challenged the Wyandotte Constitution's exclusions after a contested mayoral election, and the Kansas Supreme Court agreed with the defense that "the privilege or franchise of voting is only given to certain *white* persons."[87] In Kansas, the word *white* was not removed from the state constitution until 1918.

The transformation of Kansas from a place of Black freedom to a place of Black exclusion had first been imagined at the failed 1855 and 1857 constitutional conventions. Although the wording was not included in the final draft of the Big Springs Constitution, the political platform excluded Black people from the state altogether: "*The best interests of Kansas require a population of free white men.*"[88] Rejected by Congress and President Pierce on the grounds that it would violate the property rights of slaveholders, the failed constitution nonetheless recorded the interconnectedness of prisons and slavery in its prohibition of slavery and its exception: "There shall be no slavery in this state, nor involuntary servitude, unless for the punishment of crime."[89] The failure of the first free-state constitution was followed by a proslavery convention that resulted in the proposed 1857 Lecompton Constitution. The Lecompton Constitution would have legalized slavery and restored the right of white property to a place "higher than any constitutional sanction . . . the right of the owner of a slave to such slave and its increase is the same and as inviolable as the right of the owner of any property whatever."[90] It would also have prohibited the legislature from regulating slavery at any point in the future, creating a structure of governance in which slavery would have become an unchangeable institution. The document was praised by President Buchanan but was ultimately defeated by Republicans in Congress.

When the promise of slavery failed to bring Kansas into the Union, the Free State Party responded with a convention held in Leavenworth in 1858, where party members drafted a document that outlawed slavery, enfranchised "every male citizen," and required the building of a state prison.[91] Embedded in the very idea of a free-state Kansas, the prison became the foundation of the state-making project because it represented the authority of law. As an indicator of the possession of power, the prison served as the ultimate symbol of the right to do justice. While abolition Kansas had once fought and died over what it meant to be free, the state of Kansas would operate in the name of the people even as it claimed the right to imprison them. Supported largely by the free-state and free-soil political parties, the Leavenworth Constitution was the first to imagine a Kansas state prison, requiring that its location and its "directors and superintendents" be "elected by the people" in a "vote of the electors at large."[92] The document's ratification was opposed by the old "border-ruffian element," which "remain[ed] in Leavenworth, and occasionally display[ed] itself."[93] The former members of the Bogus Legislature had reorganized themselves in support of the previously defeated Lecompton Constitution and in support of the principles of "Law and Order." The Law and Order Party, which met in Leavenworth as early as 1855, declared that "no man or set of men are at liberty to resist a law passed by a legislative body, legally organized, unless they choose by their actions to constitute themselves rebels and traitors, and take all the consequences that legitimately follow the failure of a revolution."[94] The party's ideas were described in relation to other proslavery civic organizations in the *New York Times*: "For some time past, it has been known that the Knights of the Golden Circle had revived their old organizations in town and county. Information gives their number in the city as about sixty and throughout the county at three hundred. They are composed principally of the old Border Ruffian element, with which we have always been pestered. All call themselves Democrats, and this faction hold the balance of power here. It is they who have the brains and money, and their votes carry elections. As a consequence, all office-strikers bow to their decision."[95]

While the Free State Party and the Law and Order Party were divided and even at war over the question of slavery's future, the prison reunited the legal imaginaries of slavery and freedom. The idea of Kansas that finally brought it into the Union put the prison, as a symbol of law and order, at the center of its state-making project. When Kansas became a "free state" in 1861, the Wyandotte Constitution simply required that "a penitentiary . . . be established."[96] The state immediately designed a prison that transferred the power of the people to the state. The location of the new state penitentiary, which was built in Leavenworth County by the architect Erasmus Carr, was selected because of the temporary use of the city jailhouse as a state prison and because of the prison's social importance in the new legal order of Kansas state. Leavenworth was selected because it "exerted a major influence in the councils of the new state of Kansas."[97] By 1867, the prison was only a "temporary wooden stockade" measuring eighty-seven by thirty-six feet and housing one hundred prisoners who were "almost naked—clad in rags."[98] The result of one's imprisonment in this institution was a legal status of civil death: "A sentence of confinement and hard labor for a term less than life, suspends all civil rights of the person so sentenced during the term thereof . . . and a person sentenced to such confinement for life, shall thereafter be deemed civilly dead."[99]

FIGURE 8. Postcard image, Kansas State Penitentiary, n.d.

This structure of civil death, which emerged from the Wyandotte conciliation, was a triumph of state power over and against the people's justice, and a betrayal of *abolition Kansas*. It inaugurated a system of governance that ended the practice of slavery but limited the franchise to "white male persons."[100] Incorporating the racial framework of slavery into its afterlife, the prison reunited the legal imaginaries of slavery and freedom.

The prison at the end of the Mason-Dixon Line was, by 1875, indistinguishable from its proslavery counterpart in Missouri. Patterned after the prison in antislavery Illinois, its castellated architecture made it a symbol of northern reformative and industrial principles. Putting its 379 prisoners to work making wagons, shoes, furniture, harnesses, marble slabs, bricks, twine, and coal, Kansas was considered a model prison. As historian Blake McKelvey has noted, "Kansas stuck doggedly to what many had considered an overambitious program and was able to report in 1880 the completion of the entire prison structure. With 688 up-to-date cells patterned after those at Joliet it was, without a rival, the best prison west of the Mississippi."[101] But prisoners in the institution published accounts of their experience, referring to the prison as *The Kansas Inferno* (1906) and *A Kansas Hell* (1890).[102] John Reynolds, who spent time in both the Kansas and Missouri state prisons, even called the indistinguishable institutions *The Twin Hells*.[103] The prison of Kansas was anchored in a routine state violence that was inflicted on the bodies of prisoners who were civilly dead—violence rooted in the use of the chain, the cuff, the iron horse, and the water crib, "a coffin-sized box that gradually filled with water while a strapped-down inmate struggled to keep from drowning."[104] Reuniting the legal imaginaries of slavery and freedom, the prison made use of popular sovereignty even as it secured for the state the practice of justice and the

practice of law and order. This was an uneven and unstable security interrupted by
the memories of border war and the legal time of Bleeding Kansas.

Although the prison that came with statehood was in some ways honored as
the end of war, custom in many instances remained more powerful than law. The
Kansas legislature found it necessary to protect the prison from the people's dissent. New laws in 1862 made it a crime to set fire to the new state prison or to
rescue a prisoner from imprisonment or execution.[105] These laws appeared necessary because the methods of the border war continued through the guise of popular justice. The proslavery element, for example, hanged John Guthrie for horse
stealing in Bourbon County; observers described how he was punished "without
authority or shadow of law and never [given] even a mock trial, as has generally
been the case."[106] Free-state vigilance committees also continued to hold court to
punish proslavery forces. A party of free-state men arrested and hanged Russell
Hinds after he returned a fugitive slave to Missouri; firsthand accounts suggest
that, drawing on the tradition of civic justice, the party "quickly convened a court,
sentenced and hanged him for this offense."[107] In proslavery Atchison, in April of
1863, "A mob took possession of the jail and courthouse for a week; they held court
and tried each prisoner, with four or five lynchings as the result."[108] Between 1850
and 1930, there were 206 killings by nonstate actors assuming the work of law in
the Territory and then state of Kansas.[109]

What was obscured by all the violence was that in the aftermath of slavery the
war was really about the prison. What was also obscured was the federal government's role in fomenting that violence. When the Lawrence Massacre began
on August 21, 1863, the Emancipation Proclamation had already been issued on
January 1. This meant that slaves in the Confederate states had gone free, but five
hundred thousand remained legally bound in the southern states that did not formally secede. This meant that slavery still existed in Missouri until the governor
issued a state proclamation in January of 1865. In the space between slavery and
freedom, federal troops in what had become the Border District (all of Kansas and
western Missouri) began arresting the mothers and sisters of known Confederates
in the region. The women were held in a former tavern in Kansas City, Missouri,
that was repurposed as a prison.[110] With seventeen inside, the building collapsed
and four women were killed. Others were permanently injured. The federal use of
a prison on behalf of Bleeding Kansas led to retaliation in Lawrence. Quantrill's
Raid was an early morning attack that killed nearly two hundred people in less
than four hours.[111] These events show how central the prison was to the war and its
memory, and as moments in the history of the carceral state they illustrate what it
meant to build a prison state.

The continuing struggle over punitive authority in the region was resolved
through a process of centralization in which the state gained authority over matters of justice by preserving the old legal rituals in new forms and by including
"the democracy" in the state practice of justice. Mobilizing the power of popular

sovereignty on behalf of the state, the new legal regime drew on the old rituals of trial, imprisonment, and execution in order to consolidate state authority over practices of justice. Leavenworth's local papers described the military execution of John Shirley for robbery in a time of martial law as "one of the most exciting, soul-thrilling scenes ever witnessed" and as the "largest concourse of people [ever] assembled in Kansas."[112] Shirley's hanging not only reinforced the spectacle of the procedure but consolidated the ritual influence of the military and martial law in Leavenworth. His execution had its beginning and end marked by the music of a military band—a "mournful dirge" for a death procession in which "silence pervaded the crowd," and a "lively air" as the body was taken down.[113] As a celebration of a successful legal ritual, the military music that ended the ceremony also symbolized the triumph of federal law and order in a space that challenged state conceptualizations of justice. It was this triumphant practice that drew crowds of Kansans to witness the spectacles. When Carl Horne was hung in February of 1863, "every crack or cranny of the high fence was soon sought out by two or three pairs of eyes, anxious to get a look at the [gallows]."[114] By 1870, newspapers reported that executions were "besieged by crowds" so that "a stranger would have imagined a popular circus was about."[115] As passive participants *in the state's justice,* citizens observed state and federal and military rituals and in doing so ultimately recognized the authority of the state through the new exclusions of participation.

These new legal rituals were distinguished by the citizen's changed relationship to the work of justice. In the older traditions, "the people" controlled the mechanisms of justice; they convened deliberative bodies and developed local rituals for carrying out sentences. But the new tradition distanced the citizen-audience from those who acted on behalf of the state. By 1870, the identity of the executioner was routinely withheld from the public eye. In Leavenworth, the executioner was "enveloped in a Black domino surmounted by a Black hood."[116] The crowds during hangings were "anxious to know who sprung the trap," but "the sharpest eyes failed to discover the identity of the masked instrument of the law's vengeance."[117] Enshrouded in mystery, the rituals were part of a larger imaginary that specified roles for public and private actors in the spectacle of execution. In Leavenworth, it was customary for the masked executioner to utter the words "May God have mercy on your soul" and to release the trapdoor on the last word.[118] Because the prisoner was hooded and his hands were secured behind him with a white handkerchief, the primary relationship that was produced and legitimated in the ceremony was between the executioner and the crowd. Unseen by the condemned, the charges were inscribed on a "grim document" that was tied with "Black crepe" and "handed to the sheriff at the proper time and ceremoniously unrolled."[119]

As the citizen became a different kind of legal participant, a direct observer who expected to read detailed accounts of executions in the morning papers, the public's perception of state authority was manufactured not only in the crowded rituals of state-imposed death but also in the recording and circulating of execution stories in local newspapers.[120] As the act of reading about executions increasingly became part of the ritual, the press reported the details of death work in excruciating detail, evaluating for its audience the success of the new legal procedures. Allowing readers to relive the experience, the newspapers reported on the diligence of the authorities and the emotions of the condemned, along with the weather, the crowd, and the ritual silence of taking down the body. Reporting whether authorities seemed nervous or whether the death warrant was read in a "clear, steady voice," local newspapers emphasized the proper roles of the participants.[121] Officials appeared confident in their own legal authority when the condemned appeared subdued and solemn in the final moments. John Shirley, who was executed during Leavenworth's martial law, was reported to have "ascended the terrible instrument of death" with confidence: his "step was firm, and not a muscle of his face showed the least indication of fear or faltering. He was not even pale."[122] William Dickson in 1870 ascended the stairs of the gallows "more firmly," the paper noted, "than any of his escort."[123]

As state authority was consolidated over time by the widening of death's audience to include readers as witnesses, newspapers extended their coverage to include the minute details of the audience reaction. In 1870, Dickson's hanging in Leavenworth ended when he "hung without a struggle for twenty-five minutes" before a silent and stunned audience, while "a corps of physicians . . . made examinations every half minute."[124] The *Leavenworth Daily Times* published the information in chart form—"a resume of the dying man's pulse rate, taken every thirty seconds."[125] The force of state death as cultural custom became such an important form of political participation (albeit a passive and even exclusionary form of participation) that the *Leavenworth Daily Conservative* celebrated punishment as a public duty, even as justice became both a state and a private practice: because of the burdens of the past, "a summary visitation of merited punishment has become a duty."[126] While the *Daily Conservative* had once been one of the most ardently antislavery papers in the state, it now celebrated the punishment of its criminals: "Punishing criminals is one of our things, and we shall adhere to it!"[127]

## THE MEANING OF LEAVENWORTH

When Kansas stood against slavery in 1854, it abolished slavery but retained the legal status of the slave in its prisons. It could have been otherwise. Abolition Kansas might have refused to honor the state practice of the prison as it had refused to honor the legality of slavery. Instead, the military, state, and federal prisons of Kansas became monuments to law and order and a reconciliation that recalled the dream of abolition justice only as part of the shamed history of "mob rule." The idea of the prison was always at the center of the federal intervention in Bleeding Kansas—it emerged first in judges' homes turned into jails, in buildings that collapsed, and in tents pitched on the prairie. When the federal idea of law and order finally took the shape of a castle with bars, walls, and cages of steel after 1861, it failed to eliminate the power of custom. Emerging from this very specific place and time, the idea of Leavenworth was the culmination of a long attempt to wrest power from the people in the name of the people, and it secured that power through the inversions of an architecture that signified democracy.

Positioning itself as the answer to its own violence, the federal prison system took root in the afterlife of Bleeding Kansas, transforming a place that had rejected federal power into a place that embraced penal citizenship as a way of life. That process of prison building as state building through the terrain of culture is etched onto the landscape and honored as a form of law and order that now constitutes its very statehood. John Brown and "the freaks" who defied federal law to abolish slavery as a legal imaginary have been tucked away in the cemetery or the madhouse, or have even been condemned as early examples of "domestic terrorism."[128] When abolition Kansas is acknowledged, its power as a form of justice is often marginalized as "essentially a myth" because only a vocal "minority" believed in slavery's illegality or because the protection of white voting rights from outside invasion eventually became paramount.[129] Others have suggested that the violence of Bleeding Kansas has been exaggerated on the grounds that there were "only" fifty-six "political killings" in Kansas Territory between 1854 and 1861, a counting that presumes that the lines between state and private violence and social and political crimes could ever truly be measured.[130] It also fails to capture the chronology of a violence that continued beyond the Civil War, particularly since the second burning of Lawrence, which took nearly two hundred lives in a single morning, occurred in 1863. Bleeding Kansas was a critical moment in a local war over the terms of democracy but also in the history of US law and the emergence of the carceral state.

The prison's central place in the legacy of Bleeding Kansas is now forgotten even in moments of its remembrance. When recalled by the major news networks during basketball games between the Kansas University Jayhawks and the Missouri University Tigers (both named after militia groups from Bleeding Kansas), sportscasters describe the popular rivalry as drama that goes "all the way back to the Civil War." The documentary film *The Border War* contains footage of a pregame celebration in which Jayhawks insult Missourians with signs that accuse them of being slave owners and racists, while Missouri fans warn that the game will mark Quantrill's Revenge. As sworn enemies, the Kansas Jayhawks and Missouri Tigers of the twenty-first century did not approve of a change in the annual event's official description from "Border War" to "Border Showdown" after 9/11, when it was decided that it was no longer appropriate to refer to intercollegiate sports as war. Former Kansas coach Don Fambrough remarked that "it's not a showdown, or a hoedown, it's a goddamn war. And they started it."[131] Because the annual tradition was ended in 2012 after nearly one hundred years because of conference changes, the teams no longer engage in a rivalry that makes the nation remember. The political consequence is that Bleeding Kansas is no longer part of a national memory despite its relation to penal federalism but is reduced to local rituals like the annual reading of the names of Lawrence's dead. The prison's absence from these resurrections and burials means that the federal apparatus that overlaid and prosecuted the landscape of abolition justice is no longer understood as an invasion. When Kansas was taught *through punishment* to reject "mob justice" and embrace the federalization of crime and punishment, the federal prison's meaning in the context of that history was reduced to the forgotten rubble of a war punished by the turning of "the people's house" into the Big House. Despite the fading of the border war from public memory, abolition Kansas remains etched on the walls of the state capitol building. John Brown's body is present, but not his warning that the free state might be turned into the prison state: "On the eve of one of the greatest wars in history,. . .I fear slavery will triumph, and there will be an end of all aspirations for human freedom. For my part I drew my sword in Kansas when they attacked us, and I will never sheathe it until this war is over. Our best people do not understand the danger. They are besotted. They have compromised so long that they think principles of right and wrong have no more any power on this earth."[132] Having been made to believe in institutions as sites of justice, the prison remained an artifact of slavery in the most radical of states on the slavery question. As part of the history of mass incarceration, the legal time of Bleeding Kansas led to the formation of the federal prison system and a cultural tradition of penal citizenship that normalized civil death and state violence.

# 4

# Prisons at the Border

## *The Political Geography of the Mason-Dixon Line*

When Leavenworth consolidated the post-Reconstruction political landscape by redesigning the terrain of civil death, it carried forward the race-making traditions of an earlier era. Leavenworth taught race not only through the arrangements of racialized bodies but also through the procedures of fugitive pursuit. In 1898, as prisoners marched from the military prison to the new construction site, fifteen prisoners ran into the woods. "Innumerable volunteers" scoured the landscape and "ransacked the woods" for fifteen "desperate characters"—"some of the worst criminals from the Indian Territory."[1] In 1901, another mass escape of twenty-seven prisoners ended in a gunfight and "the most desperate prison mutiny which ever happened in this section of the country."[2] Subsequent reports focused almost exclusively on the pursuit of Frank Thompson, the "desperate Negro ringleader," and his unidentified companions, "Indian and white."[3] Their arrests were celebrated: "Twelve men are safe, two on pine tables in the dead house, two in the hospital, and eight in the dungeon."[4] According to the local paper, "Crowds of the morbidly curious viewed the dead bodies and visited the scene of the shooting."[5] It was agreed that "nothing like the present condition of affairs has been experienced by Kansas since the border ruffian times."[6]

During the course of this community ritual, Frank Thompson was one of the last to be caught. Thompson, despite his five-foot-seven-inch frame, was described in the papers as "lurking near the Kaw" at Lawrence, a "bad southern negro, a giant in strength, cunning, brutal and with absolutely not a bit of good in him."[7] Among these men was J. N. O. P. Wood, "formerly of Leavenworth," who had once kept the prisoners of Bleeding Kansas in his house.[8] In the deputization of white citizens as legal agents, local farmers joined state forces, seeking the sixty-dollar reward for capture. Accompanied by a reporter from the *Leavenworth Times*, the search parties "hung to the hunt like grim bull dogs. . . . Farmers, sheriffs, county and city officers are scouring all timber, watching all roads and holding all bridges."[9] The "talk heard on everyside" was the bravery of the "six citizens" who "engaged" the prisoners in battle after responding to the call of the prison siren. The capture of Thompson was an act of bravery, according to the newspaper, because he once had to be "chained and shackled and secured to a stake in an open field" without a cap and "left broiling under a merciless sun" so that he could be "brought into subjection."[10] Thompson's capture made news again when he was "shot in the head, without being severely injured."[11] In this post-Reconstruction Kansas landscape, federal power and the practice of hunting for fugitives was represented as a matter of settled law and no longer an intrusion: "Uncle Sam often hangs murderers and there is a strong likelihood that the seven ringleaders, if they are caught, will stretch hemp."[12]

For his role in this mass escape, Frank Thompson received a life sentence, which was later commuted. Despite his representation as a violent and notorious prisoner, he was sent to Leavenworth from Ardmore, Central District, Indian Territory, on a seven-year sentence for larceny. His prison file acknowledges that he had no part in the killing of Guard Waldrupe but that prison officials believed that mass escape required mass punishment.[13] Although he was sent to the solitary cells nearly twenty times at Leavenworth, his offenses included laughing, talking to other prisoners, leaving the worksite, cursing at guards, and otherwise resisting the prison's structure of silence and labor. In the "stone cells," solitary prisoners were required to break rock during the daytime hours on a restricted diet. In January of 1902, Thompson was placed in one of these cells and "clothed in stripes, to wear [the] ball and chain."[14] He was once placed in the dark cells, the triangular dungeons in the basement of Building 63. Thompson's relationship to a nationalized prison system is indicated in the warden's handwritten note at the bottom of the preprinted form that inventoried prison discipline. He had once been confined at the Arkansas State Penitentiary in Little Rock, and after his release from Leavenworth he appeared, according to fingerprint evidence, as Morris Dent in the Oklahoma State Penitentiary.[15] His confinement illustrates the carceral state's focus on Black prisoners from the Indian Territory, the post-Reconstruction ritual of hunting prisoners like slaves, and the residues of slavery that were carried over into state and federal prison systems, into dungeons built like triangles and solitary cells anchored in chains.

In the post-Reconstruction landscape, the prison's relationship to the peculiar institution was embedded in the institution's aurality, in the sounds of search hounds, grim hunts, and deputized citizens. As an everyday racial regime, the prison was part of a culture that connected it to slavery in ways that exceeded targeted bodies, forms of labor, or methods of discipline. These aural connections, built into the social life of the region, are best understood historically through W. E. B. Du Bois's representation of the congenital connections between slavery and prisons in "Jesus Christ in Texas" (1920). In this short story, a "mulatto" Jesus (or perhaps Du Bois himself) interrupts the sale of convicts in the opening scene with questions about the harms of the practice and is invited to dinner by a man who hopes to build a railroad with prison labor. The dinner party's participants— the colonel-capitalist, the white housewife, the criminal court judge, the military officer, and the preacher—represent racialized capitalism, white supremacy and white womanhood, military violence, and organized religion. Although their social engagement is continually interrupted by "howl after howl," which "rose in the night, swelled, and died away," the sound of the search for escaped prisoners is such a normalized aspect of their daily lives that they only comment in passing as they dine: "Another one of those convicts escaped, I suppose. Really, they need severer measures."[16] Using the allegorical figuration of the characters to critically observe—as both Du Bois the scholar and Jesus the absolver of social sin—the collective labors that make the prison an everyday institution, Du Bois had already discovered in 1920 the legacies of the prison's appearance as common sense, as an institution that survives not just in the racial terrain of the border but in daily rituals as routine as the dinner table. What if prisons produce rather than reflect the larger order of race in society?

This chapter tries to recover, through an attention to the historical political geography of enslavement and punishment at the border, the connections between prisons and slavery that continue to anchor the practice of mass incarceration. It was no accident that prisons first emerged in the United States at the border between slavery and freedom, in "states with thriving commercial cities," including Virginia, Maryland, Kentucky, Tennessee, and Missouri.[17] As a line of prisons that emerged across the landscape, border prisons formed "a belt of states stretching from Virginia and the Carolinas to Missouri that scarcely fell in with the general penological trends of either the North or the Deep South."[18] Entrenched in the state-sponsored law of slavery, the border prisons served as the epicenter of a carceral complex that was both public and private and that structured a political geography of mass incarceration. Kansas, of course, stood at the end of this line.

When an emerging federal prison system looked to the states to house its prisoners in the post–Civil War era, it utilized mostly the institutions along the northern side of the border. The idea of the "southern prison" overtook the idea of the border prison, and the federal government looked to border prisons that had become "northern institutions" to house federal prisoners. In the context of these regional shifts, the meaning of the border prison was forgotten and the homogenization of the southern prison meant that its challenge to "penitentiary slavery" has been erased from the prison's archive. The relationship between border prisons and southern prisons reveals a moment when citizens refused to consent to state violence against the body. While some Deep South states built prisons, they largely abandoned the institutions in the early part of the nineteenth century, and some southern states refused to build prisons altogether until after the Civil War. The

Carolinas and Florida were the last to admit citizens to the prison in the late 1860s. Southern reluctance to adopt the penitentiary form was eventually resolved only by the "blackening" of the institution. When Leavenworth withdrew federal prisoners from state prisons altogether, the border prison became a forgotten artifact in the institution of slavery and the codification of "Black crime."

This chapter works to disentangle the history of the border prison from the larger story of American punishment in order to trace how the project of Black containment became a systematizing force in the history of state and federal prisons. The border prison explains the entrenched history of Black incarceration in the United States and the political geography of slavery as a form of mass incarceration. The chapter's archival work reveals how the narrative of northern rehabilitation and southern retribution has obscured the history of slaves in prisons and shifted the focus to the later horrors of the convict lease system. While the regime of convict leasing affected the whole southern landscape of rights and racial status, it did so beginning mostly but not entirely in the aftermath of the Civil War.[19] The Deep South states began experiments as early as the 1840s with a lease system that lasted for over one hundred years; in the border states, the penitentiaries were already gothic monuments by 1840. Because the history of the border prison has been overshadowed by a North-South regionalism, this chapter examines how border states used prisons to define the terms of freedom and bondage and how Leavenworth, as a nationalizing project, attached this conjoined legal status to the bodies of all prisoners in the post-Reconstruction era.

## A GOTHIC HISTORY OF SLAVES IN PRISONS

The history of slavery and prisons in the border states is structured by two overlapping systems of punishment. In the southern states as a region, buildings called "slave jails" emerged to discipline and punish enslaved people. But prisons in the border states were also used to punish slaves, either because the state bought the body of the enslaved in order to inflict punishment or because slave owners brought slaves to the state for punishment. The mixed genealogy of public and private punishments during the time of slavery marks the history of the prison as a legal arrangement. The idea of mass incarceration was born in the relationship between slavery and prisons as congenital institutions, as practices connected from birth and organized by the same kind of legal status.

The emergence of state penitentiaries at the border was driven by a political economy specific to the border region. Because border cities and towns relied on a combination of free and unfree Black labor, the region had large concentrations of both kinds of workers. In Maryland, slaves made up one-third of the state population as early as 1790, and in the southern portion of the state 54 percent of Black people were free and 44 percent were enslaved by the start of the Civil War.[20] Likewise, in Virginia, 60,000 free Black people lived alongside 58,042 slaves in 1860.[21] Border states were some of the first to adopt the prison as a mechanism for managing a dual class of free and enslaved Black people as part of this political economy of the border. In this context, the prison became a "Black" institution in the border states as places for managing the legal condition of Black freedom.

Unlike in the Deep South, where there were few free Black people and almost no Black prisoners, the border prison stood at the center of slavery as a form of mass incarceration. When freed and self-emancipated persons gathered in the border-lands in unprecedented numbers, border states developed "crime control" methods to eliminate the "corrupting" influence of freedom on those bound by law to a "slave criminality." In the "misty and elusive terrain" of the Middle Ground, slaves arrived at state penitentiaries in order to be executed, deported to other states, held for punishment upon public conviction for "slave crime," or submitted for state punishment by private individuals.[22] In these cross-currents of Black punishment, states sold prisoners who were already slaves for the profit of the public treasury but also sentenced free people to the condition of slavery upon conviction for crime. The border prisons created a legal apparatus in which a free person could be treated like a slave and a slave could be punished by the state as though he were free.

The routine presence of slaves in prisons has been obscured in the written history of the US prison.[23] The public punishment of slave-prisoners contradicted the principle in political thought that prisons and slaves were irreconcilable. This was an idea at the heart of liberal contract governance. The slave, as a subject who was not free, had no liberty to give to the state; only a free subject who failed to abide by the law brought on the loss of freedom. Although slaves were not supposed to be subject to *state* punishment, archival records in the border states, including prison ledgers, state laws, and first-person accounts, show slaves in prisons in Maryland, Virginia, Kentucky, Tennessee, and Missouri. While the practice was largely a border state project, in the Deep South states Arkansas briefly incarcerated slaves for second-degree murder before abandoning the practice in 1858, while the prison-friendly Louisiana sent more than two hundred slaves, including children, between 1835 and 1862 to a penitentiary where all prisoners were employed making shoes and clothes for slaves across the state.[24] Louisiana passed an 1848 law that made all children born to the thirty-three enslaved women incarcerated for life "the legal property of the state," and the auction of eleven children brought proceeds to the state treasurer for the "free-school fund."[25]

The combined threats of death, incarceration, deportation, and re-enslavement formed the basis of American slave punishments in nineteen-century state penitentiaries. In the border states, prisons were first used as part of the institution of slavery as sites for slave executions, which required the state's seizure of slave "property" in cases of exceptional crime. Slave executions were rooted in the idea that states were obligated to punish slave crime in instances when, as Gustave de Beaumont described it, "outraged society demands reparation."[26] Indemnification was required when the state took an enslaved person from the person claiming ownership, and state sentencing courts determined the "market value" of enslaved persons in order to compensate owners for the loss of this "property."[27] The role of southern courts in the regulation of slavery as an institution meant that southern states were "paying for the right to do justice."[28] Compensation laws existed in Delaware (1787), Maryland (1788), South Carolina (1788), Virginia (1788), North Carolina (1789), D.C. (1790–1), Kentucky (1792), Louisiana (1812), and Alabama (1819).[29] Only Tennessee, Arkansas, and Florida allowed "slave property" to be seized without compensation. The whole regulatory structure of southern slave law, which governed the state's right to take the life of a person without status, is part of the history of mass incarceration and the racialization of the penitentiary form.

The criminal jurisprudence of southern slavery shifted from executions to penitentiary punishment because slave executions in state institutions were frequent and therefore costly. Between 1785 and 1865, Virginia paid for the right to execute over 628 slaves.[30] Condemning a slave to death in Virginia required a unanimous decision of the courts of *oyer and terminer,* which heard cases of "slave crime" committed off the plantations and "issued orders for execution, loss of member, or other punishment."[31] In 1821, Kentucky paid $2,110 for "slaves executed" as required by the 1898 Slave Code.[32] Kentucky insisted that it could execute without compensation any slave brought into the state "for merchandise, or which shall be passing through."[33]

Federal law eventually ratified the right of states to seize slave property for execution and punishment but left the matter of compensation to the states. In *United States v. Amy* (1859), an enslaved woman named Amy was prosecuted in federal court on a new law requiring a ten-year prison sentence for stealing mail. Amy's position was not actually represented in the case, and her owner's lawyer argued that because the Fifth Amendment's Just Compensation Clause applied to the states, the federal government had reached into the "private" institution of slavery and should therefore compensate her owner according to the terms of Virginia law. He argued that because she was property state law required proper compensation for her prison time. Chief Justice Taney ruled that "a person, whether free or slave, is not taken for public use when he is punished for an offence against the law. . . . Society has a right to punish for its own safety, although the punishment may render the property of the master of little or no value."[34] Although the Supreme Court's ratification of slave punishments in *United States v. Amy* involved a law under which anyone could be prosecuted, states began widening the range of offenses for which only slaves could be punished and therefore increased significantly the number of slaves in prisons.

The idea of indemnification for slaves sentenced to prison time was settled law in Maryland by the early 1800s. From 1812 to 1820, slaves were routinely held in the Maryland penitentiary, and owners were compensated for the loss of their property according to the terms of the 1809 Penitentiary Act.[35] The state's very first prisoner in 1811 was the slave Bob Butler; he was accompanied by sixteen other enslaved people in an institution where half of the prisoners were Black.[36] According to the 1809 law, should a slave-prisoner "survive his or her time in confinement," he or she would be "sold by auction" upon the expiration of the sentence.[37] After 1817, prison sentences for slaves were increased, so that no "colored person" sent to the penitentiary could serve less than one year.[38] By 1818, fully 61 of Maryland's 146 prisoners were Black, 46 of them men and 16 of them women.[39] According to William Crawford, who toured US prisons in the 1840s, Maryland's compensation laws were revised in 1819 "as to require the sale of convict slaves out of the limits of the state," while the "money arising from the sale was applied to the use of the county."[40] Despite the laws on the books, which encouraged judges to sentence Black prisoners to whippings and county sales, Black prisoners "flooded into the penitentiary."[41] Maryland's system of paying specifically for prison time made it unique among the border states, but it was part of a pattern: free and enslaved Black people represented 8 percent of Kentucky's prisoners and 4 percent of Tennessee's prisoners.[42]

As prisons became deeply entwined with the business of slavery, border states shifted from incarcerating slaves to selling slaves through systems of transportation or deportation when punishing slave crime. The Missouri Revised Statutes of 1835 gave judges the option to sentence slaves to thirty-nine lashes and public sale out of the state rather than incarceration.[43] In Maryland, an 1836 law required that slaves released from prison, upon conviction for another crime, would be "sold out of the state."[44] This led to such an overall decline in Maryland's prison population that state reports in 1842 regretted the policy's adoption because of the prison's declining profitability.[45] Under Virginia's 1800 transportation law, the governor would commute death sentences to imprisonment; then, when "public feeling would permit," the slave could be released to a private trader for sale and deportation "beyond the limits of the United States."[46] Slaves awaiting "transportation" were to be kept in dormitories of "idle, temporary storage" while arrangements were made with dealers to buy "slaves from the state in lots."[47] Although state records show that nine hundred Virginia slaves were sentenced to deportation upon convictions for crime, they languished in the state prison.[48] In 1823, Virginia superintendent Edmund Pendleton wrote: "No sale of transports has been made . . . since I came into office, and the number now confined in the Penitentiary is an inconvenience of increasing magnitude. They occupy rooms which could, in the event of their removal, be appropriated to convicts, and they add to the expenses of the establishment without being either useful or profitable."[49] By 1825, four rooms in the prison were still used for the purpose of holding slaves already sentenced to deportation, and by 1827, Governor William B. Giles lamented that transportation orders were "seldom or never complied with. . . . The whole number transported [since 1824] amount to only 44."[50] Because of the structure of deportation, Black prisoners made up fully one-third of Virginia's state prison population.

In addition to execution, incarceration, and deportation, slaves became prisoners in the border states when they were brought to the state for private punishment or "safe-keeping." In Missouri, where "the slaveholder's prison" built in 1836 was used as the punitive arm of a proslavery state, the prison was used preemptively to detain slaves who might escape.[51] George Thompson in his memoirs describes meeting an unnamed Black man imprisoned because of a "suspicion on the part of the master that he would run away."[52] While the Missouri Penitentiary was in this sense both a public and a private institution, Kentucky banned the state punishment of slaves in the Penal Code of 1802 but allowed local exceptions for safe-keeping, a "custom which had existed in the institution for years, and is still practiced under the provisions of the act."[53] Kentucky regulated the practice of penitentiary slavery in 1844, with a law declaring, "It shall not be lawful for the keepers to receive into the penitentiary any slaves for safe-keeping, unless they shall keep the same confined in the cells at night, and at all times, either during the day or night, apart from the white convicts."[54] According to Dr. William Sneed's 1860 report on the "mode and management" of the Kentucky institution, the private use of the prison to confine slaves was "the shame of the State," and the 1844 guidelines abandoned: "This section has been violated time and again, and is now forgotten, and slaves are received, worked, and fed with white convicts."[55]

In addition to the use of the public prison for private punishments, border states incarcerated slaves when they participated in the movement for abolition, which was often condemned as a movement of "scurf and scum, collected from the prisons, brothels, and sink-holes of iniquity."[56] In Maryland, the enslaved abolitionist Samuel Green was sentenced to ten years in the Maryland prison for the possession of *Uncle Tom's Cabin*, a map of Canada, and a railroad schedule.[57] In Missouri, slaves entered the penitentiary as a mass of forty-two Black and white abolitionists sent to the state prison between 1830 and 1860.[58] Missouri's 1835 Criminal Code punished slave rebellions with death or a life sentence in the penitentiary, and "stealing slaves" with a prison sentence of "not less than seven years."[59] Kentucky's system of incarcerating abolitionists began in 1811, when the state imposed death for slave conspiracies and imprisonment for "stealing slaves." In the first fifteen years of the institution, six people were incarcerated for "stealing slaves" and four for "helping slaves" run away.[60] Throughout the 1840s, Kentucky increased the range of offenses related to abolition; by 1844, six prisoners had been convicted of "assisting slaves to run away," and by 1846, Kentucky required imprisonment for the new offenses of "concealing slaves" and "enticing slaves to run away."[61] By 1853, Kentucky had imprisoned twenty-nine people for "assisting" abolition and four for "stealing slaves." In Virginia, the criminal offenses of "enticing slaves to freedom" and providing false freedom papers brought five prisoners to the penitentiary between 1800 and 1838.[62] By 1848, ten of the eighty-one free Black people in the Virginia penitentiary had aided or abetted slave escapes in a place still haunted by the mass rebellion of the slave Gabriel in 1800 and his execution at the prison.[63]

The racialization of the penitentiary form in the border states was entrenched not only through a public-private regulatory structure that put slaves in prisons but also through the cultural artifacts of everyday life. Against the backdrop of slave rebellion, the punitive powers of the border prisons reached beyond the walls in places like Richmond, where the prison was present in the lives of free Black residents because it overlooked the James River from one of the city's seven hills in a poor but free Black neighborhood called Penitentiary Bottom. Prison hangings were carried out on the edges of the nearby Black burial ground.[64] The transmutation of the penitentiary form into the routine architectures of everyday life could also be seen in the design of slave quarters. In border southern cities, slave quarters were shaped like honeycombs and mimicked the structure of incarceration: "Not only were the bondsmen's quarters placed close to the main building, but the plot itself was enclosed by high brick walls. The rooms had no windows to the outside. . . . In this arrangement, the walls had an extraordinary significance. Sometimes more than a foot thick, almost always made of brick, generally very high, they transferred a residential complex into a compound."[65] Woven into the fabric of everyday life, the prison was also at work in the slave patrols that were sometimes a compulsory part of suffrage requirements. Virginia's Public Guard, for example, was established after Gabriel's rebellion to patrol the capitol, the armory, and the penitentiary, where "one sentinel [was kept] on duty" as part of a "paid militia" that, for sixty years, protected the penitentiary against slave insurrection.[66]

When the prison ritualized Black punishment in the border states through slave executions, deportations, sales, "safe-keepings," and the terrains of the everyday, the blurred lines between slavery and freedom created a form of mass incarceration. Beginning in the 1820s, border states claimed the right to sell emancipated slaves back into bondage upon conviction for crime. In Virginia, an 1823 law required that free Black people who committed crimes punishable with more than two years of prison time be "whipped and sold as a slave."[67] Since the law disallowed Black prison sentences of less than five years, this meant that almost every crime could turn free people into slaves. While the law was partially repealed in 1828, by 1860 even those born free could be sold into perpetual slavery: "If any free negro commit an offense for which he is punishable by confinement in the penitentiary, he may, at the discretion of the court before whom he is tried, be punished, in lieu of such confinement in the penitentiary, by sale into absolute slavery."[68] Through these legal mechanisms, more than thirty-five free people were sold into slavery by the state of Virginia.[69] Between 1858 and 1860, eighty-nine Black prisoners from Maryland were "sold into slavery" by the state for terms of two to sixty-five years.[70] In 1861, seventeen free Black people were sold into slavery, while sixteen slaves languished in the penitentiary.[71] Maryland's system also targeted "vagrants" and those who refused to labor according to contracts, who could be "bound or sold . . . at the direction of a magistrates' or orphans' court."[72] Using the prison as a mechanism for returning free people to the legal condition of slavery, states at the border created a freedom defined by the possibility of slavery.

Border states blurred the lines between slavery and freedom not just by turning free people into slaves but by banishing free people from the state and enslaving them if they failed to leave within time constraints set by the state. This was part of a long colonial tradition that began in 1691, when Virginia slave owners who emancipated slaves were required to arrange for their paid transportation out of the state "within six months" or face a "penalty of ten pounds sterling to the church wardens . . . to the use of the poor of the parish."[73] The state of Virginia consolidated its punitive manumission policies in 1806, when lawmakers established that all emancipated slaves were to leave the state within twelve months of manumission.[74] In the state constitution of 1850–51, Virginia reaffirmed that "slaves hereafter emancipated shall *forfeit their freedom* by remaining in the commonwealth more than twelve months after they become actually free, and *shall be reduced to slavery* under such regulations as may be prescribed by law."[75] The reduction of the free population and regulation of manumission was widely depicted as a crime-prevention strategy, while the subsequent migrations out of Virginia led Maryland, Kentucky, Ohio, and Delaware to pass laws banning free Black people from entering their boundaries. Indiana, Illinois, Missouri, North Carolina, and Tennessee also developed restrictive policies. The interstate regulation and management of Black freedom across the border relied on the narrative of "slave crime" to transfer the status of the slave to the legally free Black subject.

As states became what Du Bois called "dealers in crime," they wedded the business of slavery to the penitentiary, which took Black bodies for a cost and sold Black bodies for a profit.[76] The public and private nature of the prison in the border states reveals that slavery was foundational to mass incarceration as part of a regulatory structure deployed by the state to eliminate the threat of abolition, to manage the condition of Black freedom, and to create profitable prisons through the state sale of slaves. Border states codified the distinction between slave and free in the creation of specific slave punishments and then blurred the boundaries between them in governing the legal distinction between Black slavery and Black freedom. States used border prisons to manage slavery as part of a carceral state, while in the Deep South Black punishment was a private, administrative practice cautiously regulated by the state. In the postwar era, the regional constellation of border prisons was replaced in the political imaginary by a set of "southern prisons" that were understood as "Black institutions." The next section of the chapter explores how southern reluctance to the adoption of the penitentiary form was reconciled in the context of regional debates about punishment, property, and the law.

## SOUTHERN PENITENTIARIES AND THE CHALLENGE TO STATE VIOLENCE

In the 1840s, Louisiana, Arkansas, Mississippi, Alabama, and Texas joined the border states in building prison systems, while Florida and the Carolinas refused to adopt the penitentiary form on the grounds that it violated the honor of the citizen's body. After protracted debates about the prison's relationship to republicanism, North and South Carolina chose not to construct a penitentiary because public punishment was reserved for Black residents. Building an elaborate and expensive castle would ornament in unnecessary ways a structure that was already about Black punishment. Because of the already existing relationship between punishment and slavery, the prison was widely regarded as a form of "penitentiary slavery." When the southern tradition of prison resistance finally ended in the late 1860s, the Carolinas, Florida, and West Virginia, which had by then been set apart from Virginia, became leaders in postwar prison reform. The intertwined history of southern prisons and border prisons illustrates that the prison was not a natural institution. It required the engineered consent of a mass of southern constituencies.

In debates about the penitentiary form, white southerners were concerned with the prison's relationship to republicanism, religion, and taxes. In the republicanism that anchored southern society, the state's right to the body of the southern gentleman was restricted: touching the body defiled its sovereignty and therefore dishonored a citizenry that served as the only authorized source of state power. While governors, legislatures, planters, and grand juries urged southern voters to approve state prisons on the grounds that they would republicanize the prison and dignify the body, evangelical ministers and their congregations opposed "prison reform" on the grounds that it was contrary to God's justice. Because of this insistence that the prison undermined the retributive rendering of an eye for an eye and usurped a form of authority reserved for God, southern voters, when offered the choice, rejected the prison on the grounds that it made men subject to the will of the state rather than the will of God. Southern white citizens rejected the prison in twenty-three failed legislative attempts in North Carolina and eighty-two grand jury petitions in South Carolina between 1846 and 1857.[77] Other southern states had rejected the prison in referendums in Alabama in 1834 and the Tennessee General Assembly before 1829, when representatives of the eastern Tennessee districts rejected "time in a penitentiary for most major crimes" because of local opposition to increased taxes for a state penitentiary.[78] Tennessee state senator Charles F. Keith suggested that taxes on slaves might generate prison funds with "6.75 cents levied per hundred acres of land *and per slave*."[79]

The prison was also rejected on the grounds that, in subjecting the body to the state, it created a system of abject dependence through the assignment of infamous status. The prison was condemned as an antirepublican institution not just because it temporarily subjected the citizen to the will of a violent state but because it consigned the prisoner to the permanence of infamy. This gothic status was widely integrated into southern state constitutions in the decades before the Civil War, resulting either from the commission of a morally outrageous crime (infamy from fact) or from the infliction of degrading punishments (*infamia juris* or infamy from law). State laws in the early 1800s distinguished penalties for infamous and noninfamous crimes and then disenfranchised the infamous, who could not give testimony or vote. In the North, infamous status was generally attached to crimes so horrifying or outrageous that they were preserved in the public memory. In the South, infamy was generally attributed to punishment or the status of having been punished.[80] As discussed in chapter 1, punishment brought such a loss to the status of persons that they ceased to have legal standing. This meant that in the South Black citizens were sometimes beaten on the streets during elections precisely because it removed them from eligibility for the franchise. In North Carolina, for example, white citizens "undertook mass whippings" of Black residents because state law excluded from the franchise anyone "whipped as punishment for petty crime."[81] In 1866, army officer Robert Avery documented the practice of former Confederates, who began to "seize negroes, procure convictions for petty offenses punishable at the whipping post, and thus disqualify them forever from voting in North Carolina."[82]

The prison was an infamous institution not just in its physical violence but in the rituals of domination designed to humiliate: the shaving of the head, the donning of the stripes, the withholding of food and touch and light. When law inscribed infamy on the body, it did so to shame that body, to render it subject to power, and to defile its political status. Missouri defined infamy as the loss of status resulting from a conviction, when one became "incompetent to be a witness or juror, or to vote at any election, or to hold any office of honor, profit or trust within this state."[83] In Kentucky, infamous punishments carried such a stigma that white men injured in accidents registered their injuries with the county clerk to prevent future accusations that they had been tainted by the prison's punishments.[84] The violence of degradation ruled the "twin towers" of Kentucky's prison through what Beaumont and Tocqueville called the "indelible signs of infamy," signs that served as evidence of ineligibility for the rights of citizenship. Beaumont and Tocqueville wondered about the reconcilability of the penitentiary idea and the state's legal authorization of whippings and broken bones: "When the mutilation of his limbs reminds others incessantly of his crime . . . must we not ardently wish, that the last traces of such barbarism should disappear from all the US, and particularly those which have adopted the penitentiary system, with which they are irreconcilable, and whose existence renders them still more shocking."[85] The status of the prison as a political question with an uncertain future was rooted in the racialization of the penitentiary form and the refusal of a degraded citizenship. The prison's violence degraded the whole right of citizenship, lowering southern whites to the status of the infamous.

In this context, antiprison arguments about the state's right to inflict punishment were grounded in an analysis of the prison as a form of slavery. Because the prison inscribed a state of dependence on an honored white body, "penitentiary slavery" was said to violate the proper domain of the state. In North Carolina debates published in newspapers, "Bertie" captured the perspective of southern republicans who saw prisons as slavery:

FIGURE 9. "Slave pen" operated by Price, Birch & Co., Alexandria, Virginia, 1860s. Courtesy of the Library of Congress, Prints and Photographs Division, Reproduction No. LC-DIG-cwpb-01470.

What are inalienable rights? . . . It was admitted that . . . taking away any part of our labor, without our consent, amounted to slavery, and that only such slavery was worse than death; but under the Penitentiary system the free-born citizen is made to labor directly under the lash as a slave, and is this not worse than death? . . . I think instead of adopting the Penitentiary system we should rather increase our Christian humanity and benevolence in the abolition of Penitentiary slavery in other states . . . for, in my opinion, a free-born American sovereign to be placed in this degrading institution is far worse than death by any torture.[86]

Tennessee's Sampson David, who had once sponsored proprison legislation, likewise argued that "the refinements of civilization, the strength of moral conduct, and the stability of our Holy religion, all shudder and tremble for the prosperity of a state possessing within its limits a Penitentiary Wall."[87] The rejection of the penitentiary as a place of terror and torture illustrates not only its connection to slavery in nineteenth-century discourse but also the prison's subsequent naturalization as a just form of punishment.

The prison was already seen as punishment fit for a slave because of the matrix of "slave jails" that dotted the region. "Slave depositories" and "slave pens" functioned as sites of punishment that crossed the boundaries between public and private. Enslaved people were also punished in plantation jails, county jails, and city jails across the South. This matrix of carceral institutions was unified by a legal architecture in which the slave was simultaneously understood as public and private property. William Wells Brown recorded in his *Narrative* the experience of escaping from a "domestic jail" on a farm and from a "pen" for those awaiting sale, as well as his punishment at a public jail where he was sent with a note containing instructions for punishment: "It is true that in most of the slave-holding cities, when a gentleman wishes his servants whipped, he can send him to the jail and have it done."[88] Because "having it done" removed the stigma of cruel reputation and the peering eyes of urban neighbors, the practice was popular in southern cities, where local jurisdictions developed public-private institutions for the punishment of slaves.[89] When Henry Bibb escaped from Kentucky to Ohio, he was transported to an "American slave prison" and incarcerated in a network of connected institutions: the Covington Jail, the Bedford Jail, the New Orleans Jail, and the Louisville Workhouse, "a very large brick building, built on the plan of a jail or State's prison, with many apartments to it, divided off into cells . . . enclosed by a high stone wall, upon which stood watchmen with loaded guns."[90] Bibb was astounded by the Louisville Workhouse because so many "slaves, there without crime . . . for safe keeping" were held there and because "so many whites as well as colored men [were] loaded down with irons, at hard labor, under the supervision of overseers."[91] Bibb wrote that in his capture he was "dragged back" across the border to "suffer the penalty of a tyrant's law, to endure stripes and imprisonment . . . and linger out almost a living death."[92] Frederick Douglass's *Narrative of the Life* also analyzed the "clanking of fetters and the rattling of chains" coming from slave prisons across the South. In these buildings, slaves could be submitted by owners for public punishment or merely detained for a fee in "safe keeping."[93]

While the border states embraced the prison as part of the law of slavery, Deep South states like South Carolina refused to design expensive institutions of state punishment because the unbuilt prisons were already imagined as Black institutions. In South Carolina, the penitentiary was seen as an unnecessary and distinctly northern imposition because of institutions like the Charleston Workhouse. As a "slave depository," the Charleston Workhouse emerged in 1724 alongside the slave patrols, which captured any Black person "out" after nine at night to be "confined in the Cage of Charles Town till the next morning."[94] Over 150 slaves were brought to the workhouse each month for whippings at the cost of twenty-five cents, with a limit of twenty-five lashes twice a week. Time on the treadmill could be substituted for whipping.[95] In a Black majority state, slave crimes were initially tried in Magistrate Courts, which imposed sentences of death or time in the jailhouse; major felonies were tried before panels of two justices and three citizens, and convicted slaves were sent to the Workhouse.[96] According to Benjamin Perry in 1839, penitentiary punishment was unnecessary because it would be "applied to 1/2 of our population and that is not the part from which crime usually proceeds."[97] Slavery was therefore so tightly bound to the idea of public punishment that its infliction upon white southern gentlemen, for whom the duel was the "functional equivalent of litigation," was unimaginable.[98]

Antiprison southern states conceded to the penitentiary only after a war over slavery. The war recentered the prison in the American imagination. Because of the prison's relationship to the state, northern armies burned southern prisons to the ground. Georgia and Alabama were forced to rebuild prisons that were already "in a neglected state."[99] In a few instances, Union soldiers commandeered the old slave jails and used them to detain captured Confederate soldiers.[100] The ensuing legal war over the treatment of prisoners impressed upon the nation a wartime "prison horror," even as the Union victory was also a victory for the prison.[101] When the war was over, prison construction became part of the customary requirements of reentering the Union. Confederate states sought readmission to the Union by building or rebuilding prisons as symbols of capable states.

It was in this context that southern states became leaders in postwar prison reform. When secessionist South Carolina became a Black majority democracy during the period of Reconstruction, the state legislature immediately abolished the Charleston Workhouse.[102] In the development of a state apparatus for punishment, South Carolina voted to establish a prison in 1868, "in the lead of a southern surge in prison construction."[103] When President Andrew Johnson appointed Benjamin Perry as head of South Carolina's provisional government, South Carolina built an elaborate gothic structure so brutal in its violence that 279 prisoners died between 1867 and 1883.[104] Because the older structures of Black punishment were replaced by new institutions, the state prison was "overwhelmingly Black from the time it opened its doors."[105] While in South Carolina the state coopted the abolition of the Charlestown Workhouse as a symbol of slavery and built a penitentiary in its place, in North Carolina the prison was built because the 1868 Reconstruction Constitution required it. In the view of people like Bertie, the prison remained a result of "carpetbagger misrule" because it was embedded in the southern constitutions that reunified the nation and entrenched federal power over state systems of punishment.[106]

Because the prison was a symbol of national reunification and the spoils of war, the form of mass incarceration that followed the prison-building boom of the post–Civil War period consolidated ideas about the meaning of race and nation and depoliticized the prison as a project of state violence. In 1868, the West Virginia governor convinced a reluctant legislature to build an ornately gothic institution in Moundsville next to one of the largest indigenous burial grounds in the United States.[107] The institution's cells were remarkably small for the period, at five feet by seven feet, and the prison was governed by new tools of infamy: the "kicking Jenny" and the "shoo-fly" were devices of restraint meant to intensify whippings with nine strands of cowhide and wire and with straps soaked in water and sand.[108] Following the example of West Virginia, Florida borrowed a military installation to use as a prison in 1868 but passed a Penitentiary Act in 1869 to build what the state envisioned as "the best prison in the south."[109]

Southern prisons became national models because they offered instructions for legalizing and liberalizing the already existing matrix of public and private Black punishments. This was exhibited in the postwar agreement of the Thirteenth Amendment, which excepted criminals from a nation that could no longer be enslaved. In an early version of the amendment, Charles Sumner proposed that "everywhere within the limits of the United States, and of each state or Territory thereof, all persons are equal before the law, so that no person can hold another as a slave."[110] In shifting the agent claiming ownership from a person to the state, the ratified version suggested that slavery was a status that could be assigned only by the state. This idea of civil death preserved in the Thirteenth Amendment's exception was further codified in *Ruffin v. Commonwealth* [of Virginia] (1871), which established the legal identity of the prisoner as a "slave of the state"—as one with no property, certainly not of the body. He was *civiliter mortuus*: "His estate, if he has any, is administered like that of a dead man."[111] In this case, Woody Ruffin, a Virginia prisoner who was sent to work on the Chesapeake and Ohio Railroad, was accused of killing his privately employed overseer. Ruffin argued that because he was tried in the improper location of his imprisonment rather than his crime, he was denied his state constitutional right to a trial by an "impartial jury of his vicinage," a trial in the place of the alleged crime. Virginia's Reconstruction Constitution of 1871 established that "in criminal prosecutions a man hath a right to demand the cause and nature of his accusation, to be confronted with the accusers and witnesses, and to call for evidence in his favor, and he shall enjoy the right to a speedy and public trial, by an impartial jury of his vicinage."[112] Ruffin was "brought back" for punishment to Richmond, the site of the penitentiary, a place where the prison superintendent spoke openly about the gothic nature of the institution: "Such characters, for a certain portion of their confinement, should be dead, as far as it respected the world; make it terror to be villains, and crimes will be less frequent."[113]

In consolidating the power of civil death, the Virginia court also pressed Ruffin's vicinage claim to establish the prison's location—the question of the prison's nearness in space and time to the body of the prisoner. Ruffin was said to have been "in" the penitentiary, even when the state moved him outside its walls. The prison therefore attached to the "person of the convict wherever he may be carried by authority of law, (or even when he makes his escape), as certainly and tenaciously as the ball and chain which he drags after him. And if when hired upon the public works, though hundreds of miles from the penitentiary, he kills a guard stationed over him by authority of law, he is as guilty of killing a guard in a penitentiary . . . as if he had killed an officer or regular guard of that institution within its very walls."[114] As *Ruffin* attached civil death to the signs of the building, state and federal courts in the post-Reconstruction era confirmed the meaning of the prison in relation to the body. In 1880, the federal court in Tennessee confirmed that "incarceration produced degradation" because the prison was infamous, it morally degraded the prisoner, and it removed him from a future of civic participation: "This notion of moral degradation by confinement in the penitentiary has grown into a general understanding that it constitutes any offence a felony."[115] The doubly disabling status of a slave-prisoner born at the border was attached to the bodies of all prisoners, and the normalizing influence of federal courts created a "general understanding" that prisons were institutions designed to degrade.

## NATIONALIZING THE PRISON, RACIALIZING THE STATE

It was in this nationalizing moment that the prison could have been rejected in the context of the long history of the prison as a contested institution. That rejection could have crossed borders, joining the ideas of abolitionists to a southern antipenitentiary tradition turned back on itself. Instead, the gothic power of the penitentiary as a place of Black punishment was recorded in the gothic emblems of the border states and the southern institutions of the postwar period and became embedded in the course of the prison's history, in the taken-for-granted racial terrain of public punishment. The compromise of the prison's racialization could be seen in the regime of convict leasing that overtook the South as prison structures aged and state budgets fell short. Although border prisons and Deep South prisons had originally emerged as distinct regional formations, the new framework of the "southern prison" replaced those earlier architectures, so that in the postwar consensus the border prison was forgotten as a regional formation that helped design a legal framework for mass incarceration. This regional cluster of border prisons may have remained absent from the field of historical vision, but it was engrained in the racial culture of the twentieth-century institution. By 1911, when Warden Weylen of the Maryland State Penitentiary was publicly accused of "cuffing" three Black prisoners (using ropes and pulleys to suspend prisoners from cuffed hands behind the back), he insisted that "*two-thirds of the inmates* here are Negroes, and many of these are *the so-called Border State type,* confessedly the most difficult to handle . . . [who] cannot be made to understand anything unless it is beaten into them."[116]

As the border prison's place in the history of mass incarceration became a forgotten artifact of the relationship between prisons and slavery, the history of southern punishment was reorganized around the more recent regime of convict leasing. The border prison remained present, however, in the songs and stories of popular culture. While John Henry is remembered as a working-class hero who famously defeated the steam engine, laying down his life and his hammer in the process, he was also a formerly enslaved prisoner in the Virginia State Penitentiary, who, like Woody Ruffin, was sent off to build tunnels for the C&O Railroad.[117] According to the famous song that honors his life, "They took John Henry to the white house, and buried him in the sand." The song references the state penitentiary painted white and the lines of sand that were later discovered between boxes buried on the prison grounds. The song was passed down with the memory and the legacy of the border—a place where a former slave took one dollar from a grocery store and was sent to the penitentiary on a ten-year sentence of civil death, where he died famous and forgotten at the same time.

As border prisons became southern prisons, they were unified by the techniques of Black mass incarceration. The "southern prison" was an institution shaped by the structure of slavery as a legal and economic relation that was both public and private. This was because the southern prison was built at the border, where slavery was public and prisons were private, where slaves were subjected to public punishments in state institutions, and prisons could be accessed by private citizens for slave punishments. This system of public and private punishments was a dual system of control. The border prison reconciled all of these seemingly irreconcilable forms of legal status into an idea about the management of Black freedom in America. It was an idea about the techniques of Black mass incarceration that was eventually nationalized in Leavenworth's border architecture.

When Leavenworth nationalized the power of the post-Reconstruction prison as a monument to the carceral state, it stood at the end of a chain of border prisons that stretched from east to west. By the middle of the nineteenth century, prisons at the border, whether north or south—Pennsylvania, Virginia, Maryland, Kentucky, Missouri—contained large populations of Black prisoners, whether enslaved or free. Leavenworth crowned this constellation and created its own modes of radial extension as the centerpiece of an emerging federal system. That system was structured not just to target the bodies of certain populations but also to include broad participation of free citizens in its workings. When Leavenworth arranged the fugitive hunt for Frank Thompson in 1898 and then condemned him to the "ball and chain," the federal law-and-order project had already extended into the finer details of everyday life in the region in ways that continued the legacy of slavery. The prison's aural tradition of coded siren signals transmitted across the prairie—five one-minute-long blasts set ten minutes apart for a mass escape, and three shorter blasts for an all-clear—normalized support for a carceral capacity that crossed the boundaries of public and private, deputizing private citizens to assist in hunting down the fugitives.

The legacy of the border prison is therefore rooted not only in slavery's congenital connection to the institution but also in the transmission of prison culture to the masses in ways that undermine modes of resistance to the penitentiary form. As part of a carceral democracy that drew on long traditions, the rituals of the hunt for escaped prisoners increased public support for an institution that was failing, by virtue of the escape itself, before the public's very eyes. In these moments of institutional failure, the racialization of the penitentiary form and its connections in the realm of culture contributed to its institutional revivification; moments of mass escape and scandalous violence were opportunities for the state to resolidify the legitimacy of the prison as a symbol of racial democracy. Given that mass incarceration first developed in the space of the border, perhaps that border might be used as a lens for rethinking the logic of civil death and the racialized future of "democratic" punishment. By the mid-twentieth century, the majority of prisoners in the United States were white, and the prison's racialization was said to have resulted from the mass incarcerations of the late twentieth century. That legal time, however, was actually only the most recent instantiation of racialized mass incarceration. At the border, the prison was always a racial house.[118]

# 5

# Leavenworth's Political Prisoners

## Race, Resistance, and the Prison's Archive

*Farewell, O comrades, I scorn life as a slave!*
*I begged no tyrant for my life, though sweet it was;*
*Though chained, I go unconquered to my grave,*
*Dying for my own birth-right—and the world's.*

—RICARDO FLORES MAGÓN, "FAREWELL!" 1922

The Black Twenty-Fourth Infantry of the US Army, the Industrial Workers of the World (IWW), and the organizing board of the Partido Liberal Mexicano (PLM), who began the Mexican Revolution from exile in the United States, met as prisoners at Leavenworth Penitentiary in 1918. They had known one another before. The Black Twenty-Fourth Infantry, which formed in the wake of Reconstruction, was sent to patrol the US-Mexico border and to guard striking workers at Coeur d'Alene, Idaho, who became the Western Federation of Miners and later the IWW. When the Black Twenty-Fourth Infantry later rebelled against police brutality in the city of Houston, their military status was withdrawn, and they were thrown into a prison camp with the IWW at the US-Mexico border. Librado Rivera and Ricardo and Enrique Flores Magón, as radical voices of the Mexican Revolution, endured the regimentation of the border between home and exile as journalists who wrote speeches, poetry, songs, and plays beloved by the IWW.

In 1918, these movements, as ideas about freedom, were convicted in mass trials under the Espionage and Sedition Acts, which punished with twenty years of imprisonment all conspiracies intended to "willfully cause . . . or incite insubordination, disloyalty, mutiny, or refusal of duty, in the military or naval forces."[1] The United States argued that the Black Twenty-Fourth Infantry had conspired to cause mutiny among themselves by stealing their own guns, that the Mexican revolutionaries had incited US military forces to anarchism by mailing literature opposing Mexico's Diaz regime, and that the IWW had encouraged the refusal of military duty by telling its membership to register for the draft as "IWW—Opposed to War." Legislative debates reveal that the act targeted the "pernicious vermin" and "outlaw leaders" of the IWW in order to prevent the circulation of their ideas, which, it was feared, would travel "all through the South urging Negroes to rise up against white people."[2]

Although these three social movements were convicted under the 1918 Sedition Acts, which was a set of amendments to the 1917 Espionage Act, they were initially charged under both sections of the law. The Espionage Act made it a federal crime to "willfully utter, print, write, or publish any disloyal, profane, scurrilous, or abusive language about the form of the government of the United States," to "willfully urge, incite, or advocate any curtailment of production in this country of any thing or things . . . necessary or essential to the prosecution of the war," and to "by word or act support or favor the cause of any country with which the US is at war or by word or act oppose the cause of the US therein."[3] These charges, while not resulting in convictions, were designed to contain the IWW threat of "One Big Union," to target the anti-imperialist organizing of the PLM that contested the ownership of most of Mexico by US capitalists, and to punish the Twenty-Fourth Infantry, avid readers of the *Crisis*, for openly rebelling against white supremacy in the South.

When antiracist, anticapitalist, and anti-imperialist political prisoners arrived at Leavenworth in 1918, they entered a racial architecture that worked to discipline cross-racial solidarity out of existence. Political prisoners became part of a racial script that undermined movements for democracy. This chapter explains the kind of racial regime that defined Leavenworth in the early part of the twentieth century and examines two sets of social movements whose members were incarcerated en masse as political prisoners. First it explores how in the early 1900s the IWW, the Black Twenty-Fourth Infantry, and Mexican anarchist-revolutionaries were targeted because they challenged the prison as an antidemocratic institution and worked across difference to abolish it. Then it examines the political work of prisoners in the early 1970s who drew attention to the problem of mass incarceration through a series of work strikes and ethnic studies initiatives that changed how the public understood the problem of the prison. This was a cross-racial movement that introduced the idea of a time beyond the prison. These movements arrived collectively at an analysis that broke from the terms of carceral democracy and offered the theory that prisons existed primarily as a means of inflicting mass punishment on targeted groups.

## THE PRISON AS A RACIAL HOUSE

When political prisoners arrived at Leavenworth, they entered a structure of racial segregation that had begun only four years before they arrived. Because the prison's labor needs had previously prevented the arrangement of prisoners by race, the prison's racial regime had to be constructed as part of its architecture. The prison was not driven by a formal segregation policy until 1914, after members of Congress were shocked to discover in congressional hearings that Leavenworth did not segregate its prisoners:

Chairman: You mention the question of race and color. In the dining room, what distinction, if any, is made with respect to race and color?

Warden: We do not make any. . . .

Chairman: Do you not think it could be arranged?

Warden: It is very desirable to do that, if it can be done.

Chairman: You do make that distinction in celling?

Warden: Yes, sir.

Chairman: That is, you do not put in the same cell men of different races or colors?

Warden: No. I would like to arrange it . . . but, really, we are so crowded now that we have not been able to do that.

Chairman: Any Mexicans?

Warden: We have several, I think, now. We received 4 or 6 the other day. . . .

Chairman: Do you cell Mexicans, Japanese, Chinese, Indians—these races, with the colored convicts?

Warden: No sir, not when we know it. The Mexicans cell together; but we had two or three years ago, I think, a case where there was a Mexican and a Negro who was part Mexican. They were put in the same cell.[4]

Despite the absence of a formal segregation policy, the prison's racial taxonomy was considered to be part of the institution's "tradition."[5] In order to institute a culture of segregation, Leavenworth had to teach racial order to its prisoners. Its method was prison leisure. The theatrics of prison minstrelsy transmitted state pedagogy to the prisoners in its form and content.[6] In at least three performances in 1914, 1915, and 1917, performers traveled from the neighboring military prison at Fort Leavenworth "on street cars and marched to our front gate, band playing and continued with a scripted performance written, staged and produced by the military prisoners."[7] Having come "from their prison to OURS," as the prison newspaper reported, "forty soldier lads broke in" on the federal prisoners in 1914 and performed "the first minstrel show ever given by prisoners of one institution before prisoners of another."[8] The prisoners received the entertainment with "thunderous applause" that "shook the very foundations of the building" as "three hundred visitors and eleven hundred of us fell easy victim to volley after volley of original wit, songs well rendered, dancing, fancy roller skating, acrobatics, etc., etc., etc., well executed."[9]

The trick of prison leisure was that the prisoners appeared to be teaching themselves—the military prisoners wrote the script and produced the wardrobe, while the federal prisoners built the set and provided the music. Although prison minstrelsy appeared to be a collective recreational project accommodated by the institution, the minstrel shows were state scripts of racial order. The state's pedagogical project was received not only through the show's content (deriding Black culture through mimicry and celebrating a properly ordered southern past) but also through its form.[10] The shows were structured into parts—a "minstrel part" followed by the Olio or variety show and then the obligatory semicircle—and was moved along by the cast of characters. The interlocutor stationed in the center "keyed" the semicircle and pulled jokes out of his "end men" or "bones," who poked fun at prison authorities. Prison minstrelsy therefore borrowed its form from minstrelsy's practice in the outside world, which used the bones as critics of class order.[11] As actors in blackface who "ran short on black face makeup and had quite a time . . . getting it off," white military prisoners were able to deride authority because they were not themselves when they did it—the "boys from the Fort," who called themselves the White Mice Smoking Club, joked that the warden and the deputy warden were popular only because their friends were "number-less." The political function of these routines was to route critiques of the administration through comedy rather than protest.

These spectacles of prison minstrelsy taught race to the prisoners but also to the citizens. The teaching of state scripts of racial order was incentivized by prisoners' temporary reincorporation into the life of citizenship—they were allowed to "don citizens' clothes for the occasion" as they appeared in "black knickerbockers, white vests, and red coats" and "brilliant yellow and gold uniforms."[12] The military prisoners performed their prison minstrel show for the town of Leavenworth— they "came into town on a special electric car, formed a line and marched through the principal streets, band playing and streamers flying, to the Lyceum Theatre, where matinee and evening performances of the American Black Face Minstrels were given."[13] The streets of Leavenworth City were "packed solid" for the parade in blackface, and reviewers praised the show as "rattling good . . . better than many professional performances."[14]

In the production of a racial regime that crossed the social landscapes of the prison's inside and outside, the message was received not only through the spectacle of prison minstrelsy but though participation in prison sports, which also emerged in 1914 as the prison constructed a racial architecture of segregation. The prison's Black baseball team, the Booker T's, played against the Brown Socks and the Red Men. In the prison football league, the Mixed Vegetables were the white team and the Pork Chops the Black team.[15] While sports coverage in the prison newspaper, the *Leavenworth New Era,* described sports participation and spectatorship as a method of survival for prisoners at Leavenworth, prison sports, according to Charles Wharton, a former congressman imprisoned at Leavenworth in the 1930s, were "typical of Leavenworth's contradictions"—prison leisure helped prisoners survive but channeled their allegiances through a sports program governed by intrarace solidarity and cross-racial competition.[16]

Although the state pedagogical project that emerged at Leavenworth worked to naturalize racial segregation, curricular gaps in the social labor of prison leisure enabled the formation of cross-racial resistance. As prisoners witnessed, absorbed, and resisted Leavenworth's racial architecture, they also challenged the mass incarceration of political prisoners through letter-writing and legal defense campaigns. In the course of this work, political prisoners were forced to confront the state's racial pedagogy and to grapple with the idea of Leavenworth as an idea about race. In the movements that followed in the 1970s, another set of cross-border imaginaries of freedom became targets of federal efforts to control and politicize punishment. This work built on the earlier legacies of social movements at Leavenworth.

## "CITIZENS OF INDUSTRY": THE CRIMES AND PUNISHMENTS OF THE IWW

The IWW was an idea born in jail. It emerged from the labor struggles in the western United States, where labor unions like the Western Federation of Miners emerged to counter the power of the Mine Owners' Association and the Pinkerton Detective Agency in bringing a violent end to labor strikes.[17] Big Bill Haywood once noted in a United Mine Workers Convention speech that the Western Federation of Miners was "not ashamed at having been born in jail, because many great things . . . have emanated from prison cells."[18] After clashes between 1892 and 1899, Bill Haywood and others drew on the knowledge of labor struggles in the Western Federation of Miners to develop the idea of "One Big Union."[19] It was a coming together of unskilled labor and the unemployed that resulted in new ideas about freedom, work, and citizenship. Rather than identify as citizens of states that routinely used violence against starving workers, IWW workers described themselves as "citizens of industry."[20] Formally established in Chicago in 1905, the IWW articulated their work in the language of democracy—the founding convention was opened as the "continental congress of the working class."[21]

When ninety-four members of the IWW arrived at Leavenworth in September of 1918, the prison's newspaper reported that the "eyes of the nation were focused on this prison."[22] They were charged with ten thousand crimes in four mass trials in Chicago, Sacramento, Omaha, and Wichita. Each trial employed a different prosecutorial strategy.[23] In Wichita, Kansas, the prosecution set out to prove only that the defendants were members of the IWW, while in Sacramento a silent defense in protest of the deaths of two Wobblies in the Sacramento County Jail resulted in harsh sentences. In fifty-five minutes, the Chicago trial sentenced the paid employees of the union to 878 years in prison and focused on the IWW as an antiwar organization aligned ideologically with the German Kaiser. The event was accompanied by a military band and was billed as the "trial of the century." The movie theater across the street featured *The Red Viper* and *The Menace of the IWW*.[24] When the court began handing down ten- and twenty-year sentences, Benjamin Fletcher, the only Black prisoner among the Wobblies, announced to the courtroom that "Judge Landis is using poor English today. His sentences are too long."[25] By the time the IWW reached Leavenworth, five of its members had already died in the local jails.

Once at Leavenworth, the ninety-four members of the IWW began organizing for their release, but they were limited by prison rules in their communication with the outside world. Although the IWW were allowed to publish "News and Views from the Labor World" in the prison's newspaper, *Leavenworth New Era,* they were prohibited from publishing any writing in the outside press. E. F. Doree noted in a letter that "the matter of our freedom is out of our hands. We are not permitted to write for publications. We cannot conduct meetings. We are limited in the number of letters we may write. Our mail is subject to censoring. What we may do is not much."[26] Some Wobblies were able to smuggle their writings out—James Rowan, for example, published an article in the *Nation* while imprisoned at Leavenworth.[27] The insularity of the prison was also an opportunity to read and to think about strategies and principles. Earl Browder, who would later become the leader of the Communist Party, recalled in his memoirs that "in Leavenworth our university courses began. We began an intensive education. We had plenty of time on our hands."[28]

Their efforts to organize a legal defense campaign were complicated by the new organizational leadership that emerged in their absence. The imprisoned IWW believed that those who had replaced them in the IWW offices preferred seeking status as Communist Party politicians to taking on the burden of antiprison activism. Doree noted that he had read nearly every issue of *Industrial Worker* and that "to read it you would not know we were here at all."[29] Feeling a sense of erasure, Ralph Chaplin drew and distributed one of his most famous drawings—an image of himself behind bars pointing out at the free world: "Remember! WE ARE IN HERE FOR YOU, YOU ARE OUT THERE FOR US."[30] While Chaplin's circular motivated outside groups to mobilize in defense of the IWW—the Children's Crusade for Amnesty, for example, brought twenty-five children of imprisoned Wobblies to the White House—organizing efforts were complicated when the IWW was accused of starting a fire at Leavenworth. The warden told the local newspapers that "an IWW spirit" had purposefully targeted the only wooden structure in the whole prison.[31]

Within the context of their further criminalization as prison arsonists, the Wobblies at Leavenworth splintered—some believed that individualized applications for clemency could lead to their release, while others believed that an appeal for clemency was an admission of guilt and that the IWW should remain, as a matter of principle, in prison. "An Open Letter to President Harding From 52 Members of the IWW in Leavenworth Penitentiary Who Refuse to Apply for Individual Clemency" argued that while "there is not one of us who will not bear the scars of the prison until he dies," they had arrived at Leavenworth on a group conviction for conspiracy that could be remedied only by mass release.[32] The document noted that three prisoners had applied for clemency at the insistence of the fifty-two signers because they were dying of tuberculosis or going insane.[33] Their applications were denied. One successful application resulted in the temporary release of the IWW for twenty-two months but ended with their return to Leavenworth on the grounds that the government had not yet issued a formal declaration of peace. In the context of a wartime economy of crime and sedition, Bill Haywood escaped to Russia,[34] while the editors of IWW newspapers published in immigrant languages, *A Bermunkas, Darbunenku Balsas, Il Proletario, Rabochy, El Rebelde, A Luz, Allarm,* and *Solidarnose,* were deported from the United States after their release from Leavenworth.

When the Wobblies met Ricardo Flores Magón and Librado Rivera at Leavenworth, they formed a discussion group in the prison's yard called the Campus. This collective space of learning emerged because Ralph Chaplin and other members of the IWW considered the Flores Magón brothers their "personal heroes" before their arrival at Leavenworth.[35] The publication of John Kenneth Turner's work *Barbarous Mexico* (1910), which chronicled the PLM's work to link indigenous and workers' rights to the construction of the US-Mexico border, made the IWW into regular readers of the PLM's paper, *Regeneración*.[36] The paper, often credited with beginning the Mexican Revolution, was published from St. Louis and then Los Angeles because the PLM had been exiled from Mexico after they hung a large banner from the newspaper offices of *El Hijo del Ahuizote,* which read "LA CONSTITUTION HA MUERTO." As a result, they were thrown into Mexico's Belén Prison and were then prohibited under threat of further punishment from ever publishing any statements in the Mexican press. Once exiled in the United States, the PLM survived police brutality in Los Angeles, confinement in the St. Louis and Los Angeles jails, and prison sentences at Yuma Territorial Prison in Arizona and McNeil Island in Washington before arriving at Leavenworth Penitentiary in 1918.[37]

Although Ricardo Flores Magón and Librado Rivera refused to admit guilt or ask the state for mercy, any application for clemency or pardon would have been denied. Department of Justice memos reveal that although the men had committed no violence they were considered "IWW's of the most violent character."[38] Prison authorities also condemned them as "anarchist types," even though members of the PLM understood anarchism through an indigenous framework of self-determination represented by the slogan "Land and Liberty!" The mathematician Librado Rivera is described in prison records as a "Mexican who is said to have made trouble in his own country and he works with the I.W.W. and other destructive groups in the United States."[39] In reflecting on the twenty-year sentence handed down by the courts, the Department of Justice noted that while "the sentence is a long one . . . nothing else will deter a criminal of this kind," since "Punishment for short terms in the penitentiary has absolutely no effect upon them."[40] US Attorney Alfred Bettman admitted in internal documents that espionage law was not "designed to reach pamphleteering of this kind" but recommended that "any consideration of commutation" be "postponed until after they have served a considerable term."[41]

Although the PLM prisoners chose not to generate a legal defense in order to reject the very terms of US law and their own punishability, they continued to publish, through their lawyers, updates on the failing health of Ricardo Flores Magón. They resisted the insularity of civil death by writing letters and poetry even when their writing privileges were revoked. His lawyer published Ricardo's own description of his failing health in the *New Republic*:

> Once when I was young, I was kept for several weeks in a dark dungeon, so dark that I could not see my own hands. It was in the City of Mexico during that harrowing period in which Diaz swayed with a bloody hand. . . . But I could suffer all that excepting the absence of light. I need light. I need light. I need light, and I want to be free to cure my eyes. . . . I can still see the color of a flower. I can still see a sunbeam and can still glory in the sight of a smile. If I could only step into life again before it be too late.[42]

Having resisted civil death and the force of US law, Ricardo Flores Magón died at Leavenworth on November 21, 1922. Pressure from outside organizations had resulted in Ricardo's examination by prison doctors in October of 1922, when he was declared only "slightly pale from indoor confinement."[43] State documents offer conflicting accounts of his death, which is listed on the Record of Death and Internment as the result of angina pectoris (a strangling feeling in the chest caused by blocked arteries). In a telegram sent by prison officials to Magón's lawyer, his time of death is recorded as 5:00 in the morning, while an internal report from the prison physician to the warden puts his death at 4:15 in the morning: "The night attendant at the hospital was called by guard Lewis in Cell House B about 4:15 o'clock this morning. The attendant went over promptly and found Magón suffering with distress and pain about the heart, he examined him and returned to the hospital for medicine. While the attendant was returning to the hospital the guard called again and stated that Magón was dead."[44] Both Librado Rivera and Ralph Chaplin maintain that Flores Magón was moved to a different cell where they could not see him in the days before his death. Librado Rivera was called to see the body and swore until his own death in 1932 that Magón's body bore the marks of strangulation. As a result, Rivera's mail privileges were "suspended indefinitely"—he wrote three undelivered letters detained in his prison file that described Leavenworth as a "regime of terror" and insisted that the prison physician consistently misrepresented Magón's declining health.[45] When Magón's body was transported to Los Angeles and then to Mexico, thousands gathered along the train's route to honor his dreams of freedom.[46]

What Ricardo Flores Magón left behind was a critique of the prison as a form of mass incarceration. In reflecting on the state pedagogy of punishment, he asked, "What is the object aimed at by means of these banishments, and incarcerations, and even lynchings of those who cherish an ideal different to that sustained by those in power? And after thinking and thinking until my head aches I can find but one answer: to kill the ideal!"[47] Flores Magón was already analyzing the racialization of US prisons in some of his earliest political speeches. "The Intervention and the Prisoners of Texas," delivered on May 31, 1914, implored his audience to take up arms to "claim our brothers who are prisoners in Texas from the hands of bourgeois justice" and to recognize moreover that "the prisons in the United States are full of Mexicans."[48] In a 1911 speech, he referred to the "shameful rule called Law" and to the words of Praxedis G. Guerrero, "the first Mexican libertarian," who often said, "To be alive is to be a prisoner."[49] He offered a cross-border analysis of "the world" as a prison, "a much larger one than those with which we're familiar, but a prison nonetheless. The prison guards are the police and soldiers; the wardens are the presidents, kings, and emperors; the watchdogs are the legislators; and in this sense we can exactly equate the armies of prison functionaries and their acts with the armies of government functionaries and their acts. The downtrodden, the plebeians, the disinherited masses are the prisoners, obliged to work to support the army functionaries and the lazy, thieving rich."[50] When Rivera was finally released in 1923, he would not "obey the laws of the United States if released unless they agree with his conscience" and was deported to Mexico, where he was imprisoned again for his radical journalism.[51] The dreams of the PLM remain central to theories of prison abolition that take seriously the relationship between walls and borders and the potential for solidarity between the working classes of Mexico and the United States.

The IWW and the PLM were joined by the members of the Black Twenty-Fourth Infantry, who were also considered guilty at the level of the group and who built a successful movement for mass release. The Black Twenty-Fourth Infantry was created in the aftermath of the Civil War in 1868 as part of the Reconstruction troops, along with the Twenty-Fifth Infantry and the Ninth and Tenth Cavalries. Because of their relationship to the western United States (they were, unlike white troops, rarely rotated out of duty in the frontier states), they came to be known as the Buffalo Soldiers. When Black soldiers claimed the rights of citizenship through military service, conflicts between Black troops and local police were common. The Twenty-Fifth Infantry stationed at Brownsville, for example, were falsely accused of shooting and killing a white person and were dishonorably discharged as a group by Teddy Roosevelt for their "conspiracy of silence." Like the soldiers at Brownsville, the Twenty-Fourth Infantry had encountered extreme racial violence—at Salt Lake they endured the taunts of the Mormons, in Tampa, Florida, they witnessed the use of a two-year-old boy for target practice, and in Waco, Texas they experienced harassment by the police and fought back. When they were transferred to Houston to guard a military camp under construction on the outskirts of the city, Houston's white residents posted circulars warning Houston to "remember Brownsville" and refuse the service of alcohol to Black soldiers. The resistance quickly gave way to tolerance on the part of white merchants who profited from their residence. On the night of the "Houston Riot," they were to be honored at an event at Emancipation Park.

In the months before the arrival of the Twenty-Fourth Infantry, police violence in Houston and lynching in Texas had reached unprecedented levels.[52] The racism of Houston's citizens was backed by a police force known for its frequent practice of shooting at the ground to invoke terror in Black citizens. The Twenty-Fourth Infantry, as readers of the *Crisis,* encouraged Houston's Black citizens to stand up for themselves and began tearing down the "whites only" signs and the segregation screens from the public street cars and throwing them out the windows.[53] Three days before the Houston Riot, a white man stabbed Sam Blair, a Black camp employee, for cutting into the payment line; one day before the Houston Riot, the soldiers had asked to be transferred out of Houston on the grounds that they were "treated like dogs here."[54]

The next morning, the newspapers described a military attack on the city of Houston by enraged soldiers marching in formation. Houston saw sixteen white bodies and four Black bodies. It could not see its own history of racial violence. Amid calls for revenge and the restoration of white supremacy in the city, W. E. B. Du Bois, as editor of the *Crisis,* sent Martha Gruening, a white reporter from New York, to investigate. Her report, published in the November 1917 edition of the *Crisis,* revealed that the Twenty-Fourth Infantry had been disarmed after two of its members—Baltimore and Edwards—were beaten and shot by two police officers who had earned reputations for "negro baiting." The soldiers were beaten after intervening in the arrest of Sara Travers, a Black woman whose home had been invaded by police looking for "crap shooters" while she ironed in her underwear. As Travers was arrested for hostility toward police, Edwards approached the police officers but was beaten and arrested, and when Baltimore confronted the police officers that assaulted Edwards he was shot and wounded. It was the inaccurate news that Colonel Baltimore had been shot to death that brought the Twenty-Fourth Infantry to the edge of law, and it was the subsequent expression of outrage that brought the US Army to disarm the Twenty-Fourth Infantry, leaving them entirely unprotected against police violence. For these reasons, "They faced and faced fearlessly the vision of a shameful death."[55] As they walked toward Houston, one thousand white citizens gathered at the police station and were provided with police weapons.[56]

The following morning, every member of the Twenty-Fourth Infantry was arrested and sent to Camp Furlong near the US-Mexico border, where they were imprisoned with one thousand members of the IWW before their removal to Fort Bliss. As they left Houston by train, the soldiers dropped signs of their discontent scrawled on paper: "remember august 23, 1917" and "take tex and go to hell."[57] The remaining members of the Twenty-Fourth Infantry were sent south to dig ditches in Georgia and were permanently disarmed; the unit was eventually dissolved altogether.[58] Black Houston was also disarmed—police searched houses and confiscated guns. Two weeks after the uprising, Officer Sparks shot two more Black men in the city of Houston.

While the "Houston Riot" was depoliticized almost immediately in political memory (a riot is an unthinking and apolitical act of chaos, not rebellion), the Twenty-Fourth Infantry used the trial as another stage for the condemnation of

American justice. The structure of the military courts-martial, governed by a panel of judges and a judge-advocate who was both the trial organizer and prosecutor, limited any available defense to the casting of doubt on the identities of the participants. This was the same legal strategy used in the federal prosecution of the IWW. Having already established their collective guilt, the military judges were ruling simply on the question of whether these men as a mass constituted "Houston Rioters." Coming before the law as a group, the Twenty-Fourth Infantry refused to legitimize the law by participating in its proceedings. In a photo published by Du Bois in the *Crisis,* the prisoners at trial are dressed in army uniforms but surrounded by armed guards and seated behind a rope that divides them from the room, a diamond-shaped chapel at Fort Sam Houston. The photograph, taken from one point in the diamond, focuses on the rows of soldiers who sit in protest of the legal ritual—the entire front row distances themselves from the work of law with crossed legs and crossed arms. Only the seven soldiers who confessed and implicated others in exchange for lesser sentences were allowed to speak during the proceedings.

In the aftermath of the largest courts-martial in US history, a trial that was not about establishing guilt, the US Army sentenced thirteen members of the Black Twenty-Fourth Infantry to death on December 11, 1917. They were hanged within a few hours of the trial despite their request that they be shot like soldiers. Buried without the customary right to appeal and in graves marked only by numbers 1 through 13, the soldiers Baltimore, Nesbit, Brown, Wheatley, Moore, McWhorter, Davis, Divins, Breckenridge, Hawkins, Snodgrass, Johnson, and Young were confined to coffins, each with a soda bottle containing a slip of paper with the soldier's name, rank, and date of death. This was a combination of the burial of a soldier and an enemy—they remained anonymous to the world above ground but retained the identity of the soldier inside the coffin. Two subsequent mass trials resulted in two more mass executions, while sixty-two men were given life sentences at Leavenworth Penitentiary.

When the soldiers-turned-prisoners arrived at Leavenworth, they built a mass movement that resisted the insularity of the prison house door in order to reframe their collective identity from the Houston Rioters to the Houston Martyrs. After their initial work began, outside organizers were focused on the Dyer Anti-Lynching Bill, and Congress entertained the idea of paying restitution to the white people of Houston for the events of "Black mutiny." The Houston Martyrs began a letter-writing campaign to the NAACP. Nearly every letter acknowledged the failure of the antilynching bill but suggested that their cause would draw attention to the injustice of their own mass incarceration. They argued that only a mass movement could end a structure of punishment that was defined by blanket charges that applied to the group and by individualized remedies for mass injustice: "Now the [War] Department, upon being urged to consider our cases, says that only individual consideration can . . . be given to each man."[59] Their mass sentence was recalibrated, on the basis of individual behavior, from life to twenty- and thirty-year terms. When an unsigned letter reached Du Bois in November of 1920, he wrote to James Weldon Johnson that he was writing an editorial for the December issue of the *Crisis,* adding, "I think we ought to start something."[60]

Although the Houston Martyrs convinced the NAACP and the National Equal Rights League to organize a mass movement around their case, they had to proceed as individuals making applications for clemency. To build support for executive action, James Weldon Johnson hand-delivered two petitions to two US presidents—one with fifty thousand signatures to Harding in 1921 and one with one hundred thousand signatures to Cleveland in 1923, when he brought a delegation of black churches, the black press, and black women's organizations to the White House. Eventually, he orchestrated the unprecedented strategy of bringing 558 members of the NAACP to Leavenworth Penitentiary. In September of 1923, the NAACP held its annual meeting in nearby Kansas City so that delegates could visit the Houston Martyrs. Johnson's speech at the prison reiterated the organization's commitment to their cause and noted that even Warden Biddle believed they were "neither criminals nor murderers."[61] The *Crisis* referred to the Leavenworth visit as that "now famous pilgrimage" to Leavenworth by 558 delegates ("stirring addresses made") and reported to readers that the Houston Martyrs were "clean-cut specimens of manhood, their head unbowed by six years of prison."[62]

Although the Martyrs had the support of the warden, they were recalled by military authorities in January of 1925 and transferred to the neighboring Fort Leavenworth prison. This had the political effect of keeping them incommunicado—they could not write to outside groups, including the NAACP, but smuggled messages on toilet paper. This retaliatory action on the part of the military retuned to them their status as soldiers. Once stripped of that status and housed as civilians, they were now returned to military custody in order to be hidden away from the outside world. In 1927, according to a letter written by Leroy Pinkett, the National Equal Rights League convinced authorities to reduce the prison sentences by eighteen months, which made the remaining men eligible for parole.[63] After a twelve-year campaign initiated and sustained by the men themselves, the last of the Houston Martyrs, Stewart Phillips, left Leavenworth in 1936.

The movement generated new ways of working across the walls, but it was enmeshed in Leavenworth's racial architecture, which pitted prisoners against each other to undermine a sense of collective power. Some prisoners resisted that framework. Ben Fletcher of the IWW smuggled information to NAACP officials about the mistreatment of the Twenty-Fourth Infantry. He and other Wobblies committed themselves, even after they were released, to securing the freedom of the Twenty-Fourth Infantry.[64] Two members of the Twenty-Fourth Infantry accepted roles in the labor of prison discipline, which meant that they served as "isolation orderlies" in Building 63. In an "Open Letter" published by the IWW in 1922, the authors described an "atavistic" Black prisoner who "beat our boys into insensibility in the prison dungeon with a club" and then was "given his liberty."[65] Roy Connor, an IWW placed in isolation for three years for refusing to break rock, wrote in a letter to Senator Henry Cabot Lodge that was smuggled out of the prison that the permanent isolation cells were "ruled by two Negro Rioters."[66] One of these men remains unnamed, but the other was likely Roy Tyler, who Warden Biddle wrote deserved clemency because he was "on duty for a long time as [an] orderly in the isolation department . . . and . . . rendered valuable services in protecting officers when attempts were made to assault them by vicious characters."[67] Biddle reported to federal authorities that Tyler "always lines up with the side of good order and shows a commendable disposition to back the prison officials. On November 14, 1923, when Joe Martinez, a Mexican murderer killed Captain Andrew Leonard and wounded six guards by stabbing them, Tyler voluntarily entered the underground coal bunker and took a dagger from Martinez."[68]

There is also a remote possibility that one of the men was Jack Johnson. Jack Johnson had a complicated presence in the racial regime of Leavenworth, sometimes representing a figure of Black freedom and sometimes becoming part of the prison's logic. When Johnson arrived at Leavenworth as a fugitive world champion, he drove himself to the prison's gates greeted by cheering crowds. As the famous world champion, Johnson had traveled the world to avoid prison time on Mann Act charges (which meant transporting a woman across state lines for lewd or immoral purposes, or, in Johnson's case, having consensual interstate sex with white women).[69] Because of his fame, Johnson dined with the warden in his home, wore starched jackets instead of prison grays and blues, and kept a supply of liquor, cigars, and fancy foods in his possession. His relationship with the prison administration and his confidence made him the target of outraged guards who wrote him up for using the staff restroom.[70] He was allowed and encouraged to return to the ring inside Leavenworth, and in 1920 the entire prison and many of the city's local elite gathered ringside to watch him box.[71] But there was a period of three months when Johnson was borrowed from his regular job in the prison's baseball park as a sweeper and umpire and was used as an isolation orderly.[72] Johnson wrote his own account of his time in Leavenworth, but the 135-page manuscript written on a combination of prison stationery and blank New Era paper remained in federal custody until the 1990s because the warden refused to release it.[73] It reveals little about the institution's racial architecture, but Johnson's place within the labor of prison discipline illustrates how the art of division is part of the prison's project.

Although the labor of prison discipline was a mechanism for dividing prisoners, the vast majority of the IWW and the Twenty-Fourth Infantry saw the connections between their struggles and refused the logic of the prison as a racial architecture. After his release, the Wobbly H. F. Kane wrote a letter to the NAACP noting that "much has been made by some who call themselves radicals, of the fact that in Leavenworth penitentiary several of the imprisoned 24th Infantrymen have been used by prison officials to beat members of the I.W.W. who had

FIGURE 10. "Lest We Forget," drawing signed "Holloway," *Pittsburgh Courier*, January 12, 1924, Papers of the NAACP.

been accused of revolting against the inhuman prison system. . . . Prison officials, as do the employing class, try to pit white and black workers against each other whenever it is possible."[74] Kane insisted that these men were "forced to maltreat men of my organization" and that the incorporation of prisoners into the violence of the institution does not erase the legacy of the Houston Martyrs: "The grave cannot give up the dead. . . . But the fifty-four victims still living can be released from their prison cells."[75] This analysis of the connections between mass incarceration and the targeting of political prisoners against war, racism, and imperialism was generated in discussion groups in Leavenworth's yard, where Librado Rivera and the Flores Magóns taught and learned as teachers and students.[76] Out of this period came a critique not just of individualizing struggle but of the whole idea of what it meant to build a prison like Leavenworth. In the disciplinary mechanisms of Leavenworth's internal arrangements, prisoners imagined new ways of relating across difference in spite of the prison's lessons in segregation. As a staged racial encounter, Leavenworth worked to contain political possibilities and to discipline political movements that disbelieved in its power. In a cartoon image published to draw attention to the mass incarceration of the Houston Martyrs, thirteen ghosts stand with a banner that spells out that ongoing struggle, but they are pointing at Leavenworth. With arms outstretched and fingers extended, they are pointing to the prison as an antidemocratic idea about democracy.

The prison in that image was by that time a powerhouse in a carceral state that targeted citizens for political crimes. The federal prison population had exploded in the early part of the twentieth century, when Leavenworth held as many as four thousand prisoners. Much of this overcrowding resulted from the creation of new federal crimes in 1910, 1914, and 1920 that regulated interstate sexual relations, drug taxes, and automobile thefts. These new prisoners joined Native people convicted of "major crimes" and a whole generation of political prisoners who were imprisoned as a mass in the years between the world wars. There were more than one hundred Mennonite conscientious objectors imprisoned at Leavenworth in 1917, and when they protested the shaving of their beards they were sent as a mass to the isolation cells.[77] At Leavenworth and the other federal prisons, socialist, communists, and anarchists wrote letters and memoirs describing the terms of mass incarceration. Eugene Debs was sent to Atlanta, Elizabeth Gurley Flynn was sent to a newly built federal prison for women at Alderson in West Virginia, and Earl Browder was sent to Leavenworth. During the Second World War, political prisoners continued to arrive at Leavenworth, including 160 Jehovah's Witnesses who were imprisoned for their opposition to the conflict. Bayard Rustin was sent to the federal prison in Lewisburg, Pennsylvania, from 1944 to 1946 for violating the Selective Service Act.

When the mass incarceration of political prisoners accelerated in the 1950s, leaders of the Communist Party, Black civil rights movement, and the Puerto Rican independence movement became targets of federal law enforcement. A new generation of political prisoners arrived at Leavenworth, including Gus Hall, the leader of the Communist Party, who was sent to Leavenworth in 1951 on Smith Act charges along with ten other defendants. The Smith Act required federal prison time for anyone advocating the overthrow of the federal government, and by 1956, 131 more members of the Communist Party had been indicted. Leaders of the Puerto Rican independence movement were also sent to federal prisons. Lolita Lebrón was sent to Alderson, while Oscar Collazo, Irving Flores, Andrew Figueroa Cordero, and Rafael Cancel Miranda were sent to Leavenworth.[78] In the antiprison movement that emerged from these cross-currents of mass incarceration, political prisoners and their vision of a different future resonated with a later generation of Leavenworth activists who resisted the prison's lessons and built movements that contested the power of the prison and its place in democracy.

## MASS INCARCERATION IN THE 1970S:
## THE END OF A BEGINNING

Drawing on the spirit of those who came before, the mass movement that was generated in the early 1970s drew the nation's attention to the problem of the prison house door. Prison litigation was a strategic use of the law to force the courts into the struggle to end state violence. When Leavenworth's prisoners challenged the conditions of their confinement, the Tenth Circuit maintained a hands-off posture, even when confronted with the brutality of the carceral state. In *Morgan v. Willingham* (1970), the Tenth Circuit responded to the beating of a prisoner with total deference to prison administrators: "Courts do not supervise the execution of the penal sentences they impose. This function is rightly committed to the discretion of the executive, acting through the Department of Justice and the Bureau of Prisons; and judicial interference does not comport with effective administration."[79] In ratifying the prison as a structure of violence, the Tenth Circuit relied on the language of the Supreme Court: "Accepting as we do Mr. Justice Harlan's opinion in *Barr v. Matteo* . . . (1959), the immunity of these government officers is absolute if the acts complained of were committed 'within the outer perimeter of [their] line of duty,' even though maliciously done."[80] Between 1971 and 1974, prisoners mounted legal challenges to the use of the control unit, the procedural framework of the disciplinary hearing, racial discrimination, and the practice of the rectal exam. The Tenth Circuit upheld in *Long v. Harris* (1971) the use of solitary confinement as a form of "institutional security" and shielded the prison in *Shimabuku et al v. Britton* (1972) from the US Constitution by creating the conditions of its legal enclosure.[81] In challenging the prison as a form of racial discrimination, a class-action lawsuit was filed in March of 1972 on behalf of all Chicano prisoners at Leavenworth. It was promptly dismissed by the federal court.[82] *Daughtery v. Harris* (1973) held that the rectal exam was a "necessary and reasonable concomitance of appellants' imprisonment."[83]

In a series of work strikes beginning in September of 1971, the prisoners honored the struggle at Attica and the legacy of George Jackson only to find that the prison dismantled the ethnic studies curriculum that brought them together. After taking a class called "Cultural History of the Southwest," Raúl Salinas and others built Chicanos Organizados Rebeldes de Aztlán (CORA) and wrote the CORA Constitution, reframing the four hundred Chicano prisoners at Leavenworth as a "miniature nation."[84] After 165 mostly Chicano prisoners went on strike in 1971, Leavenworth's brush and clothing shops were shut down in March of 1972 during an event involving eight hundred prisoners. In a third strike in July of 1972, Salinas recorded the vote count: "July 19, 1972, vote slips—66 out of 600 in favor of resuming work."[85] During the resulting seven-day punitive lockdown, prison administrators disestablished the ethnic studies curriculum in "the purges of '72," when sixty-four of Leavenworth's legal activists were transferred to the new behavior modification program at Marion Federal Penitentiary in Illinois.[86] Salinas later recalled that he was greeted with "fists through the bars" and was deeply impressed by "all that talent on the grounds."[87] In spite of the use of "box car cells" to physically and mentally incapacitate radical activists who had used the law to force the question of the prison's contradictions, they formed the Student Union/Law Library, which developed into the Federal Prisoners for Freedom of Expression Committee (FPFEC) and the multiprison/systemwide Federal Prisoners' Coalition Intra-National.[88]

This was a mass uprising of federal prisoners across the system, using the law to turn the whole federal framework of justice back on itself. The prisoners did this by drawing on the tradition of cross-racial antiprison organizing at Leavenworth to work across the very differences that were solidified in the prison's script. As Salinas writes, "So we immersed ourselves in the Puerto Rican history and united our struggles . . . joined our struggles as one. And so through that connection and the Black Muslims that were coming in, and the Republic of New Africa, and the Black Liberation Army People, we began to talk."[89] Those conversations and the "prison rebellion years" that followed were, according to Salinas, critical moments in the history of social justice:

> We weren't just challenging the state in an irrational, inane way, but we were very clearly outlining our arena of struggle and what we had to deal with. The fact that people were becoming educated, helping each other to go into higher learning, to read books critically, to become writers and painters and . . . jail-house lawyers . . . there was a transformation taking place. And this was happening throughout the country, no doubt about that. But we were focused on our arena of struggle, which happened to be the federal joint at the time—Leavenworth federal penitentiary, and later, Marion. It was a time of organizing and turning each other on to new materials that we never had the opportunity of holding in our hands, much less read; new languages that we were learning, new concepts, new paradigms, that began to make it clear to us that it was part of a colonial mindset. This is the captives, this is the renegades, these are the ones who will not conform to the reservation or the plantation, and we must deal with them.[90]

With most of the movement locked up in Marion's program of sensory deprivation, a small group of prisoners at Leavenworth engaged in a series of actions with significant consequences. In July of 1973, after an unsuccessful food boycott, a white prisoner named William Hurst engaged in a strategy of forced negotiation. He took four hostages into the laundry room for eleven hours, holding them until the warden agreed to a public conference with prison administrators, two sympathetic members of the press, and twenty men "who had something to say." For the next two hours, the men sought rights to education and due process, and the abolition of solitary confinement and the rectal examination. They also sought an end to the federal prison system's use of behavior modification programs, including the Special Treatment and Rehabilitative Program (Project START) at the Springfield Medical Center in Missouri, and the Behavior Research Center under construction at Butler, North Carolina. Warden Daggett rarely spoke, but at the meeting's end he ordered fifteen prisoners placed in the control unit. Six men remained in the hole for more than six months and were indicted in February of 1974 on riot and assault charges. The public's relationship to this moment in the prison's history was complicated by Hurst's involvement in a "militant" organization known as the Church of the New Song (CONS) and an unrelated event that occurred alongside the actions of the men that became the Leavenworth Brothers. The administration blamed Hurst's actions on his membership in CONS, which "attracted to its membership men primarily interested in the prisoner rights movement and penal reform, including some of the most militant-minded."[91] The public was unsure how to interpret the actions of other prisoners that day, who wore "pillow cases or other white pieces of cloth with eye holes cut in them" and attacked and killed a guard.[92] Even though all murder charges were eventually dropped in the Leavenworth Brothers cases for "lack of evidence," the administration linked the crime and the protest as part of the same political problem.[93]

In the political trials that followed, public sentiment turned against Leavenworth and its gothic inversions concealed in democratic symbols. In proceedings broken up by the racial logic of the prison, the six men on trial were tried in groups. Hurst, who had been held separately from the other men at a local jail, died mysteriously of suicide, but not before insisting that white prisoners had a revolutionary duty not to become "the enforcers of the status quo of prison life."[94] In refusing to become part of the labor of prison discipline, Hurst organized the prison takeover with mostly Black prisoners, including Jessie Evans, Odell Bennett, Alf Hill Jr., and Alfred Jasper. They were each sentenced to an additional eighty years in prison for conspiring to incite a riot and assaulting prison personnel in trials they condemned as frauds.[95] As the *Afro-American* reported, behavior that prison officials "attributed to Jasper on July 31, was in an Aug 6 report attributed to another inmate named Coleman."[96] The Leavenworth Brothers Offense/Defense Committee emerged from the local Veterans of Foreign Wars chapter because each of the four Black defendants was a veteran and member of the VFW. By linking the struggle for prisoners' rights with the struggle for veterans' rights, the Leavenworth Brothers used their trial to put the prison on trial.

Having been shut out of the courts, prisoners at Leavenworth invited the public to the prison in a letter-writing campaign to the *Kansas City Star*. In two hundred letters, Leavenworth was described as the "next Attica" and as a crisis that could still be given another ending:

> In retrospect to Attica, the conditions here are almost identical. The races have been brought together through their persecution. I beg of you to hear our charges in the backward house of dehumanization before it is too late. I ask you to take the initiative to act as interveners and to move for changes to begin now, not after the crisis as in Attica or McAlester, Ok. This is not a threat or is it meant to be one, but is only the certainty of the doom that fills the air inside the walls of Leavenworth Penitentiary.[97]

As a result of their organizing efforts, *Kansas City Star* reporters Harry Jones and J. J. Maloney publicly condemned the institution as "one of the worst prisons in the federal system" and contrasted the federal prison's use of the rectal search with the neighboring military prison's use of the metal detector.[98] In the case of the Leavenworth Brothers, District Court Judge Wesley Brown continued to dismiss the legal claims of Leavenworth's prisoners as "ill-disguised attempt[s] by recalcitrant, abusive, litigious criminals to vex and harass the courts and prison officials with contrived and exaggerated personal grievances."[99]

As the federal courts continued to isolate the prison as a kind of legal island, prisoners continued to draw attention to the contradictions of the prison house door. Federal prison administrators finally saw in Leavenworth the tools of the prison's undoing. In September of 1974, the director of the Bureau of Prisons, Norman Carlson, suddenly announced that Leavenworth was obsolete and would be closed within ten years. He noted Leavenworth's aging structure and suggested that "no one would have kept a high school or hospital open that long."[100] But instead of being shut down permanently, it underwent structural and systemic renovations that breathed new life into an old institution.

# Postscript: "Walls Turned Sideways Are Bridges"

## *Abolition Dreams and the Prison's Aftermath*

By the time mass incarceration is said to have begun in the 1970s, Leavenworth had already created a massive carceral complex and transformed the meaning of democracy. It was supposed to be the beginning of the carceral state, but because the state had always been carceral the 1970s was the latest manifestation of an already developed and institutionally grounded law-and-order politics. During the federal prison system's "rebellion years," people living on the edges of democracy and behind prison walls had convinced the nation that Leavenworth's architecture was a regime of state violence that should be brought to an end. By the time of mass incarceration, Leavenworth had already died and been brought back to life. Carlson promised that the city of Leavenworth would be considered for a smaller replacement prison.[1]

Leavenworth's reemergence as the flagship institution of the federal prison system relied on a remodeling of its internal architecture. The Bureau of Prisons claimed it was closing Leavenworth because of its antiquated structure rather than because of the regime of racial and legal violence that was exposed by the efforts of antiprison organizers, so in 1975 authorities simply imagined a different sort of Leavenworth. When the institution was forced to change, it abandoned the old dungeons of Building 63, which was torn down and replaced by a remodeled Cellhouse C with "silent cells, a mini-Marion on site—bars rather than the double doors and pie-shaped cells. . . . The physical environment has been brightened by painting the interior of the cellblocks green, blue or yellow to replace the usual gray."[2] In the aesthetic of this new architecture, the idea of Leavenworth was recalled to life by a state with new priorities in the project of mass incarceration. When the Bureau of Prisons announced the end of Leavenworth's life, it was without a way forward beyond the prison, so embedded in this concession was the resurrection of the carceral state.

The project of federal punishment took on new political and cultural functions, increasing in capacity and insularity, becoming a site for the legal enclosure of federal prisons from public regulation and a site for the mass incarceration of immigrants. In new forms of legal incorporation, immigrant detainees were assigned the "hopelessly outdated" cell houses that radiated from the back of the prison's dome.[3] By the early 1980s, the mass incarceration of immigrants in federal prisons brought 719 Cuban prisoners to Leavenworth from Atlanta, which the Cubans had tried to burn down. There were three thousand Cubans in federal custody, and while some had actually violated criminal laws, most were seeking political asylum and remained in federal custody only because Fidel Castro refused to take them back. When Castro agreed to renegotiate the terms of mass deportation and the resulting "riots" ended in mass transfers to Leavenworth, the prisoners were denied family visits, recreational facilities, educational classes, jobs, religious services, and exercise.[4] They were double celled and given one shower per week. In this newly established immigration jail inside the nation's flagship institution, the "four-point restraint," or practice of chaining detainees to their beds, was a routine part of "institutional security."[5]

Leavenworth's resurrection consolidated its power in political and economic terms. As part of a whole way of life, the sustained public commitments to federal power that had overturned an earlier set of traditions could not simply be abandoned. In a region that once went to war over the impositions of federal law and order, state power relied on the incorporation of the people into the prison's rituals. The prison was mapped into the town's existing gridlines, and it deputized citizens of a carceral democracy to do its work. In addition to the cultural aspects of the relationship, the closure of the nation's first prison would mean a loss to the local community of nine hundred jobs, 6.5 percent of the workforce, and $5.9 million in revenue.[6] Losing Leavenworth would also have diminished the city's political power in the state, since Kansas districting laws count prisoners as residents in order to bolster the region's power in elections.[7]

As Leavenworth found new institutional priorities as a joint political, economic, and cultural project, it was adapted to meet new racial designs in a very old racial script. In the 1980s and 1990s, the federal prison system experienced what administrators described as "race wars." As part of that regime of violence, Thomas Silverstein, a member of the Aryan Brotherhood, killed a member of the DC Blacks prison gang named Raymond "Cadillac" Smith at the federal prison in Marion, Illinois. When he killed a guard named Merle Clutts in 1983, he was sent to Atlanta and then to Leavenworth in 1987, where he was given a "no human contact order" in a "special isolation cell" made of steel in the prison basement.[8] Lights remained on and officers stood guard around the clock. The cell was originally constructed to house organized crime bosses on "protective" status, and it was "buried underneath the rotunda in a section of the basement [not] used for years. It was so isolated that you could not hear any of the familiar sounds of prison life—no human voices, toilets flushing, doors clanging shut, televisions blaring. Nothing."⁹ The adaptation of old architectures meant that the public demolition of Building 63 took place alongside the private reliance on new methods of state deprivation.

Despite the public announcement of its closure in 1974, Leavenworth remains open today as an icon open to prisoners but closed to the public. Signs across the street from the institution state firmly in red letters that no photos of the institution should be taken. The last researcher allowed inside was the journalist Pete Earley, who wrote *The Hot House* with unfettered access between 1987 and 1989. Calls for Leavenworth's closure have abated, and it seems an institution without end. If its limestone could somehow be disassembled and forged into something new, what shape would it take? What happens when prison walls are taken down? What remains? What does it mean to imagine the end of the prison as the beginning of democracy rather than to tinker in the realm of reform?

There was a time when even James Bennett, head of the Bureau of Prisons for most of the twentieth century, imagined a time beyond the prison.¹⁰ In explaining his vision of the prison's end, he suggested that state terror could somehow be removed from the building—that prisons could be redesigned into residential rather than custodial kinds of buildings. When Leavenworth's walls almost came down, one of the most important lessons from that moment was that state terror cannot be removed from the prison. Leavenworth was an idea about many things, but it was an idea about the end of gothic violence that served only to ratify a structure of civil death and to normalize the terms of carceral democracy. It created the very terms of the violence it claimed to remedy. In the moment when it was almost abolished, Leavenworth fortified itself, drawing on the secrets of its architecture and the enormity of its shadow across the prairie to reassert its sense of permanence.

To understand the prison's revivification as a democratic institution, we return analytically to the border. At this most gothic place, the border prisons of the nineteenth century were crumbling architectures by the 1970s. They had stood for over a century as emblems of a carceral state at the border between slavery and freedom. Their closures re-marked space in different ways. The Virginia State Penitentiary, where slaves were admitted to a prison system designed for free subjects, was reduced to a barren green lawn on the side of the highway until it was paved for a company parking lot. The prison was demolished in 1999, when state prisoners brought the bricks down one by one. No traces remain of John Henry or the "white house." The original Maryland Penitentiary, established in 1811, remains open today as the oldest operating prison in the world. Maryland's second prison, built in 1879, was condemned in 2007 with a national reputation as the "killing fields." When the governor shuttered the prison because of its "antiquated design," hundreds came to tour the institution before its demolition.¹¹ Prisoners took apart the prison house door and salvaged the parts for the state.

While some of the original institutions of the gothic generation have been taken down brick by brick, others have become sites of memorialization or have developed into prison museums for dark tourism. Eastern State is now the site of art exhibits, daily tours, and even a haunted house. The Missouri State Penitentiary is now a tourist site with an online store where one can order a real piece of brick from the institution. Missouri and West Virginia are also part of ghost-hunting expeditions depicted on television. These relationships between the prison and society reinscribe the gothic imaginary, even as they normalize the prison's continuation in the realm of culture. Prison tourism registers the production of a long cultural memory that remains in the institution's afterlife. It is also part of the long tradition of prison reform, a winding and labyrinthine structure that, once entered, is difficult to escape.

The exit from mass incarceration requires an exit from prison reform and a reconceptualization of mass incarceration from a moment in time to a form of political status. The number of people in prison can be reduced to a "normal" use of cages and wall, but the walls will still stand as articulations of state violence. The buildings can be taken apart, but they will be given new life if they remain bound to the idea of civil death as a status assigned to the body. In taking down the gothic formulation of civil death brick by brick, prison abolition, as an idea with a very long life, requires learning from the history of mass incarceration about the processes that entrenched the carceral state. This book has tried to think beyond the prison's architecture and to reimagine terrains of democracy and justice that come from the abolitionist tradition. Having examined how the state articulates the meaning of mass imprisonment over time, it ends by asking what it would mean to redesign a theory of the state not bound to the project of the prison.

# ACKNOWLEDGMENTS

This book is dedicated to the memory of my grandmother, Patricia Benson. It was in the materials that she left behind that I first understood the many threads of this story. Having grown up at the Kansas-Missouri border, I learned at her kitchen table the meaning of the border war and our place within it. Many years later, as a young graduate student, I rediscovered the meaning of that story when one of my teachers pushed me to locate myself in the history of my work on punishment. This led to over a decade of archival work at the Kansas-Missouri border. This book was a project with many beginnings; much of the early thinking for it took place in Gina Dent's office, a place where I could be brave in articulating my ideas, and where she spent many hours thinking with me about the meaning of Bleeding Kansas. I see now, looking back, that you let me be excited about things you already knew, and you taught me how to read historical and legal documents and to find joy in that work. I'm thankful that you let me get lost in the details but always brought me back to the big picture. I know that I am not an easy person to mentor. I also have tremendous gratitude for Angela Davis, who turned this project inside out so many times and who always returned my thinking to questions of democracy. I would also like to thank Paul Frymer for always rooting for the Kansas Jayhawks, in theory and practice. Ronnie Lipschutz thought with me about the project in its earliest stages.

I wrote much of this book under redwood trees and in a hummingbird garden and could not have found the energy to write with such a heavy teaching load had it not been for those moments. I'll always be thankful for that time. Susy Zepeda has gone to the woods with me on more than one occasion, and I could not be more thankful for her friendship. I would also like to thank Heather Turcotte, Cindy

Bello, Nick Mitchell, Jasmine Syedullah, Sandra Alvarez, and Soma de Bourbon for engaging the project in its earliest days. And I thank teachers, mentors, and colleagues at UC Santa Cruz and UCLA, including Kelly Lytle Hernandez, Neda Atanasoski, Bettina Aptheker, and Eric Porter.

In more recent years, I have been supported by many people at San José State University, including Alessandro De Giorgi, Tony Platt, Bill Armaline, Ken Peter, and Lawrence Quill. I would also like to thank Danijela Dudley for reminding me to laugh. I was able to finish important archival work because of generous research support from Chair Melinda Jackson and the Department of Political Science at SJSU. This research was also funded by the UC President's Postdoctoral Program. I am also indebted to the researchers who have written to me over the years inquiring about Leavenworth's archives. This helped make the process of writing less lonely, and I especially wish to thank Laura Browder for sharing her grandfather's writing with me. I would also like to thank the many students along the way who have endured long stories about Leavenworth and have engaged these ideas generously and critically, including Ernest Chavez, Eduardo Bautista, Chelsea Van Aken, and Jen Rushforth.

This work would not have been possible without the assistance of archivists at the National Archives in College Park, Maryland, and Kansas City, Missouri. I would like to extend special thanks to Steve Spence and Gregory Schmidt at the National Archives, and Anne Diestel at the archives of the Bureau of Prisons. I am also grateful to the many archivists whose names I do not know at the Leavenworth Public Library and the Kansas State Historical Society. At UC Press, Maura Roessner let me write an unconventional book, while Sabrina Robleh and Elisabeth Magnus helped the book come together.

This has been a difficult book to write, and my family has endured my many questions about our family's relationship to this history. I wish to thank my parents, grandparents, aunts, uncles, and cousins for putting up with me. I have tried to tell this story honestly but radically as a story about the possibilities of justice. It is not an invitation to view Kansas's history as a curiosity, a singular and aberrant story. That story has already been written. Instead, this book is an invitation to disrupt that tradition. My hope is that the book does justice to the history of abolition. For years of support during the challenges of writing, I would like to acknowledge Rachael Huffman. I would also like to thank Libby Franklin, who taught me when we were young that dramatically crumpling up pieces of yellow-lined paper is a perfectly normal part of the writing process. PMF was the best writing companion a gal could ever have, and Matt, who has taught me so many things, kept me company on long days of writing, always encouraging me to be my best self.

# NOTES

## ABBREVIATIONS

NA KC     National Archives, Central Plains Region Branch, Kansas City, MO
NA II      National Archives II, College Park, MD
RG         Record Group

## INTRODUCTION

1. "Work on West Cell Wing," *Leavenworth New Era,* April 13, 1917. In the reproduction of the bicameral approach, cell block A, the "House" side, was built to hold eight or twelve people per cell, while cell block B, the "Senate" side, held only two.

2. Charles S. Wharton, *The House of Whispering Hate, by Charles S. Wharton, Ex-Congressman, Ex-Lawyer, Ex-Convict* (Chicago: Madelaine Mendelsohn, 1932), 3; Joe Jackson, *Leavenworth Train: A Fugitive's Search for Justice in the Vanishing West* (New York: Carroll and Graf, 2001), 2.

3. David Theo Goldberg, *The Racial State* (Oxford: Blackwell, 2002).

4. Katherine Beckett and Naomi Murakawa, "Mapping the Shadow Carceral State: Toward an Institutionally Capacious Approach to Punishment," *Theoretical Criminology* 16, no. 2 (Spring 2012): 221–44.

5. Jack Cope (under the supervision of G. Cuthbertson), *1300 Metropolitan Avenue: A History of the United States Penitentiary at Leavenworth* (Leavenworth, KS: US Printing Office, 1963), 11. Cope was a federal prisoner given the task of researching the prison's history.

6. William Eames and Thomas Young, *Specifications for the United States Penitentiary, Leavenworth, Kansas* (St. Louis, MO: William Eames and Thomas Young, 1910). As an architectural firm, Eames and Young operated from 1885 to 1927. The firm developed a national reputation for commercial, governmental, and residential buildings in St. Louis,

Seattle, San Francisco, and Atlanta. They also designed structures for World Expositions in 1898 and 1904. See Ronald R. McCarty, "Eames and Young," in *The Grove Encyclopedia of American Art*, ed. Joan Marter (Oxford: Oxford University Press, 2011), 124.

7. "United States Penitentiary Is Getting a Dome," *Leavenworth Times*, July 20, 1927.

8. "Urged to Act at Once," *Leavenworth Standard*, April 7, 1896.

9. LaDow to Eames, September 21, 1908, Papers of R. V. LaDow, RG 129, NA II; Eames and Young to R. V. LaDow, August 29, 1908, Papers of R. V. LaDow, RG 129, NA II.

10. Eames to LaDow, August 29, 1908, Papers of R. V. LaDow, RG 129, NA II; Cope, *1300 Metropolitan Avenue*, 11.

11. Letters to the Attorney General, June 4, 1897, Records of the Attorney General, File 2256, RG 60, NA II.

12. William Eames and Thomas Young, "Federal Prison, Atlanta Georgia," *American Architect*, June 2, 1920, 697.

13. Leonard Peltier, *Prison Writings: My Life Is My Sun Dance* (New York: St. Martin's Griffin, 1999), 154–55.

14. Warden McClaughry to Attorney General, November 30, 1905, Box 13, Papers of R. V. LaDow, RG 129, NA II.

15. "Visiting Record Again Broken at Federal Prison," *Leavenworth Times*, June 24, 1910.

16. Warden McClaughry to Attorney General, November 30, 1905, Box 13, Papers of R. V. LaDow, RG 129, NA II; Gustave de Beaumont and Alexis de Tocqueville, *On the Penitentiary System in the United States and Its Application in France* (New York: Augustus Kelley, 1970), 30.

17. Warden McClaughry to Attorney General, November 30, 1905, Box 13, Papers of R. V. LaDow, RG 129, NA II.

18. Warden to Cecil Clay, September 5, 1907, Box 13, Papers of R. V. LaDow, RG 129, NA II.

19. "Visitors Won't Be Shown into Federal Prison," *Leavenworth Times*, June 28, 1910.

20. *Escape Signal—Five Waving Blasts*, pamphlet, April 20, 1906, Miscellaneous Records Concerning the Leavenworth Penitentiary, Box 1, RG 129, NA II.

21. The name of the Kansas State Penitentiary was changed to Lansing Correctional Facility (LCF) in 1990. Although it is now located in the neighboring town of Lansing, the land on which the prison was built used to be in Leavenworth, and because the border between Leavenworth and Lansing is undetectable the area is often described as Lansing-Leavenworth.

22. As one of the nation's earliest prison towns, by 1909, the military, state, and federal prisons and local jails were already the city's major employers. Frank M. Gable, "The Kansas Penitentiary," *Kansas Historical Collections* 14 (1915–18): 379–437. For accounts of the emergence of "prisons towns" in the wake of the 1990s prison boom in California, see Joelle Fraser, "An American Seduction: Portrait of a Prison Town," in *Prison Nation*, ed. Tara Herivel and Paul Wright (New York: Routledge, 2003), 73–84, and Ruth Wilson Gilmore, "Crime, Croplands and Capitalism," in *Golden Gulag* (Berkeley: University of California Press, 2007).

23. Joel Walsh, "Leavenworth Touted as Site for New Federal Prison," *Lawrence Journal World*, July 4, 2007.

24. See the 2009–10 Visitors Guide of the Leavenworth Convention and Visitors Bureau and Chamber of Commerce. The Leavenworth First City Museum features exhibits on prison

history, and the Lansing Historical Museum on state prison grounds narrates the history of the town through its prisons and sells memorabilia, books, documentaries, and postcards.

25. Nicole Kelley, "Group Decries Boyda's Earmark for Prison Museum," *Lawrence Journal World*, July 11, 2007; "Fake Prison Gets Real Tax Dollars: Congress Earmarks $100,000 for Kansas Prison Museum," CBS News, September 28, 2007, www.cbsnews.com/stories/2007/09/28/eveningnews/main3310451.shtml.

26. Angela Y. Davis, *Are Prisons Obsolete?* (New York: Seven Stories, 2003), 15.

27. Thomas Dumm, *Democracy and Punishment: Disciplinary Origins of the United States* (Madison: University of Wisconsin Press, 1987), 87. See also Gina Dent, cited in A. Davis, *Are Prisons Obsolete?*, 17.

28. Michelle Brown, *Culture of Punishment* (New York: New York University Press, 2009), 9.

29. Ibid., 16.

30. Mike Davis, "Hell Factories in the Field: A Prison Industrial Complex," *Nation*, February 20, 1995; Angela Y. Davis, "Masked Racism: Reflections on the Prison Industrial Complex," *Colorlines Magazine*, September 10, 1998.

31. Michelle Alexander, *The New Jim Crow* (New York: New Press, 2010).

32. R. Gilmore, *Golden Gulag*. See Heather Thompson's economic analysis in "Why Mass Incarceration Matters: Rethinking Crisis, Decline, and Transformation in Postwar American History," *Journal of American History* 97, no. 3 (December 2010): 703–34.

33. Naomi Murakawa, *The First Civil Right: How Liberals Built Prison America* (New York: Oxford University Press, 2014); Vesla Weaver, "Frontlash: Race and the Development of Punitive Crime Policy," *Studies in American Political Development* 21, no. 2 (Fall 2007): 230–65; James Foreman Jr., "Racial Critiques of Mass Incarceration: Beyond the New Jim Crow," *New York University Law Review* 87, no. 1 (2012): 21–69.

34. Elizabeth Hinton, *From the War on Poverty to the War on Crime: The Making of Mass Incarceration in America* (Cambridge, MA: Harvard University Press, 2016); Kelly Lytle Hernandez, "'Persecuted Like Criminals': The Politics of Labor Emigration and Mexican Migration Controls in the 1920s and 1930s," *Aztlán: A Journal of Chicano Studies* 34, no. 1 (Spring 2009): 219–39; Nicholas De Genova and Nathalie Peutz, *The Deportation Regime: Sovereignty, Space and the Freedom of Movement* (Durham, NC: Duke University Press, 2010); Kitty Calavita, *Immigrants at the Margins: Law, Race and Exclusion in Southern Europe* (Cambridge: Cambridge University Press, 2005); Alessandro De Giorgi, "Immigration Control, Post-Fordism, and Less Eligibility: A Materialist Critique of the Criminalization of Immigration across Europe," *Punishment and Society* 12, no. 2 (April 2010): 147–67; Erica R. Meiners, *For the Children? Protecting Innocence in a Carceral State* (Minneapolis: University of Minnesota Press, 2016); Victor Rios, *Punished: Policing the Lives of Black and Latino Boys* (New York: New York University Press, 2011).

35. Beckett and Murakawa, "Mapping."

36. Jonathan Simon, *Governing through Crime* (Oxford: Oxford University Press, 2007); Vesla Weaver and Amy Lerman, "Political Consequences of the Carceral State," *American Political Science Review* 104, no. 4 (November 2010): 817–33; Marie Gottschalk, "Democracy and the Carceral State in America," *Annals of the American Academy of Political and Social Science* 651 (January 2014): 288–95; Andrew Dilts, *Punishment and Inclusion: Race, Membership, and the Limits of American Liberalism* (New York: Fordham University Press,

2014); Albert W. Dzur, *Punishment, Participatory Democracy, and the Jury* (Oxford: Oxford University Press, 2012).

37. Shanisse Kleuskens, Justin Piche, Kevin Walby, and Ashley Chen, "Reconsidering the Boundaries of the Shadow Carceral State," *Theoretical Criminology* 20, no. 4 (Winter 2016): 566–91.

38. On American political development and its origins as a subfield, see Karen Orren and Stephen Skowronek, *The Search for American Political Development* (Cambridge: Cambridge University Press, 2004), and Richard M. Valelly, Suzanne Mettler, and Robert C. Lieberman, *The Oxford Handbook of American Political Development* (Oxford: Oxford University Press, 2016).

39. Marie Gottschalk, *Caught: The Prison State and the Lockdown of American Politics* (Princeton, NJ: Princeton University Press, 2015).

40. Georg Rusche and Otto Kirchheimer, *Punishment and Social Structure* (New York: Columbia University Press, 1939).

41. David Garland, "Introduction: The Meaning of Mass Imprisonment," in *Mass Imprisonment: Social Causes and Consequences*, ed. David Garland (Thousand Oaks, CA: Sage Publications, 2001), 1–2.

42. David Garland, *The Culture of Control: Crime and Social Order in Contemporary Society* (Chicago: University of Chicago Press, 2001), 2.

43. Megan Ming Francis, *Civil Rights and the Making of the Modern American State* (Cambridge: Cambridge University Press, 2014), 12.

44. William J. Novak, "The Myth of the 'Weak' American State," *American Historical Review* 113, no. 3 (June 2008): 754. See also Desmond King and Robert Lieberman, "Ironies of State Building: A Comparative Perspective on the American State," *World Politics* 61, no. 3 (July 2009): 547–88; Daniel Kato, *Liberalizing Lynching: Building a New Racialized State* (Oxford: Oxford University Press, 2016).

45. Heather Schoenfeld, *Building the Prison State: Race and the Politics of Mass Incarceration* (Chicago: University of Chicago Press, 2018), 19.

46. Margaret Werner Calahan, *Historical Correction Statistics in the United States, 1850–1984* (Rockville, MD: US Department of Justice Bureau of Justice Statistics, 1986).

47. Angela Y. Davis, "The Prison: A Sign of Democracy?," lecture presented at the Center for Cultural Studies, University of California, Santa Cruz, November 28, 2007.

48. Khalil Gibran Muhammad, *The Condemnation of Blackness: Race, Crime, and the Making of Modern Urban America* (Cambridge, MA: Harvard University Press, 2010).

49. On the history of the federal prison system, see Paul W. Keve, *Prisons and the American Conscience: A History of U.S. Federal Corrections* (Carbondale: Southern Illinois University Press, 1991); Mary Bosworth, *The U.S. Federal Prison System* (Thousand Oaks, CA: Sage Publications, 2002); and John M. Eason's critically important work in *Big House on the Prairie: Rise of the Rural Ghetto and Prison Proliferation* (Chicago: University of Chicago Press, 2017).

50. Angela Y. Davis and Gina Dent, "Prison as a Border: A Conversation on Gender, Globalization, and Punishment," *Signs* 26, no. 4 (Summer 2001): 1235–41; Julia Sudbury, *Global Lockdown: Race, Gender, and the Prison-Industrial Complex* (New York: Routledge, 2006); Ana Muñiz, *Police, Power, and the Production of Racial Boundaries* (New Brunswick, NJ: Rutgers University Press, 2015); Alessandro De Giorgi, "Back to Nothing: Prisoner Reentry and Neoliberal Neglect," *Social Justice* 44, no. 1 (Winter 2017): 83–120.

51. Dominique Moran, *Carceral Geography: Spaces and Practices of Punishment* (Burlington, VT: Ashgate, 2015), 3, 125.

52. R. Gilmore, *Golden Gulag*; Robert Perkinson, *Texas Tough: The Rise of America's Prison Empire* (New York: Metropolitan Books, 2010); Mona Lynch, *Sunbelt Justice: Arizona and the Transformation of American Punishment* (Stanford, CA: Stanford University Press, 2010); Mishuana Goeman, "From Place to Territories and Back Again: Centering Storied Land in the Discussion of Indigenous Nation-Building," *International Journal of Critical Indigenous Studies* 1, no. 1 (2008): 23–34. West Virginia's prison, discussed in chapter 4, was also built next to an indigenous burial mound in the town of "Moundsville."

53. Dumm, *Democracy and Punishment*, 3.

54. Keally McBride, *Punishment and Political Order* (Ann Arbor: University of Michigan Press, 2007), 122; Lisa Lowe, *The Intimacies of Four Continents* (Durham, NC: Duke University Press, 2015), 2.

55. Dumm, *Democracy and Punishment*, 5.

56. A. Davis, "Prison."

57. See the work of local historian J. H. Johnston, which relies heavily on newspaper sources, in *Leavenworth Penitentiary: A History of America's Oldest Federal Prison* (Leavenworth, Kansas: J. H. Johnston, 2005). Former correctional officer Kenneth LaMaster has published a collection of photographs in *Images of America: U.S. Penitentiary Leavenworth* (Chicago: Arcadia, 2008). Journalists Joe Jackson and Pete Earley have also written about Leavenworth's prisoners, escapes, and employees. See Joe Jackson's *Leavenworth Train* and Pete Earley's *The Hot House: Life inside Leavenworth Prison* (New York: Bantam, 1992).

58. On the methodology of subjectivizing the state, see M. Jacqui Alexander, *Pedagogies of Crossing: Meditations on Feminism, Sexual Politics, Memory, and the Sacred* (Durham, NC: Duke University Press, 2005), and James C. Scott, *Seeing Like a State* (New Haven, CT: Yale University Press, 1999).

59. General Agent Frank Strong to Attorney General, May 17, 1895, Department of Justice Central Year Files (folded), 2256–1891, RG 60, NA II.

60. Ibid.

61. An Act to Establish a Site for the Erection of a Penitentiary on the Military Reservation, 29 Stat. 380, Chapter 400, Section 1 (1896).

62. US Department of Justice, *Annual Report of the Attorney-General of the United States, 1906* (Washington, DC, 1906).

63. On the settler colonial state, see Audra Simpson, *Mohawk Interruptus: Political Life across the Borders of Settler States* (Durham, NC: Duke University Press, 2014); Patrick Wolfe, "Settler Colonialism and the Elimination of the Native," *Journal of Genocide Studies* 8, no. 4 (Winter 2006): 387–409; Jodi Byrd, *The Transit of Empire: Indigenous Critiques of Colonialism* (Minneapolis: University of Minnesota Press, 2011); Aileen Moreton-Robinson, "Virtuous Racial States," *Griffith Law Review* 20, no. 3 (Winter 2011): 641–58; Paul Frymer, *Building an American Empire: The Era of Territorial and Political Expansion* (Princeton, NJ: Princeton University Press, 2017); Kelly Lytle Hernandez, *City of Inmates: Conquest, Rebellion, and the Rise of Human Caging in Los Angeles, 1771–1965* (Chapel Hill: University of North Carolina Press, 2017).

64. On the study of the slave state, see Stanley W. Campbell, *The Slave Catchers: Enforcement of the Fugitive Slave Law, 1850–1860* (Chapel Hill: University of North Carolina Press,

1970); Angela Y. Davis, "From the Prison of Slavery to the Slavery of Prison: Frederick Douglass and the Convict Lease System," in *The Angela Y. Davis Reader*, ed. Joy James (Malden, MA: Blackwell, 1998), 74–95; Saidiya V. Hartman, *Scenes of Subjection: Terror, Slavery, and Self-Making in Nineteenth-Century America* (Oxford: Oxford University Press, 1997); Dennis Childs, *Slaves of the State: Black Incarceration from the Chain Gang to the Penitentiary* (Minneapolis: University of Minnesota Press, 2015).

65. Childs, *Slaves of the State.*

66. Kim Gilmore, "Slavery and Prison: Understanding the Connections," *Social Justice* 27, no. 3 (Fall 2000): 195–205. On the history of Angola, see Ernest Kikuta Chavez, "My Brother's Keeper: Mass Death in the Carceral State," *Social Justice* 43, no. 2 (Spring 2016): 21–36.

## 1. THE ARCHITECTURE OF LIBERALISM AND THE ORIGINS OF CARCERAL DEMOCRACY

1. A. Davis and Dent, "Prison as a Border," 1236.

2. William Blackstone, *Commentaries on the Laws of England*, quoted in Pippa Holloway, *Living in Infamy: Felon Disenfranchisement and the History of American Citizenship* (Oxford: Oxford University Press, 2013), 4.

3. Francis Lieber, *A Popular Essay on Subjects of Penal Law* (Philadelphia: Philadelphia Society for Alleviating the Miseries of Public Prisons, 1838), 48.

4. General Agent Frank Strong to Attorney General, November 12, 1885, Letters to the Attorney General, RG 60, NA II. For an analysis of Haviland's work on the Rhode Island State Prison and its cultural landscape, see James C. Garman, *Detention Castles of Stone and Steel: Landscape, Labor, and the Urban Penitentiary* (Knoxville: University of Tennessee Press, 2005).

5. General Agent Frank Strong to Attorney General, November 12, 1885, RG 60, NA II.

6. Ibid.

7. Ibid.

8. General Agent Frank Strong to Attorney General, April 30, 1886, Letters to the Attorney General, RG 60, NA II.

9. General Agent Frank Strong to Attorney General, May 20, 1886, Letters to the Attorney General, RG 60, NA II.

10. David J. Rothman's analysis minimizes the outward appearance of the penitentiary form, in *The Discovery of the Asylum: Social Order and Disorder in the New Republic* (London: Little, Brown, 1990), 83.

11. Norman B. Johnston, "John Haviland," in *Pioneers in Criminology*, ed. Hermann Mannheim (Montclair, NJ: Patterson Smith, 1971), 106.

12. James V. Bennett, introduction to *Handbook of Correctional Institution Design and Construction*, by US Bureau of Prisons (Washington, DC: US Bureau of Prisons, 1949).

13. US Bureau of Prisons, *Handbook of Correctional Institution Design.*

14. Bill Cunningham, *Castle: The Story of a Kentucky Prison* (Kuttawa, KY: McClanahan, 1995), 24.

15. Haviland to Tellkampf, October 11, 1842, Memo Book 6, Haviland Papers, quoted in Norman Bruce Johnston, "The Development of Radial Prisons: A Study in Cultural Diffusion" (PhD diss., University of Pennsylvania, 1958), 198. See also Albert Ten Eyck

Gardner, "A Philadelphia Masterpiece: Haviland's Prison," *Metropolitan Museum of Art Bulletin* 14, no. 4 (December 1955): 103–8.

16. Haviland's archives are housed at the University of Pennsylvania. The sixteen daybooks were rediscovered in 1951 in the Somerset County Archives in England by H. M. Colvin. See "News," *Journal of the Society of Architectural Historians* 10 (October 1951): 32.

17. Norman B. Johnston, "John Haviland, Jailor to the World," *Journal of the Society of Architectural Historians* 23, no. 2 (May 1964): 105.

18. Matthew Baigell, "John Haviland" (PhD diss., University of Pennsylvania, 1965), 277–78. On Haviland's work in the Egyptian mode, see Richard G. Carrott, *The Egyptian Revival: Its Sources, Monuments, and Meaning, 1808–1858* (Berkeley: University of California Press, 1978).

19. N. Johnston, "John Haviland," 107. For Haviland's biography, see Joseph Jackson, *Early Philadelphia Architects and Engineers* (Philadelphia, 1923); and Agnes Addison Gilchrist, "John Haviland before 1816," *Journal of the Society of Architectural Historians* 20, no. 3 (October 1961): 136–37.

20. Robin Evans, *The Fabrication of Virtue: English Prison Architecture, 1750–1840* (New York: Cambridge University Press, 1982), 187.

21. Matthew Baigell, "John Haviland in Philadelphia," *Journal of the Society of Architectural Historians* 25, no. 3 (October 1966): 200.

22. James Elmes, *Hints for the Improvement of Prisons* (London: W. Bulmer, 1817), 14.

23. *Encyclopedia Londonis* (1826), quoted in Norman Johnston, *The Human Cage: A Brief History of Prison Architecture* (New York: Walker, 1973), 26–27.

24. George W. Smith, *A Defence of the System of Solitary Confinement of Prisoners Adopted by the State of Pennsylvania* (Philadelphia: Philadelphia Society for Alleviating the Miseries of Prisoners, 1833), 22. See also Wayne Andrews, *American Gothic: Its Origins, Its Trials, Its Triumphs* (New York: Vintage, 1975), 72.

25. *Book of Minutes of the Building Commissioners,* quoted in N. Johnston, *Human Cage*, 31.

26. Quoted in Michael Meranze, *Laboratories of Virtue: Punishment, Revolution, and Authority in Philadelphia, 1760–1835* (Chapel Hill: University of North Carolina Press, 1996), 133–34. Meranze notes that in this original version of Rush's *An Enquiry into the Effects of Public Punishments* his gloomy narrative dominates, but in later revisions published as *Essays* he abandoned much of this narrative.

27. Talbot Hamlin, *Benjamin Henry Latrobe* (New York: Oxford University Press, 1955), 246.

28. Meranze, *Laboratories of Virtue,* 133–34.

29. Quoted in ibid., 328.

30. Evans, *Fabrication of Virtue,* 169.

31. Charles Dickens, *American Notes* (New York: Fromm, 1985).

32. Warden's speech, quoted in Meranze, *Laboratories of Virtue,* 311–12.

33. Meranze, *Laboratories of Virtue,* 311–12.

34. Warden's speech, quoted in ibid., 312.

35. W. David Lewis, *From Newgate to Dannemora: The Rise of the Penitentiary in New York, 1796–1848* (Ithaca, NY: Cornell University Press, 1965), 111. The original statue was "made of wood and subject to the ravages of weather and worms . . . and finally replaced in 1848 by a replica made of sheet copper" referred to as Copper John.

36. Beaumont and Tocqueville, *On the Penitentiary System,* 40.

37. Gershom Powers, "A Letter . . . in Answer to a Letter of the Honorable Edward Livingston, Albany, 1829," quoted in Lewis, *From Newgate to Dannemora*, 114.

38. Beaumont and Tocqueville, *On the Penitentiary System*, 41–42.

39. A. Davis, "Prison."

40. Charles L. Crow, *American Gothic* (Cardiff: University of Wales Press, 2009), 15.

41. Linda Bayer-Berenbaum, *The Gothic Imagination: Expansion in Gothic Literature and Art* (London: Associated University Presses, 1982), 24.

42. Ibid., 27.

43. Martin Tropp, *Images of Fear: How Horror Stories Helped Shape Modern Culture, 1818–1918* (Jefferson, NC: McFarland, 1999), 81.

44. See Botting's discussion of the distinction between gothic terror and gothic horror in British and American literature in Fred Botting, *Gothic: The New Critical Idiom* (Routledge: London: 2014), 68–69.

45. M. Brown, *Culture of Punishment*, 9, 16.

46. Slavoj Zizek's *Looking Awry*, cited in Eric Savoy, "The Rise of American Gothic," in *Cambridge Companion to Gothic Fiction*, ed. Jerrold E. Hogle (Cambridge: Cambridge University Press, 2002), 181.

47. John Bender, *Imagining the Penitentiary: Fiction and the Architecture of the Mind in Eighteenth-Century England* (Chicago: University of Chicago Press, 1987), 202.

48. Ibid., 8.

49. Ibid., 14.

50. Bayer-Berenbaum, *Gothic Imagination*, 19; Botting, *Gothic*, 39.

51. Botting, *Gothic*, 39.

52. George P. Marsh, "The Goths in New England: A Discourse Delivered," August 15, 1843, quoted in Faye Ringel, "Building the Gothic Image in America: Changing Icons, Changing Times," *Gothic Studies* 4, no. 2 (November 2002): 146.

53. General Assembly, Virginia, June 1619, *Colony Laws of Virginia*, quoted in Ronald J. Prestritto, *Founding the Criminal Law: Punishment and Political Thought in the Origins of America* (DeKalb: Northern Illinois University Press, 2000), 49.

54. Ibid., 49.

55. Randall G. Shelden, *Controlling the Dangerous Classes: A Critical Introduction to the History of Criminal Justice* (Boston: Allyn and Bacon, 2001).

56. John Howard, *An Account of the Principal Lazarettos in Europe* (London, 1789), quoted in N. Johnston, *Human Cage*, 28.

57. John Rochester Thomas, *History of Prison Architecture* (New York: J. J. Little, 1892), 29–30.

58. Hans-Jurgen Lusebrink and Rolf Reichardt, *The Bastille: A History of a Symbol of Despotism and Freedom* (Durham, NC: Duke University Press, 1997), 74.

59. Michel Foucault, *Discipline and Punish*, trans. Alan Sheridan (New York: Random House, 1977), 232. On the idea of the prison as a site of production, see John K. Simon, "Michel Foucault on Attica: An Interview," *Social Justice* 18, no. 3 (Fall 1991): 26–34.

60. Foucault, *Discipline and Punish*, 232–33.

61. Ringel, "Building the Gothic Image," 145.

62. Wayne Andrews, *American Gothic*, 40.

63. Mark Twain, *Life on the Mississippi* (1883; repr., New York: Dover, 2000), chap. 40.

64. Lewis Barnard, "Old Arkansas State Penitentiary," *Arkansas Historical Quarterly* 13, no. 3 (Autumn 1954): 323.

65. Ringel, "Building the Gothic Image," 145.

66. Joe Jackson, *Leavenworth Train*, 196.

67. Baigell, "John Haviland," 2; N. Johnston, "Development of Radial Prisons," 198.

68. Lisa Benton-Short and John Rennie Short, *Cities and Nature* (New York: Routledge, 2013), 29; L'Enfant memorandum accompanying his "Map of Dotted Lines," quoted in Frederick Gutheim and Antoinette J. Lee, *Worthy of the Nation: Washington, DC, from L'Enfant to the National Capital Planning Commission* (Baltimore: Johns Hopkins University Press, 2006), 23.

69. Scott W. Berg, *Grand Avenues: The Story of the French Visionary Who Designed Washington, DC* (New York: Pantheon Books, 2007), 139.

70. Hamlin, *Benjamin Henry Latrobe*, 532.

71. Baigell, "John Haviland," 26, 254.

72. N. Johnston, "Development of Radial Prisons," 185–97; Hamlin, *Benjamin Henry Latrobe*, 125.

73. Hamlin, *Benjamin Henry Latrobe*, xviii.

74. Keally McBride, *Punishment and Political Order* (Ann Arbor: University of Michigan Press, 2007), 122.

75. Thomas Hobbes, *Leviathan*, ed. C. B. Macpherson, Penguin Classics (Harmondsworth: Penguin, 1986), 230.

76. John Locke, *Second Treatise* (1690; repr., Indianapolis: Hackett, 1980), 250.

77. Dumm, *Democracy and Punishment*, 3.

78. Lowe, *Intimacies of Four Continents*, 2.

79. Dumm, *Democracy and Punishment*, 3.

80. Ibid., 5–6.

81. Despite the narrative of criminals within, many of the former felons-convict, as they were called, became members of the community, including George Washington's schoolteacher and two-thirds of the teachers of Maryland. On the impact of the British Transportation Act of 1717, see James Davie Butler, "British Convicts Shipped to American Colonies," *American Historical Review* 2, no. 1 (October 1896): 12. See also A. Roger Ekirch, *Bound for America: The Transportation of British Convicts to the Colonies, 1718–1775* (Oxford: Clarendon Press, 1987).

82. Dr. Samuel Johnson, English author of the *Dictionary of the English Language*, referred to Americans as a race of convicts; Butler, "British Convicts," 12. On the Australian history of convict transportation, see Robert Hughes, *The Fatal Shore* (New York: Alfred A. Knopf, 1987); Jon Stratton, "Two Rescues, One History: Everyday Racism in Australia." *Social Identities* 12, no. 6 (November 2006): 657–81; Cassandra Pybus and Hamish Maxwell-Stewart, *American Citizens, British Slaves: Yankee Political Prisoners in an Australian Penal Colony, 1839–1850* (East Lansing: Michigan State University Press, 2002); and A. G. L. Shaw, *Convicts and the Colonies: A Study of Penal Transportation from Great Britain and Ireland to Australia and Other Parts of the British Empire* (London: Faber and Faber, 1966).

83. Cong. Globe, 33rd Cong., 2nd Sess. (January 25, 1855): 389.

84. Ibid. See also Edith Abbott, and Alida C. Bowler, *Report on Crime and the Foreign Born*, National Commission on Law Observance and Enforcement [Wickersham Commission] (Washington, DC: Government Printing Office, 1931) 35.

85. Cong. Globe, 39th Cong., 1st Sess. (1866): 1492.

86. Immigration Law of 1875 (Page Law), 18 Stat. 477 (1875), Chapter 141, Section 5.

87. Cong. Rec., 54th Cong., 1st Sess. (1895–96): 531. The Congressional Record Index of the same session indicates several discussions of convict transportation to the United States.

88. Keve, *Prisons*, 13.

89. US Department of Justice, *Annual Report of the Attorney-General of the United States, 1896* (Washington, DC, 1896).

90. Cong. Rec., 51st Cong., 1st Sess. (January 22, 1891): 784 and 885. The speakers are House Democrat Stewart of Georgia and House Democrat Rogers of Arkansas.

91. Ibid., 785.

92. Paul Keve, *The McNeil Century: The Life and Times of an Island Prison* (Chicago: Nelson-Hall, 1984).

93. US Department of Justice, *Annual Report of the Attorney-General* [1896].

94. Letters to the Attorney General, DOJ Central Files (Folded) Box 549, RG 60, NA II.

95. Ibid.

96. Stewart Jail Works Company to R. V. LaDow, October 23, 1909, Papers of R. V. LaDow, RG 129, NA II.

97. Adam's Steel and Wireworks Prison and Jail Construction to R. V. LaDow, October 23, 1909, Papers of R. V. LaDow, RG 129, NA II.

98. Allison Poe, *Poe Brothers or the Sequel to a Conspiracy* (Wynnewood, OK, 1910).

99. "Estimates of Appropriations for the Fiscal Year 1910 . . . ," Papers of R. V. LaDow, Box 12, RG 129, NA II.

100. *Appeal to Reason*, July 15, 1911.

101. T. A. Kating to the President of the United States, April 20, 1913, RG 129, NA KC; *Appeal to Reason*, April 15, July 15, and December 15, 1911. The *Appeal* relied on the experiences of prisoners who wrote in after their release to describe the violence.

102. James V. Bennett, *I Chose Prison* (New York: Alfred A. Knopf, 1970), 61.

103. Pub. L. No. 71–218, 46 Stat. 325 (1930).

104. US Bureau of Prisons, *Handbook of Correctional Institution Design*.

105. Ibid.

106. McBride, *Punishment and Political Order*, 1.

## 2. TERRITORIAL POLITICS

1. "Still Grinding," *Wichita Star*, September 7, 1889.

2. "Wanted Poison," *Wichita Star*, September 15, 1888.

3. "United States Court," *Wichita Daily Eagle*, September 8, 1889.

4. When the federal government had to select a group of federal prisoners housed in state prisons, it created lists of possible transfers and of the work skills they might bring to the institution. These lists remain in File 2256, Department of Justice Central Files, RG 60, NA II.

5. Inmate File No. 3760 (John Grindstone), RG 129, NA KC.

6. R. V. LaDow to Attorney General, February 7, 1898, File 2256, Department of Justice Central Files, RG 60, NA II.

7. At the military prison, he was previously known as Prisoner No. 12. On Grindstone's assignment as first prisoner, see LaMaster, *US Penitentiary Leavenworth*, 31.

8. Grindstone suffered from pulmonary tuberculosis and died following an operation in 1904. See "Record of Death and Internment," Inmate File No. 3760 (John Grindstone), RG 129, NA KC.

9. Major Crimes Act, 48th Cong., 2nd Sess., Chapter 341, 23 Stat. 385 (1885).

10. Prison Ledger, RG 129, NA KC.

11. On the Canton Asylum for Insane Indians in Canton, South Dakota, which operated from 1903 to 1934, see Scott Riney, "Power and Powerlessness: The People of the Canton Asylum for Insane Indians," in *The Sioux in South Dakota History*, ed. Richmond L. Clow (Pierre: South Dakota State Historical Society Press, 2007), 41–64.

12. James J. Fisher, "Prison Files Show Its Earliest Inmates," *Kansas City Star*, August 15, 1995.

13. LaMaster, *US Penitentiary Leavenworth*, 32.

14. Inmate File No. 349 (Nannie Perkins), RG 129, NA KC.

15. Inmate File No. 420 (Minnie Jones), RG 129, NA KC.

16. Inmate File No. 436 (Eliza Grayson), RG 129, NA KC.

17. Warden J. W. French to Attorney General, May 15, 1896, File 2257, Department of Justice Central Files, RG 60, NA II. See also the warden's letters of May 25, 1896, and June 6, 1896.

18. Warden R. W. McClaughry to Department of Justice, June 1906, RG 60, NA II.

19. Warden French to Attorney General, December 12, 1897, Department of Justice Central File 2256, RG 60, NA II.

20. Inmate File No. 2040 (Mary Snowden), RG 129, NA KC.

21. *Seattle Star*, October 2, 1906, and *Boston Evening Transcript*, September 10, 1906.

22. It is possible that she was at Leavenworth for as long as three days. A note added to her file states that she was transferred to the Kansas Prison on June 14, a date that is then crossed through and replaced with June 15. Another form records her transfer date as June 16, 1906. Cardish was finally moved to the Training School for Girls in Geneva, Illinois, where she remained until her twenty-first birthday. Warden to Cecil Clay, July 3, 1906, and Cecil Clay to Warden McClaughry, September 10, 1906, Inmate File No. 5250 (Lizzie Cardish), RG 129, NA, KC.

23. James J. Fisher, "Records Tell," *Kansas City Star*, January 11, 1998. Federal prison records confirm his age.

24. Emphasis mine. Deputy Warden Lemon to Warden McClaughry, January 8, 1910, RG 129, NA II.

25. US Department of Justice, *Annual Report of the Attorney-General of the United States for the Year 1906* (Washington, DC, 1906), 43.

26. R. W. McClaughry to R. V. LaDow, January 15, 1908, Correspondence of R. V. LaDow, Box 17, RG 129, NA II.

27. US Marshal at Fort Smith, Arkansas, to Attorney General, October 18, 1896, Records of the Attorney General, RG 60, NA II.

28. Warden French to Attorney General Harmon, October 7, 1895, Letters to the Attorney General, RG 60, NA II.

29. Sarah Deer, "Federal Indian Law and Violent Crime," in *Color of Violence: The IN-CITE! Anthology*, ed. INCITE! Women of Color Against Violence (Cambridge: South End Press, 2006), 32–41; Dian Million, "Policing the Rez: Keeping No Peace in Indian Country," *Social Justice* 27, no. 3 (Fall 2000): 101–19; Ross, *Inventing the Savage*; Lisa M. Poupart,

"Crime and Justice in American Indian Communities," *Social Justice* 29, nos. 1/2 (Spring/ Summer 2002): 144–59; Waziyatawin, *What Does Justice Look Like: The Struggle for Liberation in Dakota Homeland* (St. Paul, MN: Living Justice Press, 2008).

30. Hartman, *Scenes of Subjection*; Joan Dayan, "Legal Slaves and Civil Bodies," in *Materializing Democracy: Toward a Revitalized Cultural Politics,* ed. Dana Nelson and Russ Castronovo (Durham, NC: Duke University Press, 2002), 53–93.

31. See Monique Fordham, "Within the Iron Houses: The Struggle for Native American Religious Freedom in American Prisons," *Social Justice* 20, nos. 1/2 (Spring/Summer 1993): 167, and Little Rock Reed, "The American Indian in the White Man's Prisons: A Story of Genocide," in *The New Abolitionists: (Neo)Slave Narratives and Contemporary Prison Writings,* ed. Joy James (Albany: SUNY Press, 2005), 133–50. A book of the same name (*The American Indian in the White Man's Prisons*) was also published by Little Rock Reed, Lenny Foster, and Art Solomon (Taos, NM: UnCompromising Books, 1993). On Montana, see Ross, *Inventing the Savage*; on Nebraska, see Elizabeth S. Grobsmith, *Indians in Prison: Incarcerated Native Americans in Nebraska* (Lincoln: University of Nebraska Press, 1994); on Oklahoma, see Oklahoma Department of Charities and Corrections, *First Annual Report of the Commissioner of Charities and Corrections of the State of Oklahoma* (Guthrie, OK: Leader Printing, 1908), and *Second Report of the Commissioner of Charities and Corrections* (Oklahoma City: Warden Printing, 1910), and related materials written by Kate Barnard, in the Oklahoma State Archives.

32. Kathleen Du Val, *The Native Ground: Indians and Colonists in the Heart of the Continent* (Philadelphia: University of Pennsylvania Press, 2006); John Joseph Matthews, *The Osages: Children of the Muddy Waters* (Norman: University of Oklahoma Press, 1981). See also William E. Unrau, *The Kansa Indians: A History of the Wind People, 1673–1873* (Norman: University of Oklahoma Press, 1971).

33. Amy Kaplan, "Where Is Guantánamo?" in *Legal Borderlands: Law and the Construction of American Borders,* ed. Mary Dudziak and Leti Volpp (Baltimore: Johns Hopkins University Press, 2006), 239–66; Leti Volpp, "The Indigenous as Alien," *UC Irvine Law Review* 5, no. 289 (2015): 289–326.

34. Treaty of 1805 (Ioway Treaty), in *Territorial Papers of the United States*, ed. Clarence E. Carter, vol. 13, *The Territory of Louisiana-Missouri, 1803–1806* (Washington, DC: US Government Printing Office, 1948), 245–47.

35. Treaty of 1825 (Prairie du Chien Treaty), August 19, 1825, in *Documents of United States Indian Policy,* ed. Francis Paul Prucha (Lincoln: University of Nebraska Press, 1990): 42.

36. Mary Dudziak and Leti Volpp, "Introduction: Legal Borderlands," in Dudziak and Volpp, *Legal Borderlands*. This work builds on the analysis of law that first emerged in the work of Gloria Anzaldúa in *Borderlands/La Frontera* (San Francisco: Aunt Lute Books, 1999).

37. "From Kansas: Situation, Character and Prospects of Leavenworth City—General Speculation," *New York Times,* December 11, 1858; Jeremy Bentham, *The Panopticon Writings* (London: Verso, 1995).

38. See Elvid Hunt, *History of Fort Leavenworth, 1827–1937* (Fort Leavenworth, KS: Command and General Staff School Press, 1937), 20, 30.

39. US War Department, *Report of the Secretary of War*, November 24, 1828, in appendix to *Register of the Debates in Congress, Comprising the Leading Debates and Incidents of the Second Session of the Twentieth Congress* (Washington, DC: Gales and Seaton, 1830), 9.

40. Ibid.

41. White Cloud's codefendant is variously referred to as Mira Natutais and Mera Naute.

42. William E. Foley, "Different Notions of Justice: The Case of the 1808 St. Louis Murder Trials," *Gateway Heritage*, Winter 1988–89, 2–13.

43. *Missouri Gazette*, July 26, 1808, and August 2, 1808, quoted in Martha Royce Blaine, *The Ioway Indians* (Norman: University of Oklahoma Press, 1995), 100.

44. Jefferson to Governor Lewis, August 24, 1808, in *Writings of Thomas Jefferson*, 5:353.

45. On the history of capture, see Soma de Bourbon, "Indigenous Genocidal Tracings: Slavery, Transracial Adoption, and the Indian Child Welfare Act" (PhD diss., UC Santa Cruz, 2013).

46. Testimony of Walking Cloud/Pompakin, Fort Leavenworth, August 3, 1835, quoted in Blaine, *Ioway Indians*, 157.

47. Correspondence of Indian Agent Andrew Hughes with William Clark, 1831, RG 75, National Archives, quoted in Blaine, *Ioway Indians*, 201. See Greg Olson's *The Ioway in Missouri* (Columbia: University of Missouri Press, 2008), and his "Navigating the White Road: White Cloud's Struggle to Lead the Ioway along the Path of Acculturation," *Missouri Historical Review* 99, no. 2 (2005): 93–114. See also Lance M. Foster, *The Indians of Iowa* (Iowa City: University of Iowa Press, 2009), 9, and the documentary film *Lost Nation: The Ioway* (dir. Kelly Rundle, Fourth Wall Films, 2008). On how White Cloud resisted the prisonization of the Great Nemaha Reserve by refusing to send his children to boarding schools and by traveling to England, where he developed a critique of debtors' prisons that shaped his views of crime and colonialism, see Blaine, *Ioway Indians*, 190 and 234.

48. Extract from Minutes of Treaty Council, July 7, 1830, quoted in Blaine, *Ioway Indians*, 159.

49. Ibid.

50. See Treaty of 1825 (Prairie du Chien Treaty), in Prucha, *Documents*, 42.

51. *United States Gazette*, June 29, 1833, quoted in Donald Jackson, introduction to *Black Hawk: An Autobiography*, ed. Donald Jackson (Chicago: University of Illinois Press, 1987), 10.

52. US Bureau of Indian Affairs, *Report of the Commissioner of Indian Affairs for the Year 1862* (Washington, DC, 1863), 109.

53. Hunt, *History of Fort Leavenworth*, 74.

54. Trade and Intercourse Act, June 30, 1834, 23rd Cong., 1st Sess., Chapter 161.

55. Ibid.

56. Cheryl Harris, "Whiteness as Property," *Harvard Law Review* 106, no. 8 (June 1993): 1707–91. See also the work of Aileen Moreton-Robinson, *The White Possessive: Property, Power, and Indigenous Sovereignty* (Minneapolis: University of Minnesota Press, 2015).

57. Trade and Intercourse Act, June 30, 1834.

58. President Jefferson to William Henry Harrison, February 27, 1803, in Prucha, *Documents*, 22. On Jefferson's policies, see Anthony F. C. Wallace, *Jefferson and the Indians: The Tragic Fate of the First Americans* (Cambridge, MA: Harvard University Press, 1999).

59. Indian Agent Richardson to Superintendent Mitchell, January 10, 1852, Central Superintendency, Letters Received, Office of Indian Affairs, National Archives, quoted in Blaine, *Ioway Indians*, 245.

60. Agency Farmer John Foreman to Commissioner of Indian Affairs, November 25, 1849, quoted in Blaine, *Ioway Indians*, 245.

61. Trade and Intercourse Act, June 30, 1834; emphasis mine.

62. Report of the Committee on Indian Affairs, March 15, 1836, Senate Document 246, 24th Cong., 1st Sess., 1, quoted in James P. Ronda, "'We Have a Country': Race, Geography, and the Invention of Indian Territory," *Journal of the Early Republic* 19, no. 4 (Winter 1999): 746.

63. US Bureau of Indian Affairs, *Report . . . for 1862*, 11.

64. Rita Napier, "Economic Democracy in Kansas: Speculation and Townsite Preemption in Kickapoo," *Kansas Historical Quarterly* 40, no. 3 (Fall 1974): 349–69; Paul Gates, *Fifty Million Acres: Conflicts over Kansas Land Policy* (Norman: University of Oklahoma Press, 1997).

65. Mari Sandoz, *Crazy Horse: The Strange Man of the Oglalas* (1942; repr., Lincoln: University of Nebraska Press, 1992), 91.

66. Ibid., 83. George Hyde suggests that Spotted Tail had his wife and at least one daughter with him during his imprisonment in George E. Hyde, *Spotted Tail's Folk: A History of the Brulé Sioux* (1961; repr., Norman: University of Oklahoma Press, 1987), 74n3.

67. See Spotted Tail's interview with the Nebraska reporter Alfred Sorenson, published in the *Omaha World-Herald*, September 21, 1930.

68. Stephen A. Douglas to J. H. Crane et al., December 17, 1853, quoted in William E. Unrau, *The Rise and Fall of Indian Country, 1825–1855* (Lawrence: University of Kansas Press, 2007), 125.

69. Joseph Herring's *The Enduring Indians of Kansas: A Century and a Half of Acculturation* (Lawrence: University Press of Kansas, 1990) criticizes Miner and Unrau's inattention in *The End of Indian Kansas* to Native American agency in the decision to relocate or resist. See Catherine Price's important review of this work in "Communities in Peril: Native Americans of Nineteenth-Century Kansas and Nebraska," *Reviews in American History* 20, no. 4 (December 1992): 459–63.

70. Deborah A. Rosen, "Colonization through Law: The Judicial Defense of State Indian Legislation, 1790–1880," *American Journal of Legal History* 46, no. 1 (January 2004): 26–54; Robert A. Trennert, "The Business of Indian Removal: Deporting the Potawatomi from Wisconsin, 1851," *Wisconsin Magazine of History* 63, no. 1 (Fall 1979): 36–50.

71. See Brice Obermeyer, *Delaware Tribe in a Cherokee Nation* (Lincoln: University of Nebraska Press, 2009), and Denise Low, *The Turtle's Beating Heart: One Family's Story of Lenape Survival* (Lincoln: University of Nebraska Press, 2017).

72. Gates, *Fifty Million Acres*, 7.

73. United States v. John Ward, 1 Kan. 601 (1863).

74. Hunt v. Kansas, 4 Kan. 60 (1866). See Deborah A. Rosen, *American Indians and State Law: Sovereignty, Race, and Citizenship, 1790–1880* (Lincoln: University of Nebraska Press, 2007).

75. Dred Scott v. Sandford, 60 U.S. 393 (1857). See also the later state case of Rubideaux v. Vallie, 12 Kan. 28 (1873), which assigned Native people the combined legal status of criminals, citizens, and aliens.

76. Kansas Indians, 72 U.S. 737 (1867). See also "Status of Indians before State and Federal Courts," *Columbia Law Review* 14, no. 7 (1914): 587–90.

77. Tony R. Mullis, *Peacekeeping on the Plains: Army Operations in Bleeding Kansas* (Columbia: University of Missouri Press, 2004), 63, 84, 91–99; Robert M. Utley, *Frontiersman in Blue: The United States Army and the Indian, 1848–1865* (New York: Macmillan, 1967), 116–17; George Walton, *Sentinel of the Plains: Fort Leavenworth and the American West* (Englewood Cliffs, NJ: Prentice-Hall, 1973); and Hunt, *History of Fort Leavenworth*, 92.

78. Waziyatawin, *In the Footsteps of Our Ancestors* (St. Paul, MN: Living Justice Press, 2006) and *What Does Justice Look Like?* See also Gary Clayton Anderson and Alan R. Woolworth, *Through Dakota Eyes: Narrative Accounts of the Minnesota Indian War of 1862* (St. Paul: Minnesota Historical Society Press, 1988); Carol Chomsky, "The United States-Dakota War Trials: A Study in Military Justice," *Stanford Law Review* 43, no. 1 (November 1990): 13–98; and Corrine L. Monjeau-Marz, *The Dakota Indian Internment at Fort Snelling, 1862–1864* (St. Paul, MN: Prairie Smoke Press, 2005).

79. See David A. Nichols, *Lincoln and the Indians: Civil War Policy and Politics* (St. Paul: Minnesota Historical Society Press, 2012).

80. US Bureau of Indian Affairs, *Annual Report of the Commissioner of Indian Affairs to the Secretary of the Interior for the Year 1872* (Washington, DC, 1872), 41.

81. Lt. Gen. Phil Sheridan to Gen. William T. Sherman, October 29, 1878, quoted in *The Northern Cheyenne Exodus in History and Memory*, ed. James N. Leiker and Ramon Powers (Norman: University of Oklahoma Press, 2011), 72.

82. US Bureau of Indian Affairs, *Annual Report . . . for the Year 1872*, 15.

83. Ibid., 11–12, 15.

84. Carol Chiago Lujan and Gordon Adams, "U.S. Colonization of Indian Justice Systems: A Brief History," *Wicazo Sa Review* 19, no. 2 (Autumn 2004): 9–23.

85. See, for example, Grace E. Meredith's *Girl Captives of the Cheyenne* (1927; repr., Mechanicsville, PA: Stackpole Books, 2004), written by a niece by marriage, and Jeff Broome, *Dog Soldier Justice: The Ordeal of Susanna Alderdice in the Kansas Indian War* (Lincoln: University of Nebraska Press, 2003).

86. Subject Files, Cheyenne Prisoners, Oklahoma State Historical Society, Oklahoma City. See also Louise Boyd James, "Burying the Hatchet: The German Family Makes Peace with the Cheyenne," *Persimmon Hill*, Autumn 1991.

87. On Grey Beard's capture and transportation to Fort Leavenworth, see "The Adobe Walls Fight," *Leavenworth Daily Times*, November 17, 1877.

88. On Fort Marion ledger art, see Edwin L. Wade, "The Artistic Legacy of Fort Marion: Beyond the Prison Gate," *Southwest Art*, July 1993; F. Hilton Crowe, "Indian Prisoner-Students at Fort Marion: The Founding of Carlisle Was Dreamed in St. Augustine," *Regional Review* 5, no. 6 (December 1940): 5–8, 30; and Joyce M. Szabo, *Imprisoned Art, Complex Patronage: Plains Drawings by Howling Wolf and Zotom at the Autry National Center* (Santa Fe, NM: School for Advanced Research Press, 2011). On ledger art at Fort Marion created by Dakota, Kiowa, Comanche, Apache and Cheyenne prisoners, see Ross Frank's Plains Indian Ledger Art Project (PILA) at https://plainsledgerart.org. On the Dakota Prisoner of War Letters, see Clifford Canku and Michael Simon, *The Dakota Prisoner of War Letters* (St. Paul: Minnesota Historical Society Press, 2013).

89. See John Sipes Cheyenne Family Oral Histories, Prairie Chief Family, quoted in "Gray Beard, Cheyenne Fort Marion POW," http://home.epix.net/~landis/graybeard.html. See also John H. Moore, "Cheyenne Political History, 1820–1894," *Ethnohistory* 21, no. 4 (Fall 1974): 354.

90. Pratt to Miles, May 9, 1875, Berthrong Collection Cheyenne Prisoners, quoted in "Gray Beard, Cheyenne Fort Marion POW."

91. The Cheyenne homeland encompasses parts of what is now Wyoming, Colorado, Nebraska, and Kansas. See Treaty of Fort Laramie, September 17, 1851, in Prucha, *Documents*, 83. For the Fort Wise Treaty, signed February 15, 1861, see "Treaty with the Arapahoe and Cheyenne" First People, https://www.firstpeople.us/FP-Html-Treaties/TreatyWith-TheArapahoAndCheyenne1861.html On the treaty history of the Cheyenne, see G.B. Grinnell, *The Fighting Cheyenne* (New York: Scribner, 1915), 383–98; and Elliot West, *The Contested Plains: Indians, Goldseekers, and the Rush to Colorado* (Lawrence: University Press of Kansas, 1998).

92. *Report of the Joint Committee on the Conduct of War, at the Second Session Thirty-Eighth Congress* (Washington, DC, 1865).

93. Jerome Greene, *Washita: The U.S. Army and the Southern Cheyenne, 1867–1869* (Norman: University of Oklahoma Press, 2004).

94. Although this chapter uses the term *Dakota, Oceti Sakowin* is a term that encompasses Lakota/Dakota/Nakota. The term *Sioux* is part of the legacy of colonialism and descended from the Algonquin *Naudoweissious*, meaning "enemy," while Dakota signifies "league" or "ally." See Waziyatawin Angela Wilson, *Remember This! Dakota Decolonization and the Eli Taylor Narratives* (Lincoln: University of Nebraska Press, 2005), 249n7. For a discussion of the larger terrain of identification, see Ed McGaa/Eagle Man, *Crazy Horse and Chief Red Cloud* (Minneapolis, MN: Four Directions, 2005).

95. On the unlawful arrest and murder of Crazy Horse, see Edward Kadlecek and Mabell Kadlecek, *To Kill an Eagle: Indian Views on the Death of Crazy Horse* (Boulder, CO: Johnson, 1983), and Larry McMurtry, *Crazy Horse: A Life* (New York: Penguin, 1999). On Custer's death and the Lakota victory at Greasy Grass (Little Big Horn), see Ruth Hopkins, "Fighting with Spirit: How Greasy Grass Was Won," *Last Real Indians* (blog), January 20, 2016, https://lastrealindians.com/fighting-with-spirit-how-greasy-grass-was-won-by-ruth-hopkins/lastrealindians/.

96. See also Alan Boye, *Holding Stone Hands: On the Trail of the Cheyenne Exodus* (Lincoln: University of Nebraska Press, 1999); John H. Monnett, *Tell Them We Are Going Home: The Odyssey of the Northern Cheyenne* (Norman: University of Oklahoma Press, 2001).

97. On the political significance of the actions of Buffalo Calf Road and Black Coyote, see Rosemary Agonito and Joseph Agonito, "Resurrecting History's Forgotten Women: A Case Study from the Cheyenne Indians," *Frontiers: A Journal of Women Studies* 6, no. 3 (Autumn 1981): 8–16. See Christina Rose, "Native History: Chief Little Wolf Surrenders, Establishes Reservation," *Indian Country Today*, March 25, 2017.

98. US Bureau of Indian Affairs, *Annual Report . . . for the Year 1872*, 15.

99. Todd D. Epp, "The State of Kansas versus Wild Hog et al.," *Kansas History* 5, no. 2 (Summer 1982): 139–46.

100. Annual Report of the Indian Agent D.B. Dyer at the Cheyenne and Arapaho Agency, July 22, 1885, in Moore, "Cheyenne Political History," 344–45.

101. The treaties also resulted in the loss of land as punishment. See Treaty with the Creeks, June 14, 1866; Treaty with the Cherokee, July 19, 1866; and Treaty with the Choctaw and Chickasaw, April 28, 1866, all in *Indian Affairs: Laws and Treaties*, ed. Charles J. Kappler (Washington, DC, 1904).

102. Treaty with the Cherokee, in Kappler. See also Jeffrey Burton, *Indian Territory and the United States: Courts, Government, and the Movement for Oklahoma Statehood, 1866–1906* (Norman: University of Oklahoma Press, 1995), 20.

103. The Cherokee National Prison reopened in 2013 as a museum. On the history of Cherokee legal frameworks, see Rennard Strickland, *Fire and the Spirit: Cherokee Law from Clan to Court* (Norman: University of Oklahoma Press, 1975).

104. Sidney Harring notes in *Crow Dog's Case* that the Creeks "held to the end that imprisonment was not a fit punishment for Creek people." See Sidney L. Harring, *Crow Dog's Case: American Indian Sovereignty, Tribal Law, and United States Law in the Nineteenth Century* (Cambridge: Cambridge University Press, 1994), 59. See also Act of the Chickasaw Nation, October 12, 1876, Section 6; Act of the Choctaw Nation, November 20, 1867; Muskogee Laws, Chapter 4, Article 1, Sections 1–3, in *Constitution and Laws of the Muskogee Nation*, comp. L. C. Perryman (Muskogee Indian Territory: Phoenix Printing, 1890), https://www.loc.gov/law/help/american-indian-consts/PDF/28014185.pdf. See also Burton, *Indian Territory*.

105. United States v. Rogers, 45 U.S. 567 (1846).

106. Ibid.

107. Parker tried 13,490 cases resulting in 8,500 convictions over the course of twenty-one years. His court sentenced 160 people to death and executed 79.

108. See David V. Baker, "American Indian Executions in Historical Context," *Criminal Justice Studies* 20, no. 4 (December 2007): 335. For a detailed list of those condemned to death, see "Men Executed at Fort Smith: 1873–1896," Fort Smith National Historic Site, https://www.nps.gov/fosm/learn/historyculture/executions-at-fort-smith-1873-to-1896.htm. The largest included six executions on September 3, 1875, and January 16, 1890.

109. See the archives of the *Cherokee Advocate* at the Oklahoma Historical Society. On the idea of the lawless frontier and Parker's role in containing it, see Michael J. Brodhead, *Isaac Parker: Federal Justice on the Frontier* (Norman: University of Oklahoma Press, 2003); Jack Gregory and Rennard Strickland, eds., *Hell on the Border: He Hanged Eighty-Eight Men* (Muskogee, OK: Indian Heritage Association, 1971); and Glenn Shirley, *Law West of Fort Smith: A History of Frontier Justice in the Indian Territory, 1834–1896* (Lincoln: University of Nebraska Press, 1957).

110. On the criminalized position of Black, Native, and "Black Indian" identities in the emergent spaces of Indian Territory and Oklahoma Territory, see Mozell Hill's "The All-Negro Communities of Oklahoma: The Natural History of a Social Movement," *Journal of Negro History* 31, no. 3 (1946): 254–68. It draws from Toni Morrison's *Paradise*, which critically fictionalizes the prisonization of the landscape: a "prison calling itself a town" (Toni Morrison, *Paradise* [1997; repr., New York: Vintage, 2014], 308). See also Daniel F. Littlefield Jr. and Lonnie E. Underhill, "Negro Marshals in the Indian Territory," *Journal of Negro History* 56, no. 2 (April 1971): 77–87; Sharon Jessee, "The Contrapuntal Historiography of Toni Morrison's Paradise: Unpacking the Legacies of the Kansas and Oklahoma All-Black Towns," *American Studies* 47, no. 1 (Spring 2006): 81–112; Daniel F. Littlefield Jr. and

Lonnie Underhill, "Black Dreams and 'Free' Homes: The Oklahoma Territory," *Phylon* 34, no. 4 (December 1973): 342–57; and David Chang, "From Indian Territory to White Man's Country: Race, Nation, and the Politics of Land Ownership in Eastern Oklahoma" (PhD diss., University of Wisconsin-Madison, 2002).

111. "State of Affairs in Indian Territory," *Red Man* 9 (October 1889), cited in Daniel F. Littlefield, *Seminole Burning: A Story of Racial Vengeance* (Jackson: University of Mississippi Press 1996), 22. The term *Sooner* described white settlers who crossed the Kansas and Oklahoma borders to claim land *before* national legislative prohibitions against squatting in "Indian Territory" were rescinded. The Oklahoma Sooner remains the mascot of the University of Oklahoma.

112. Ibid.

113. William Warner (R-MO), in Cong. Rec., 50th Cong., 1st Sess., 19 (1888): 6750, quoted in Burton, *Indian Territory*, 115.

114. See US Bureau of Indian Affairs, *Annual Report . . . for the Year 1872*, 243. On the organization and corruption of Quapaw administrative governance, see Albert L. Hurtado, "The Modocs and the Jones Family Indian Ring: Quaker Administration of the Quapaw Agency, 1873–1879," in *Oklahoma's Forgotten Indians,* ed. Robert E. Smith (Oklahoma City: Oklahoma Historical Society, 1981), 86–107.

115. See US Bureau of Indian Affairs, *Annual Report of the Commissioner of Indian Affairs to the Secretary of the Interior for the Year 1875* (Washington, DC, 1875), 85. For an account of Quapaw sovereignty in the region, including how by 1760 the Quapaw were "occasionally welcoming runaway slaves," see Du Val, *Native Ground*, 67–81. The Modoc, for example, were eventually "placed" away from the Quapaw on the Shawnee side of the Agency in order to avoid the influence of the Quapaw.

116. See US Bureau of Indian Affairs, *Annual Report . . . for the Year 1872*, 243.

117. Appendix B: Trial of Modoc Prisoners, Testimony of Captain Jack," in Francis Landrum, *Guardhouse, Gallows, and Graves: The Trial and Execution of Indian Prisoners of the Modoc Indian War by the U.S. Army* (Klamath Falls, OR: Klamath County Museum, 1988), 127.

118. See Cheewa James, *Modoc: The Tribe That Wouldn't Die* (Happy Camp, CA: Naturegraph, 2008).

119. Doug Foster, "Imperfect Justice: The Modoc War Crimes Trial of 1873," *Oregon Historical Quarterly* 100, no. 3 (Fall 1999): 278.

120. "Indian Hero, Dead One Hundred Years, Awaits Final Resting Place," *Los Angeles Times*, March 21, 1977.

121. "The Army and American Indian Prisoners," Alcatraz Island, California, National Park Service, last updated November 14, 2016, https://www.nps.gov/alca/learn/historyculture/the-army-and-american-indian-prisoners.htm.

122. Jeff C. Davis to Major Herbert Curtis, July 7, 1873, in Landrum, *Guardhouse, Gallows, and Graves,* 30.

123. Richard Dillon, *Burnt-Out Fires: California's Modoc Indian War* (Englewood Cliffs, NJ: Prentice-Hall, 1973).

124. The pass was issued by A.M. Rosborough, County Judge of Siskiyou, California, April 6, 1868, and was reproduced in Keith Murray's *The Modocs and Their War* (Norman: University of Oklahoma Press, 1959), 42.

125. "General Davis on the Modoc Question," in Landrum, *Guardhouse, Gallows, and Graves*, 17.

126. Quoted in D. Foster, "Imperfect Justice," 253.

127. See ibid., 282 and n. 90; and LaMaster, *US Penitentiary Leavenworth*, 10.

128. For a reproduction of the transcripts, "taken directly from the handwritten document on file at the Nez Perce tribal headquarters," see Allen P. Slickpoo and Deward E. Walker, *Noon Nee-Me-Poo (We, the Nez Perces): Culture and History of the Nez Perces* ([Lapwai, ID: Nez Perce Tribe of Idaho, 1973), 83.

129. See Joseph's account in an interview published in the *North American Review* in April of 1879. The transcript was later published as Chief Joseph, *That All People May Be One People* (Kooskia, ID: Mountain Meadow Press, 1995). See Scott M. Thompson, *I Will Tell of My War Story: A Pictorial Account of the Nez Perce War* (Seattle: University of Washington Press, 2000), and two books written by Lucullus V. McWhorter, *Hear Me, My Chiefs! Nez Perce Legend and History* (1952; repr., Caldwell, ID: Caxton Press, 2001, and *Yellow Wolf: His Own Story* (1940; repr., Caldwell, ID: Caxton Press, 1991. On the Palouse people who were sent to Leavenworth alongside the Nez Perce, see Clifford E. Trafzer, "The Palouse in Eekish Pah," *American Indian Quarterly* 9, no. 2 (Spring 1985): 169–82.

130. Berlin N. Chapman and Berlin B. Chapman, "Nimiipuus in Indian Territory: An Archival Study," *Oregon Historical Quarterly* 50, no. 2 (June 1949): 100.

131. Ibid., 102–5.

132. Ibid., 107.

133. US War Department, *Annual Report of the Secretary of War on the Operations of the Department, for the Fiscal Year Ending June 30, 1877* (Washington, DC, 1877), 631.

134. In 2004, the route to Fort Leavenworth was included in the Nez Perce National Historic Trail, which commemorates Nez Perce survival. See Crystal White, "Honoring Nez Perce History in the Heartland," lecture presented at Lewis-Clark State College, Lewiston, ID, September 28, 2005, and Melissa McEntire, "Post Part of Nez Perce Historic Trail," *Fort Leavenworth Lamp*, November 24, 2004. See also Fred Bond's account in *Flatboating on the Yellowstone, 1877* (New York: New York Public Library, 1925).

135. "Joseph's Band," *Leavenworth Daily Times*, November 27, 1877. See also "City News," *Leavenworth Daily Times*, November 25, 1877.

136. While Chief Joseph later recalled the existence of a small cluster of graves, the military has not located the gravesite. Pearson and others have been careful not to reveal knowledge of the burial locations of Native people, given the history of unearthed and stolen remains. It remains possible that Doctor Comfort, the medical doctor at Leavenworth, stole the bodies of those who died at Leavenworth, since he had previously unearthed Ponca remains and sent them to museums. See Pearson's account of the testimonies in J. Diane Pearson, *The Nez Perce in the Indian Territory: Nimiipuu Survival* (Norman: University of Oklahoma Press, 2008), 92. Isaac McCoy was likewise said to have opened Kansa Indian graves on the Delaware Reservation, "one mile west of Fort Leavenworth," in the 1830s. See Unrau, *Kansa Indians*, 17.

137. US War Department, *Annual Report . . . Year Ending June 30, 1877*, 631.

138. Chapman and Chapman, "Nimiipuus in Indian Territory," 109–10.

139. Alan Osborne, "The Exile of the Nez Perce in Indian Territory, 1878–1885," *Chronicles of Oklahoma* 56 (Winter 1978–79): 453.

140. Because of the missionary governance of the Lapwai Reservation, Christian prisoners went to the Lapwai Reservation in Idaho, while Chief Joseph's band was sent to Washington to live with the Colville, Nespelem, and Palus peoples.

141. See US Department of the Interior, Office of Indian Affairs, "Rules Governing the Court of Indian Offenses," March 30, 1883, https://rclinton.files.wordpress.com/2007/11/code-of-indian-offenses.pdf. See also Ross's important study of the Courts of Indian Offenses in *Inventing the Savage*.

142. Annual Report, Board of Indian Commissioners (1891), cited in Harring, *Crow Dog's Case*, 188.

143. US Bureau of Indian Affairs, *Annual Report of the Commissioner of Indian Affairs to the Secretary of the Interior for the Year 1884* (Washington, DC, 1884), xiv.

144. See Spotted Tail's interview with reporter Alfred Sorenson in the *Omaha World-Herald*, September 21, 1930.

145. Hyde, *Spotted Tail's Folk*, 312.

146. Harring, *Crow Dog's Case*, 112. Crow Dog's descendant, Leonard Crow Dog, was imprisoned at Leavenworth in 1975 for resisting US interference in Native justice practices. See his important account of Native resistance to punishment in *Crow Dog: Four Generations of Sioux Medicine Men* (New York: Harper, 1995).

147. Ex Parte Crow Dog, 109 U.S. 556 (1883). See also affirmative US rulings on the prosecution in Colorado of white intraracial crime on the Ute Reservation in United States v. McBratney, 104 U.S. 621 (1881), and the right of Montana to prosecute Black crime on the Crow Indian Reservation in Draper v. United States, 164 U.S. 240 (1896).

148. Major Crimes Act (1885).

149. Ibid.

150. United States v. Clapox, 33 F. 575 (1888).

151. Ibid.

152. 26 Stat. 81–100, quoted in Burton, *Indian Territory*, 143.

153. US Department of Justice, *Annual Report of the Attorney-General for the Year 1897* (Washington, DC, 1897), xxv. This figure represents approximately sixty thousand Native people and sixty thousand white squatters.

154. "The Muskogee Story," *Peace Officer* 31, no. 4 (January 1961). The first federal jail in McAlester was just west of Fifth and Choctaw Streets. See Baird Martin, "There Are Many Roads Enroute to Present," *McAlester News-Capital and Democrat*, April 1988, clipping in Subject Files, Oklahoma State Historical Society.

155. Frederick Howard Wines, "A Republic of Criminals," *New York Times*, February 6, 1898. See also US Department of Justice, "Letter from the Attorney General in Response to Senate Resolution of January 13, 1896, Relative to Jails in the Indian Territory," 54th Cong., 1st Sess., Senate Document No. 202, 1–4, in *Congressional Serial Set: Reports, Documents, and Journals of the U.S. Senate and House of Representatives* (Washington, DC, 1896).

156. Acting Attorney General to Eames and Young, May 27, 1904, Letters from the General Agent, vol. 4, RG 60, NA II.

157. On the theory and practice of refusal, see Simpson, *Mohawk Interruptus*, and Glen Sean Coulthard, *Red Skin, White Masks: Rejecting the Colonial Politics of Recognition* (Minneapolis: University of Minnesota Press, 2014).

158. "Letter from Commissioner of Indian Affairs to Phoenix Superintendent," June 26, 1906, reprinted in "Fires of Incendiary Origin," in *Native American*, July 7, 1906.

## 3. FEDERAL PUNISHMENT AND THE LEGAL TIME OF BLEEDING KANSAS

1. M. Sue Kendall, Rethinking Regionalism: John Steuart Curry and the Kansas Mural Controversy (Washington, DC: Smithsonian, 1985), 131.

2. Patricia A. Junker, *John Steuart Curry: Inventing the Middle West* (Manchester, VT: Hudson Hills, 1998). When the Kansas legislature prevented him from finishing the mural in 1941, Curry left the third panel unfinished, refused to sign the first two, and fled his Native Kansas for New York. He is said to have died of a broken heart.

3. Code Noir, or Edict Concerning the Negro Slaves in Louisiana (1724), in Alcee Fortier, *History of Louisiana*, vol. 1, *Early Explorers and the Domination of the French* (New York: Manzi, Joyant, 1904).

4. Harriet C. Frazier, *Runaway and Freed Missouri Slaves and Those Who Helped Them, 1763–1865* (Jefferson, NC: McFarland Press, 2010), 28.

5. Christopher Phillips, "'The Crime against Missouri': Slavery, Kansas, and the Cant of Southerners in the Border West," *Civil War History* 48, no. 1 (2002): 60–81.

6. Frazier, *Runaway and Freed Missouri Slaves*, 126. See also Harrison Anthony Trexler, *Slavery in Missouri, 1804–1865* (Baltimore: Johns Hopkins University Press, 1914), and Diane Mutti-Burke, *On Slavery's Border: Missouri's Small-Slaveholding Households, 1815–1865* (Athens: University of Georgia Press, 2010).

7. George Thompson, *Prison Life and Reflections: Or, A Narrative of the Arrest, Trial of Work, Burr, and Thompson* (Hartford, CT: Alanson Work, 1855), 350. See also George Thompson, *The Prison Bard: Or, Poems on Various Subjects* (Hartford, CT: William H. Burleigh, 1848).

8. See Frazier, *Runaway and Freed Missouri Slaves*, as well as her *Slavery and Crime in Missouri, 1773–1865* (Jefferson, NC: McFarland, 2009).

9. Clyde S. Kilby, "Three Anti-slavery Prisoners," *Journal of Illinois State Historical Society* 52, no. 3 (1959): 423; William A. Richardson, "Dr. David Nelson and His Times," *Journal of Illinois State Historical Society* 13 (1920): 433–63; W. Sherman Savage, "The Contest over Slavery between Illinois and Missouri," *Journal of Negro History* 28, no. 3 (1943): 311–25; Merton Lynn Dillon, "The Anti-slavery Movement in Illinois: 1824–1835," *Journal of Illinois State Historical Society* 47, no. 2 (1954): 149–66; Paul Finkelman, "Slavery, the 'More Perfect Union,' and the Prairie State," *Illinois Historical Journal* 80 (1987): 248–69.

10. Twain's novel describes a situation in which the family name of a Missouri resident from Old Virginia is disgraced when the family's son appeals to the law to address his having been kicked by two Italian travelers. His father is disgusted with his son's failed masculinity and his inability to settle the conflict through a duel. Mark Twain, *Pudd'nhead Wilson* (1894; repr., New York: Norton, 1980).

11. Hattie Mabel Anderson, "The Evolution of a Frontier Society in Missouri, 1815–1828," in *A Study in Frontier Democracy: The Social and Economic Bases of the Rise of the Jackson Group in Missouri, 1815–1828* (Columbia: Missouri Historical Review, 1940), 13, 14, 18.

12. G. Thompson, *Prison Life and Reflections*, 259.

13. Ibid., 85.

14. Ibid., 33.

15. Frazier, *Runaway and Freed Missouri Slaves*, 126.

16. Ibid.

17. The palimpsest is a framing concept that is usually described as a piece of parchment that has been written on again and again in a series of incomplete erasures, so that it bears visible traces of its earlier form. See M. Jacqui Alexander, *Pedagogies of Crossing*, and Rosalind Shaw, *Memories of the Slave Trade* (Chicago: University of Chicago Press, 2002).

18. Letter from C. E. Cory, quoted in Genevieve Yost, "History of Lynchings in Kansas," *Kansas Historical Quarterly* 2 (1933): 187. See also Martha Caldwell, "Introduction: Records of the Squatter Association, Whitehead District, Doniphan County," *Kansas Historical Quarterly* 13, no. 4 (1944): 16.

19. W. H. T. Wakefield, "Squatter Courts in Kansas," *Kansas Historical Collection* 5 (1896): 72.

20. Records of the Kickapoo Town Association, Miami Claim Association, and Leavenworth Association, Kansas State Historical Society.

21. Records of the Squatter Association, Whitehead District, Doniphan County, Kansas State Historical Society.

22. Napier, "Economic Democracy in Kansas," 350.

23. W. E. B. Du Bois, *Black Reconstruction in America* (1935; repr., New York: Free Press, 1999), 42. Du Bois refers here to the language used by James Buchanan in his Inaugural Address, March 4, 1857.

24. It is important to note that scholars like Paul Gates have argued quite carefully that economic pursuits guided people to Kansas more than the conflict over slavery. See Gates, *Fifty Million Acres*.

25. C. Phillips, "'Crime against Missouri,'" 74. This is a quote from David Rice Atchison, a Missouri senator, for whom the proslavery town of Atchison, Kansas, was named.

26. Ibid., 75. See also John McNamara, *In Perils by Mine Own Countrymen: Three Years on the Kansas Border by a Clergyman of the Episcopal Church* (1856; repr., Ann Arbor: University of Michigan Library, 2005), 41–43. Some of the names of these organizations included the Sons of the South, the Blue Lodges, and the Self-Defensives.

27. McNamara, *In Perils*, 49.

28. C. Phillips, "'Crime against Missouri,'" 72. The origins of the phrase are uncertain but may be associated with the status of the Christmas goose as the "ultimate holiday gift."

29. C. E. Cory, "Slavery in Kansas," *Kansas Historical Collections* 7 (1902): 233.

30. McNamara, *In Perils*, 53.

31. Jonathan Markovitz's *Legacies of Lynching* excises "lynching in the west" because there were more acts of mob violence in the South (Minneapolis: University of Minnesota Press, 2004), 37. Much of the literature also separates vigilante justice from the study of customary law, including Stewart E. Tolnay and E. M. Beck, *A Festival of Violence: An Analysis of Southern Lynchings, 1882–1930* (Champaign: University of Illinois Press, 1995); W. Fitzhugh Brundage, *Lynching in the New South: Georgia and Virginia, 1880–1930* (Cambridge, MA: Harvard University Press, 1988); Christopher Waldrep, *The Many Faces of Judge Lynch: Extralegal Violence and Punishment in America* (New York: Palgrave, 2002); and Jennet Kirkpatrick, *Uncivil Disobedience* (Princeton, NJ: Princeton University Press, 2008). Amy Louise Wood's *Lynching and Spectacle: Witnessing Racial Violence in America* (Chapel Hill: University of North Carolina Press, 2009) and Grace Hale's important work

*Making Whiteness: The Culture of Segregation in the South, 1890–1940* (New York: Vintage, 1999) analyze the relationship between "spectacle lynchings" and private acts of terror.

32. This figure draws from "Lynching in the United States," *Crisis*, February 1922. See James Weldon Johnson, "Lynching—American's Disgrace," in *The Selected Writings of James Weldon Johnson*, vol. 2, *The Social, Political and Literary Essays*, ed. Sondra Kathryn Wilson (New York: Oxford University Press, 1995), 72; Ida B. Wells, *A Red Record: Tabulated Statistics and Alleged Causes of Lynchings in the United States, 1892–1893–1894* (Chicago: Donohue and Henneberry, 1895), *Southern Horrors: Lynch Law in All Its Phases* (New York: New Age, 1892) and *Mob Rule in New Orleans: Robert Charles and His Fight to the Death* (Chicago, 1900).

33. For Yost's interviews with early Kansas settlers, see her "History of Lynchings."

34. *Burlington Republican*, December 14, 1908, quoted in Yost, "History of Lynchings," 185.

35. Yost, "History of Lynchings," 184.

36. "Slavery in Kansas: A Slaveholder's View of the Prospects of Slavery in Kansas," *New York Times*, October 25, 1854; Cory, "Slavery in Kansas," 232.

37. McNamara, *In Perils*, 143.

38. Wakefield, "Squatter Courts in Kansas," 74.

39. Ibid., 74.

40. Hunt, *History of Fort Leavenworth*, 92.

41. Wakefield, "Squatter Courts in Kansas," 74. Wakefield quotes a statement from an interview with an early settler.

42. Ibid.; Yost, "History of Lynchings," 185.

43. An Act to Punish Offences against Slave Property, in "Enrolled Kansas Territorial Laws (1855)," Kansas State Historical Society, Topeka, KS. While the Historical Society retains microfilms of the original documents handwritten in legal cursive, the bills may also be found in the appendix to McNamara, *In Perils*, and in Pearl T. Ponce, ed., *Kansas's War: The Civil War in Documents* (Athens: Ohio University Press, 2011), 9–10.

44. General Stringfellow, Secretary of the Self-Defensives, quoted in Cory, "Slavery in Kansas," 232. For an account of the proslavery Stringfellow's assault on the free-state governor Andrew Reeder in 1857, see Charles Clark, "Benjamin F. Stringfellow," *Bogus Legislature*, n.d., accessed October 31, 2018, http://kansasboguslegislature.org/mo/stringfellow_b_f.html.

45. Cory, "Slavery in Kansas," 236.

46. "Slave Bill of Sale, Thomas Johnson," May 24, 1856, Territorial Kansas Online, Kansas State Historical Society, www.territorialkansasonline.org /~imlskto/cgi-bin/index.php/ index.php?SCREEN=show_document&document_id=102891&FROM_PAGE=. Johnson, who purchased the fourteen-year-old Martha, was a Methodist minister, and Johnson County is named after him.

47. Cory, "Slavery in Kansas," 236. The primary archives in the history of slavery are the New Deal Federal Writers' Project and the Library of Congress Folk Histories, which document the lives of former slaves in nineteen volumes of interviews. Although volume 6 contains three interviews with former slaves who lived in Kansas at the time of the interviews, none were actually enslaved in Kansas in the years before the civil war. See Federal Writers' Project, Work Projects Administration, *Slave Narratives: A Folk History of Slavery in the United States From Interviews with Former Slaves*, vol. 6, *Kansas Narratives* (Washington, DC, 1941). For the only known recorded statement of a person enslaved in Kansas,

see "Reminiscence of Marcus Lindsay Freeman, a Former Slave," 1895, Territorial Kansas Online, Kansas State Historical Society, www.territoralkansasonline.org/~imlskto/cgi-bin/index.php?SCREEN=show_document&document_id=102302.

48. Letter from T.C. Wells, April 3, 1856, in Ponce, *Kansas's War*, 12.

49. J. Bowles to F.B. Sanborn, 1859, "The Liberty Line . . . ," in *Freedom's Crucible: The Underground Railroad in Lawrence and Douglas County, Kansas, 1854-1865*, ed. Richard B. Sheridan (Lawrence: University of Kansas Division of Continuing Education, 1998), 8.

50. On June 2, 1848, Sam Fulcher, Dorcas Fulcher, Walker, Mary, Julia, and four children escaped slavery in Missouri into Iowa. It was the basis of *Daggs v. Frazier*, a case that defined slavery's relationship to compensation laws. Robert J. Willoughby, "'I'll Wade in Missouri Blood': *Daggs v. Frazier*: A Case of Missouri Runaway Slaves," *Missouri Historical Review* (January 2005): 115-38. In 1850, in Lewis County, Missouri, more than thirty enslaved people escaped from Missouri to Kansas, armed with knives, clubs, and three guns. See Herbert Aptheker, *American Negro Slave Revolts* (New York: International Publishing, 1963), 341, and Melton A. McLaurin, *Celia, a Slave* (New York: Avon, 1991), 56.

51. Quintard Taylor, *In Search of the Racial Frontier: African-Americans in the American West, 1528-1990* (New York: Norton, 1998), 97.

52. Sheridan notes that this number may be as high as fifteen thousand when including Black troops who were out of the state. Richard B. Sheridan, "From Slavery in Missouri to Freedom in Kansas: The Influx of Black Fugitives and Contrabands into Kansas, 1854-1865," *Kansas History* 12, no. 1 (1989): 93.

53. Nell Irvin Painter, *Exodusters: Black Migration to Kansas after Reconstruction* (New York: Alfred A. Knopf, 1977), 247. See also John G. Van Deusen, "The Exodus of 1879," *Journal of Negro History* 20, no. 2 (April 1936): 111-29; Glen Schwendemann, "Wyandotte and the First 'Exodusters' of 1879," *Kansas Historical Quarterly* 26, no. 3 (Autumn 1960): 233-49; and Thomas C. Cox, *Blacks in Topeka, Kansas, 1865-1915* (Baton Rouge: Louisiana State University, 1982).

54. H.C. Bruce, *The New Man: Twenty-Nine Years a Slave, Twenty-Nine Years a Free Man* (York, PA: Anstadt and Sons, 1895). Bruce was a fugitive slave who became free by way of escape to Leavenworth.

55. Benjamin Singleton founded Singleton's Colony in 1879 near Dunlap, Morris County, Kansas, on the former Cherokee Reservation, where he lived until 1880. While the Majority Report published by the Democrats claimed that the "wholesale attempt to transfer a people" was "injurious to the people of the South," the Minority Report included testimony from Henry Adams about a committee of between 150 and 500 members who went "into every state in the South where we had been slaves" and built a movement of people interested in mass migration to Kansas that was at one point "98,000 strong." See Select Committee on Negro Exodus, "Report of the Majority" and "Report of the Minority," both in *Report and Testimony of the Select Committee to Investigate the Causes of the Removal of the Negroes from the Southern to the Northern States* (Washington, DC, 1880), 6-7 and 3 respectively, Kansas State Historical Society, Kansas Memory website, https://www.kansasmemory.org/item/210634.

56. In *Rachel v. Walker* (1836), Rachel petitioned the St. Louis Circuit Court and Missouri Supreme Court that her transportation to Michigan freed her given the ban on slavery in the Northwest Territory. The Missouri Supreme Court ruled that Rachel was free because

her transportation to a free space by the military officer who claimed ownership over her amounted to a willful act of emancipation. Her petition is available online through the Missouri Digital Heritage archives; see Rachel v. William Walker (1836), www.sos.mo.gov/ archives/education/aahi/beforedredscott/rachel-petition.asp. See also McLaurin, *Celia, a Slave,* 112.

57. "Citizens of Lawrence!" handbill, 1859 or 1860, Kansas State Historical Society, Kansas Memory website, www.kansasmemory.org/item/90349. The reference to the invasion of one's castle comes from the castle doctrine in US law (a remnant of English common law), which gives the property owner the right to protect that property. Its recent application in US law has hinged on the question of whether a property owner has the legal right to shoot someone for entering without permission. See Christopher Reinhart, "Castle Doctrine and Self-Defense," Office of Legal Research Report 2007-R-0052, January 17, 2007, www.cga. ct.gov/2007/rpt/2007-r-0052.htm.

58. Richard Cordley, "The Convention Epoch in Kansas History," *Kansas Historical Collections* 5 (1896): 42–47.

59. *Kansas Tribune,* September 15, 1855.

60. W. E. B. Du Bois, *John Brown* (1909; repr., New York: International Publishers, 1962), 139.

61. The use of the judge's house as a prison led him to claim payment owed in court documents after the war. See J. N. O. P. Wood, "J. N. O. P Wood Territorial Loss Claim: Report of Hiram Jackson Strickler, Commissioner to Audit Claims of Citizens in the Kansas Territory," Claim No. 321, 1859, Kansas State Historical Society, Kansas Memory website, www.kansasmemory.org/item/1749.

62. G. W. Brown to Eli Thayer, June 4, 1856, published in Ponce, *Kansas's War,* 15.

63. Stanley Harrold, *Border War: Fighting over Slavery before the Civil War* (Chapel Hill: University of North Carolina Press, 2010); Robert K. Sutton, *Stark Mad Abolitionists: Lawrence, Kansas, and the Battle over Slavery in the Civil War Era* (New York: Skyhorse, 2017); Thomas Goodrich, *War to the Knife: Bleeding Kansas, 1854–1861* (Lincoln: University of Nebraska Press, 1988); Jeremy Neely, *The Border between Them: Violence and Reconstruction on the Kansas-Missouri Line* (Columbia: University of Missouri Press, 2007); Jonathan Earle and Diane Mutti Burke, eds., *Bleeding Kansas, Bleeding Missouri: The Long Civil War on the Border* (Lawrence: University of Kansas Press, 2013).

64. Richard B. Sheridan, introduction to Sheridan, *Freedom's Crucible,* xxx.

65. Du Bois, *John Brown,* 139.

66. Ibid.

67. Tony Horwitz, *Midnight Rising: John Brown and the Raid That Sparked the Civil War* (New York: Henry Holt, 2011).

68. R. Blakeslee Gilpin, *John Brown Still Lives! America's Long Reckoning with Violence, Equality, and Change* (Chapel Hill: University of North Carolina Press, 2011), 2. Brown's view is echoed in the work of his contemporary biographer James Redpath in his dedication to Brown in *The Roving Editor; Or, Talks with Slaves in the Southern States* (1859; repr., University Park: Pennsylvania State University Press, 1996).

69. Du Bois, *John Brown,* 154.

70. Ibid., 134–35.

71. Ibid., 196.

72. Ibid., 197.

73. See Du Bois, *Black Reconstruction in America*, 29, and *John Brown*, 125.

74. McLaurin, *Celia, a Slave*, 112.

75. The concept of fugitive justice comes from Stephen Best and Saidiya Hartman's "Fugitive Justice," *Representations* 92 (2005): 1–15. In contrast to the hypervisible *Dred* decision, Missouri's jurisprudence was also shaped by cases like *State of Missouri v. Celia, a Slave* (1855), an unreported case buried for over a century in a county courthouse filing cabinet. Missouri law serves again as an instance of the jurisprudence of slavery throughout the nation because Celia killed her master in retribution against sanctioned sexual violence. Celia was hanged for violating the law of slavery, and her resistance was confined to a drawer.

76. Nancy Smith, "The 'Liberty Line' in Lawrence, Kansas Territory," in Sheridan, *Freedom's Crucible*, 5.

77. Ephraim Nute to Unidentified Recipient, February 24, 1859, John Brown Collection, Kansas State Historical Society, Kansas Memory website, https://www.kansasmemory.org/item/4980.

78. Ibid.

79. Ibid.

80. Richard B. Sheridan, "Editor's Commentary," in Sheridan, *Freedom's Crucible*, 129.

81. John Doy, *The Narrative of John Doy* (New York: Thomas Holman, 1860), 44.

82. James B. Abbott, "The Rescue of Dr. John W. Doy," in Sheridan, *Freedom's Crucible*, 22. See also Doy, *Narrative of John Doy* (New York: Thomas Holman, 1860).

83. The Topeka, Lecompton, and Leavenworth constitutions were presented to Congress but were rejected as undemocratic because each side boycotted the other's elections.

84. Joseph G. Waters, "Fifty Years of the Wyandotte Constitution," *Kansas Historical Collections* 11 (1910): 48; and Cordley, "Convention Epoch," 42.

85. See Nicole Etcheson's work on the role of liberalism and whiteness in the making of Kansas, *Bleeding Kansas: Contested Liberty in the Civil War Era* (Lawrence: University of Kansas Press, 2004).

86. Du Bois, *John Brown*, 137. See also the important work of James A. Rawley, *Race and Politics: "Bleeding Kansas" and the Coming of the Civil War* (Lincoln: University of Nebraska Press, 1969).

87. Anthony v. Halderman, 7 Kan. 50, 1871 WL 696 (Kan.) (1871).

88. William G. Cutler's *History of the State of Kansas* (Chicago: A. T. Andreas, 1883), 425. While this statement was included in the party's platform, it was not included in the actual constitution.

89. Topeka Constitution, November 12, 1855, approved December 15, 1855, Article 1, Section 6, Kansas State Historical Society, Kansas Memory website, https://www.kansasmemory.org/item/221061.

90. Lecompton Constitution, November 7, 1857, Article 7, Kansas State Historical Society, Kansas Memory website, https://www.kansasmemory.org/item/207409.

91. Leavenworth Constitution, April 3, 1858, Article 1, Section 6—Slavery; Article 2, Section 1—Franchise; and Article 8, Section 4—Prisons, Kansas Historical Society, Kansas Memory website, www.kansasmemory.org/item/90817.

92. Leavenworth Constitution, November 7, 1857, Article 8, Section 4—Prisons.

93. In Leavenworth, 903 of its citizens had voted for the Topeka Constitution, while 673 voted against it. See "From Kansas: Leavenworth City Republican," *New York Times*, October 13, 1859.

94. "What 'Law and Order' Means in Kansas," *New York Times*, February 22, 1856. See also Charles Clark, "Law & Order Party," Kansas Bogus Legislature, n.d., accessed October 31, 2018, http://kansasboguslegislature.org/laworder/.

95. "Interesting from Kansas: Popular Outbreak at Leavenworth," *New York Times*, February 10, 1863. The Knights of the Golden Circle were a secret society who sought to annex Mexico, Central and South America, Cuba, and the Caribbean as part of a "golden circle" of slave territory.

96. Wyandotte Constitution, July 29, 1859, Article 7, Kansas Historical Society, Kansas Memory website, www.kansasmemory.org/item/90272. The minutes of the Wyandotte meeting indicate no further discussion on the subject. Harry G. Larimer, *Kansas Constitution Convention, A Reprint of the Proceedings and Debates of the Convention which Framed the Constitution of Kansas at Wyandotte in July 1859* (Topeka: Kansas State Printing Plant, 1920), 665 and 688–89.

97. Gable, "Kansas Penitentiary," 379.

98. Ibid., 385, 388.

99. An Act Regulating Crimes and Punishments of Crimes against the Persons of Individuals, March 6, 1862, Chapter 33, Section 291.

100. Wyandotte Constitution, July 29, 1859, Article 5—Suffrage, Section 1. On the future of race in Kansas, see Randall B. Woods, "Integration, Exclusion, or Segregation? The 'Color Line' in Kansas: 1878–1900," *Western Historical Quarterly* 14 (1983): 181.

101. Blake McKelvey, *American Prisons: A History of Good Intentions* (Montclair, NJ: Patterson Smith, 1977), 104.

102. *The Kansas Inferno: A Study of the Criminal Problem by a Life Prisoner* (Wichita, KS: Wonderland, 1906); John N. Reynolds, *A Kansas Hell: Or, Life in the Kansas Penitentiary* (Atchison, KS: Bee, 1889).

103. John N. Reynolds, *The Twin Hells: A Thrilling Narrative of Life in the Kansas and Missouri Penitentiaries* (Chicago: M. A. Donahue, 1890).

104. Perkinson, *Texas Tough*, 107.

105. An Act Regulating Crimes and Punishments of Crimes against the Persons of Individuals," March 6, 1862, Chapter 33, Sections 43 and 44, and Chapter 33, Sections 156–61, Kansas State Historical Society, Kansas Memory website, www.kansasmemory.org/item/208567.

106. Alpheus Hiram Tanner to Unknown Recipient, in Yost, "History of Lynchings," 186.

107. Yost, "History of Lynchings," 186.

108. *Kansas City Journal*, March 1902, in Yost, "History of Lynchings," 185.

109. There were nineteen documented lynchings in 1850, ninety-six in 1860, thirty-nine in 1870, twenty-nine in 1880, sixteen in 1890, four in 1900, one in 1910, one in 1920, and one in 1930, most for murder, fewer for horse stealing, and fewest for rape. Half took place during the first fifteen years of statehood. Robert J. Kaiser, "Capital Punishment in Kansas," May 1, 1963, Subject Files of the Warden, RG 129, NA KC.

110. Michael Fellman, *Inside War: The Guerrilla Conflict in Missouri during the American Civil War* (New York: Oxford University Press, 1990); See also Silvana

R. Siddali, ed., *Missouri's War: The Civil War in Documents* (Athens: Ohio University Press, 2009), 155.

111. See Richard Cordley, *A History of Lawrence, Kansas* (Lawrence, KS: Lawrence Journal Press, 1895); Thomas Goodrich, *Bloody Dawn: The Story of the Lawrence Massacre* (Kent, OH: Kent State University Press, 1991); Duane Schultz, *Quantrill's War: The Life and Times of William Clarke Quantrill* (New York: St. Martin's, 1996); Matthew Christopher Hulbert, *The Ghosts of Guerrilla Memory: How Civil War Bushwhackers Became Gunslingers in the American West* (Athens: University of Georgia Press, 2016).

112. *Leavenworth Daily Conservative*, May 6, 1863; *Leavenworth Bulletin*, May 6, 1863. See also Harvey Hougen, "The Strange Career of the Kansas Hangman: A History of Capital Punishment in the Sunflower State to 1944" (PhD diss., Kansas State University, 1979), 65.

113. *Leavenworth Daily Conservative*, May 7, 1863.

114. *Leavenworth Daily Conservative*, February 14, 1863.

115. *Leavenworth Daily Times*, August 10, 1870.

116. Ibid., and *Leavenworth Daily Times*, August 11, 1870.

117. *Leavenworth Daily Times*, August 10, 1870, and *Leavenworth Daily Times*, August 11, 1870.

118. *Leavenworth Daily Conservative*, July 15, 1866.

119. *Leavenworth Daily Conservative*, February 14, 1863.

120. Hougen, "Strange Career." See also Louise Barry, "Legal Hangings in Kansas," *Kansas Historical Quarterly* 18 (1950): 279–301.

121. *Leavenworth Daily Conservative*, February 14, 1863.

122. *Leavenworth Daily Conservative*, May 7, 1863.

123. *Leavenworth Daily Times*, August 10, 1870.

124. Ibid.

125. Ibid. With Senate Bill 18, entitled "An Act to Regulate the Infliction of the Death Penalty," Kansas State Historical Society, Kansas Memory website, www.kansasmemory.org/item/208598, hangings became a private affair, with only the prosecuting attorney, the clerk of the court, two physicians, and twelve "reputable citizens" present. The 1872 bill unintentionally suspended the death penalty in Kansas because it required that people sentenced to death be held at the state penitentiary until the governor signed the death warrant. No governors signed between 1872 and 1907, when the death penalty was repealed altogether. After attempts in 1927, 1931, and 1933 to reinstate the death penalty, Kansas brought back in 1935 the practice of "hanging by the neck until dead." House Bill 10 and House Bill 11, An Act Relating to Crimes Punishable by Death, 1935, Kansas State Historical Society, Kansas Memory website, www.kansasmemory.org/item/208793.

126. *Leavenworth Daily Conservative*, April 23, 1863; *Leavenworth Daily Conservative*, April 27, 1863, and May 3–6, 1863.

127. *Leavenworth Daily Conservative*, April 23, 1863; *Leavenworth Daily Conservative*, April 27, 1863, and May 3–6, 1863. The *Leavenworth Daily Conservative* was one of the most antislavery papers in the state and was owned by Susan B. Anthony's brother Daniel.

128. See, for example, David S. Reynolds, *John Brown, Abolitionist* (New York: Vintage, 2005).

129. See Albert Castel, "Civil War Kansas and the Negro," *Journal of Negro History* 51, no. 2 (1966): 125; Etcheson, *Bleeding Kansas*; Kristen Tegtmeier Oertal, *Bleeding Borders: Race,*

*Gender, and Violence in Pre-Civil War Kansas* (Baton Rouge: Louisiana State University Press, 2009).

130. Dale E. Watts, "How Bloody Was Bleeding Kansas? Political Killings in Kansas Territory, 1854–1861," *Kansas History: A Journal of the Central Plains* 18, no. 2 (Summer 1995): 124.

131. For a history of the border war in sports, see the documentary film *The Border War: The Rivalry between Kansas and Missouri* (dir. Erik Ashel, Metro Sports, 2008).

132. John Brown, interview by William Addison Philips, January 1859, Lawrence, KS, quoted in Richard J. Hinton and George B. Gill, "John Brown and the Rescue of Missouri Slaves," in Sheridan, *Freedom's Crucible*, 88.

## 4. PRISONS AT THE BORDER

1. "Thirteen Convicts Still at Large," *Leavenworth Times*, June 3, 1898; "Prison Guards Disarmed, Fifteen Convicts Escape," *Leavenworth Times*, June 2, 1898.

2. "Convict Desperadoes," *Leavenworth Times*, November 8, 1901.

3. "Search Is Grim and Relentless," *Leavenworth Times*, November 10, 1901.

4. Ibid.

5. "Fight with Convicts," *Leavenworth Times*, November 9, 1901, and "Search Is Grim and Relentless," *Leavenworth Times*, November 10, 1901.

6. "Thirteen Convicts Still at Large," *Leavenworth Times*, June 3, 1898.

7. "Fight with Convicts," *Leavenworth Times*, November 9, 1901.

8. Ibid.

9. "Fatigued Guards Still on Watch for 2 Prisoners," *Leavenworth Times*, April 23, 1910.

10. "Fight with Convicts," *Leavenworth Times*, November 9, 1901.

11. "Captured the Ringleader," *Leavenworth Times*, November 12, 1901.

12. "May Hang Half a Dozen Men," *Leavenworth Times*, November 17, 1901.

13. Warden to Mr. James A. Finch, May 9, 1910, Prison File No. 2064, RG 129, NA KC.

14. Frank Thompson, Prison File Nos. 2064 and 5594, RG 129, NA KC.

15. Thompson's federal prison record indicates that he was incarcerated in Oklahoma in 1912 as Morris Dent (Oklahoma Prisoner No. 3529) until his fingerprints were matched to those of Frank Thompson in Leavenworth's fingerprint files. Frank Thompson, Prison File Nos. 2064 and 5594, RG 129, NA KC.

16. W. E. B. Du Bois, "Jesus Christ in Texas," in *Darkwater: Voices from within the Veil* (New York: Oxford University Press, 2007), 62.

17. Perkinson, *Texas Tough*, 72.

18. McKelvey, *American Prisons*, ix.

19. On the political significance of convict leasing in the post–Civil War era, see Sarah Haley, *No Mercy Here: Gender, Punishment, and the Making of Jim Crow Modernity* (Chapel Hill: University of North Carolina Press, 2016); Mary Ellen Curtin, *Black Prisoners and Their World, Alabama, 1865–1900* (Charlottesville: University Press of Virginia 2000); A. Davis, "From the Prison"; Matthew J. Mancini, *One Dies, Get Another: Convict Leasing in the American South, 1866–1928* (Columbia: University of South Carolina Press, 1996); Alexander C. Lichtenstein, *Twice the Work of Free Labor: The Political Economy of Convict*

*Labor in the New South* (New York: Verso, 1996); and David Oshinsky, *"Worse Than Slavery"*: *Parchman Farm and the Ordeal of Jim Crow Justice* (New York: Simon and Schuster, 1996).

20. Barbara Jeanne Fields, *Slavery and Freedom on the Middle Ground: Maryland during the Nineteenth Century* (New Haven, CT: Yale University Press, 1985), 1, 6.

21. Philip J. Schwarz, *Twice Condemned: Slaves and the Criminal Laws, 1705–1865* (Baton Rouge: Louisiana State University Press, 1988), 62.

22. Fields, *Slavery and Freedom,* xii.

23. Even in his excellent book on southern penitentiaries, Edward Ayers writes that "penitentiaries in a republican society simply were not for slaves. Slaves had no rights to respect, no civic virtue or character to restore, no freedom to abridge. . . . After 1818, only Louisiana consistently admitted slaves to its prison as an alternative to hanging." Edward L. Ayers, *Vengeance and Justice: Crime and Punishment in the 19th-Century American South* (Oxford: Oxford University Press, 1984), 61. Maryland and Arkansas are sometimes said to have briefly held slaves. See Marvin E. Gettleman, "The Maryland Penitentiary in the Age of Tocqueville," *Maryland Historical Magazine* 56 (1961): 276, and Thorsten Sellin, *Slavery and Penal System* (New York: Elsevier, 1976), 144.

24. McKelvey, *American Prisons,* 47. Joint Committee Report, 1854, cited in Jeff Forret, "Before Angola: Enslaved Prisoners in the Louisiana State Penitentiary," *Louisiana History* 54, no. 2 (Spring 2013): 133–34, 137–38.

25. Brett Josef Derbes, "Secret Horrors: Enslaved Women and Children at the Louisiana State Penitentiary, 1833–1862," *Journal of African American History* 98, no. 2 (Spring 2013): 277.

26. Gustave de Beaumont, "Note on the Social and Political Condition of the Negro Slave and of Free People of Color," in *Marie Or, Slavery in the United States: A Novel of Jacksonian America,* trans. Barbara Chapman (Baltimore: Johns Hopkins University Press, 1958), 197. The novel was first published in France in 1835 and was not translated into English until 1958.

27. Wallace Shugg, *A Monument of Good Intentions: The Story of the Maryland Penitentiary, 1804–1995* (Baltimore: Maryland Historical Society, 2000), 17.

28. Beaumont, "Note," 195.

29. Frazier, *Runaway and Freed Missouri Slaves,* 95.

30. Peter C. Hoffer, introduction to *Criminal Proceedings in Colonial Virginia,* ed. Peter Hoffer and William B. Scott (Athens, GA: American Historical Association, 1984), xliv–lii.

31. Schwarz, *Twice Condemned,* 17.

32. Statement of Moneys Paid from Treasury, quoted in William C. Sneed, *A Report on the History and Mode of Management of the Kentucky Penitentiary from Its Origin, in 1798 to March 1, 1860* (Frankfurt: J. B. Major, 1860), 119.

33. An Act of November 26, 1801, in *A Digest of the Statute Law of Kentucky,* ed. William Littell and Jacob Swigert (Frankfort, KY: Kendall and Russell, 1922), 1159.

34. United States v. Amy, 24 Fed. 792 (C.C. Va. 1859).

35. Laws of Maryland, Chapter 138, Section 21, November 1809.

36. See images of the Maryland State Penitentiary ledger books in Shugg, *Monument to Good Intentions,* 2.

37. Laws of Maryland, Chapter 138, Section 21, November 1809.

38. Jim Rice, "'This Province, So Meanly and Thinly Inhabited': Punishing Maryland's Criminals, 1681–1850," *Journal of the Early Republic* 19, no. 1 (Spring 1999): 35.

39. Shugg, *Monument to Good Intentions*, 12.

40. William Crawford, *Report of William Crawford on the Penitentiaries of the United States* (London: House of Commons, 1834), 99.

41. Rice, "'This Province,'" 35.

42. Ayers, *Vengeance and Justice*, 61.

43. Missouri Revised Statutes (1835), Crimes and Punishments, Article 9.

44. Maryland—Penitentiary, *Report of the Committee on Prison Manufactures, Maryland Penitentiary, Sept. 1842* (Baltimore: Lucas and Deaver, 1842), 3–6.

45. Ibid., 3.

46. Code of Virginia (1860), quoted in Paul W. Keve, *History of Corrections in Virginia* (Charlottesville: University of Virginia Press, 1987), 47.

47. Keve, *History of Corrections*, 47–48. See Records of the Old Dominion's Auditor's Office and Treasury Office, cited in Schwarz, *Twice Condemned*, 40. The records contain compensation lists of amounts paid to owners for the value of executed or transported slaves and represent the fullest archive of the commutation of death sentences into transportation sentences.

48. "A List of Slaves and Free Persons of Color Received into the Penitentiary for Sale and Transportation from the 25th June 1816 to the 1st February 1842," box 10, Condemned Slaves, Virginia State Library, Richmond, cited in Schwarz, *Twice Condemned*, 28. See also Philip J. Schwarz, "The Transportation of Slaves from Virginia, 1801–1865," *Slavery and Abolition: A Journal of Comparative Studies* 7 (1986): 215–40.

49. "Report of the Committee to Examine the State of the Penitentiary," *Journal of the House of Delegates of the Commonwealth of Virginia*, 1822–23, quoted in Keve, *History of Corrections*, 48.

50. Message of Governor William B. Giles to the General Assembly, December 3, 1827, quoted in Keve, *History of Corrections*, 49.

51. G. Thompson, *Prison Life and Reflections*, 350. See also G. Thompson, *Prison Bard*.

52. G. Thompson, *Prison Life and Reflections*, 350.

53. Sneed, *Report on the History*, 377.

54. Ibid.

55. Ibid.

56. "Great Excitement in Atchison—An Abolitionist Preacher Shipped on a Raft," *Squatter Sovereign*, August 21, 1855, in *Kansas in Newspapers*, ed. Nyle H. Miller, Edgar Langsdorf, and Robert W. Richmond (Topeka: Kansas State Historical Society, 1963), 26.

57. Shugg, *Monument to Good Intentions*, 62.

58. Frazier, *Runaway and Freed Missouri Slaves*, as well as her *Slavery and Crime*.

59. Revised Statutes of the State of Missouri (1835), Crimes and Punishments Article 1, Section 7, and Article 3, Section 31.

60. Sneed, *Report on the History*, 223, 256.

61. Ibid., 347. In the 1830s, the number of people in prison for helping slaves run away stayed at 4, while by 1853, the number had increased to 11 out of a total prison population of 185.

62. Schwarz, *Twice Condemned*, 302.

63. *Journal of the House of Delegates of the Commonwealth of Virginia*, 1847–48, 20, 22, cited in John Henderson Russell, *The Free Negro in Virginia, 1619–1865* (Baltimore: Johns Hopkins University Press, 1913), 165n165.

64. Michael B. Chesson, *Richmond after the War, 1865–1890* (Richmond: Virginia State Library, 1981), 123–24.

65. Richard C. Wade, *Slavery in the Cities: The South, 1820–1860* (New York: Oxford University Press, 1964), 40, 59.

66. *Calendar of Virginia State Papers* (1803) 8:352, quoted in Keve, *History of Corrections*, 32; Keve, *History of Corrections*, 31.

67. Act of 1822–23, quoted in Russell, *Free Negro in Virginia*, 106.

68. Code of Virginia (1860), 46:815–16.

69. Russell, *Free Negro in Virginia*, 106.

70. Fields, *Slavery and Freedom*, 35.

71. Jeffrey R. Brackett, *The Negro in Maryland: A Study of the Institution of Slavery* (Baltimore: Johns Hopkins University, 1889), 232.

72. Fields, *Slavery and Freedom*, 35. For an account of southern labor contract laws as a post-Reconstruction method of reinstituting slavery, see Amy Dru Stanley, *From Bondage to Contract: Wage Labor, Marriage, and the Market in the Age of Slave Emancipation* (Cambridge: Cambridge University Press, 1998).

73. A. Leon Higginbotham Jr., *In the Matter of Color: Race and the American Legal Process* (New York: Oxford University Press, 1978), 48. Free Black people in the state of Virginia had been subject to deportation upon manumission since 1680, when Virginia's colonial criminal laws required the transportation of emancipated persons beyond state lines, prompting neighboring Maryland to lament that "many of her beggarly blacks have been vomited upon us." Brackett, *Negro in Maryland*, 176–77.

74. Virginia Statutes, 1806, Chapter 63, cited in June Purcell Guild, *Black Laws of Virginia: A Summary of the Legislative Acts of Virginia Concerning Negroes* (New York: Negro Universities Press, 1969), 209.

75. Guild, *Black Laws of Virginia*, 209.

76. W. E. B. Du Bois, "The Spawn of Slavery: The Convict-Lease System in the South," in *African American Classics in Criminology and Criminal Justice*, ed. Shaun L. Gabbidon, Helen Taylor Greene, and Vernetta D. Young (Thousand Oaks, CA: Sage Publications, 2002), 85.

77. Mancini, *One Dies, Get Another*, 200–201; Ayers, *Vengeance and Justice*, 55.

78. Ayers, *Vengeance and Justice*, 49.

79. Marvin E. Schultz, "Running the Risks of Experiments: The Politics of Penal Reform in Tennessee, 1807–1829," *Tennessee Historical Quarterly*, 52, no. 2 (Summer 1993): 86, 89.

80. Holloway, *Living in Infamy*, 14.

81. Ibid., 33.

82. Robert Avery to Jonathan C. Robinson, December 17, 1866, quoted in Holloway, *Living in Infamy*, 33.

83. Missouri Revised Statutes (1835), Crimes and Punishments, Article 9, Section 37.

84. Boynton Merrill Jr., *Jefferson's Nephews: A Frontier Tragedy* (New York: Avalon, 1978), 232.

85. Beaumont and Tocqueville, *On the Penitentiary System*, 17; Bill Cunningham, *Castle: The Story of a Kentucky Prison* (Kuttawa, KY: McClanahan, 1995), 8.

86. "Bertie," *North Carolina Standard*, April 22, 1846.

87. M. Schultz, "Running the Risks," 92.

88. William Wells Brown, *Narrative of William W. Brown*, in *Slave Narratives*, ed. William L. Andrews and Henry Louis Gates Jr. (New York: Library of America, 2000), 396, 398.

89. R. Wade, *Slavery in the Cities*, 94–95.

90. Henry Bibb, *Narrative of the Life and Adventures of Henry Bibb,* in William Andrews and Gates, *Slave Narratives*, 489–490.

91. Ibid., 489–90.

92. Ibid., 470–71.

93. Frederick Douglass, *Narrative of the Life,* in William Andrews and Gates, *Slave Narratives*, 364.

94. Parish Transcripts, South Carolina, Box 1, Folder 1, p. 25, New York Historical Society, quoted in Peter Wood, *Black Majority: Negroes in Colonial South Carolina from 1670 through the Stono Rebellion* (New York: Alfred Knopf, 1974), 273n6; See also Howell Meadoes Henry, *The Police Control of the Slave in South Carolina* (Emory, VA, 1914).

95. R. Wade, *Slavery in the Cities*, 96.

96. *Census of the City of Charleston, South Carolina, for the Year 1848* (Charleston, SC: J. B. Nixon, 1849), 52, cited in R. Wade, *Slavery in the Cities*, 302n80.

97. Benjamin Perry, *Counter-report on the Report of the Special Committee . . . on the Subject of the Penitentiary,* South Carolina House of Representatives, 1839, quoted in Michael Stephen Hindus, *Prison and Plantation: Crime, Justice, and Authority in Massachusetts and South Carolina, 1767–1878* (Chapel Hill: University of North Carolina Press, 1980), 229.

98. Hindus, *Prison and Plantation*.

99. McKelvey, *American Prisons*, 47.

100. Jonathan W. White, "When Emancipation Finally Came, Slave Markets Took on a Redemptive Purpose," *Smithsonian Magazine*, February 26, 2018, https://www.smithsonianmag.com/history/when-emancipation-finally-came-slave-markets-took-redemptive-purpose-180968260/.

101. Benjamin G. Cloyd, *Haunted by Atrocity: Civil War Prisons in American Memory,* Making the Modern South (Baton Rouge: Louisiana State University Press, 2010), 37.

102. See Du Bois's chapter on South Carolina in *Black Reconstruction in America*. The workhouse jail was "immortalized" by the testimony of Angelina and Sarah Grimke in Theodore Weld's *American Slavery as It Is* (New York: American Anti-Slavery Society, 1839).

103. Hindus, *Prison and Plantation*, 229.

104. See Michal Trinkley and Debi Hacker, *The Penitentiary Cemetery, Columbia, South Carolina* (Columbia, SC: Chicora Foundation, 2009); Albert D. Oliphant, *The Evolution of the Penal System in South Carolina from 1866 to 1916* (Columbia, SC: State Company, 1916); John Charles Thomas, "The Development of 'an Institution': The Establishment and First Years of the South Carolina Penitentiary, 1795–1881" (MA thesis, University of South Carolina, 1983).

105. Hindus, *Prison and Plantation*, 229.

106. Mancini, *One Dies, Get Another*, 202.

107. Jonathan C. Clemins, *West Virginia Penitentiary*, Images of America (Charleston, SC: Arcadia, 2010).

108. Ibid., 22–23.

109. Vivien M. L. Miller, *Hard Labor and Hard Time: Florida's "Sunshine Prison" and Chain Gangs* (Gainesville: University Press of Florida, 2012).

110. Cong. Globe, quoted in Childs, *Slaves of the State*, 66.

111. Ruffin v. Commonwealth, 62 Va. 790 (1871).

112. Virginia State Constitution, Article 1, Section 8.

113. Keve, *History of Corrections*, 56.

114. Ruffin v. Commonwealth, 62 Va. 790 (1871).

115. United States v. Coppersmith, 4 Fed. 199 (C.C. Tenn., 1880).

116. Shugg, *Monument to Good Intentions*, 90. Emphasis mine.

117. Scott Reynolds Nelson. *Steel Drivin' Man: John Henry, the Untold Story of an American Legend* (New York: Oxford University Press, 2006).

118. Wahneema Lubiano, *The House That Race Built* (New York: Vintage, 1997).


## 5. LEAVENWORTH'S POLITICAL PRISONERS

1. Sedition Act, May 16, 1918, 40 Stat. 553 (1918). For an analysis of civil liberties during the First World War, see Stephen M. Kohn, *American Political Prisoners: Prosecutions under the Espionage and Sedition Acts* (Westport, CT: Praeger, 1994); Frances H. Early, *A World without War: How US Feminists and Pacifists Resisted World War I* (Syracuse, NY: Syracuse University Press, 1997); Paul Murphy, *World War I and the Origin of Civil Liberties in the United States* (New York: Norton, 1979); William H. Thomas, *Unsafe for Democracy: World War I and the US Justice Department's Covert Campaign to Suppress Dissent* (Madison: University of Wisconsin Press, 2008); William Preston, *Aliens and Dissenters: Federal Suppression of Radicals, 1903–1933* (Urbana: University of Illinois Press, 1994); H. C. Peterson and Gilbert C. Fite, *Opponents of War, 1917–1918* (Madison: University of Wisconsin Press, 1957); and George Harrison, *The IWW Trial: The Story of the Greatest Trial in Labor's History* (New York: Arno Press, 1969).

2. The speakers are Senator Lee S. Overman of North Carolina and Congressman William Green of Iowa, quoted in Kohn, *American Political Prisoners*, 8.

3. Espionage Act, June 15, 1917, 40 Stat. 217 (1917).

4. Cong. Rec., 62nd Cong., 1st Sess., House Committee on Expenditures in the Department of Justice, June 13–June 24, and July 1, 1912.

5. Acting Director Wilkinson, memorandum to all institutions, August 7, 1964, quoted in Desmond King, *Separate and Unequal: Black Americans and the US Federal Government* (Oxford: Clarendon Press, 1995), 142–43, 166. The federal prison system desegregated over the course of twenty years between 1944 and 1964 in the wake of the US Supreme Court's decision in *Brown v. Board of Education* (1954). King notes that federal prisons desegregated differently in housing, dining, and recreation. In 1964, after urging by "extremist conscientious objectors" to allow the "indiscriminate intermingling of the white and colored groups," the official policy was that "no inmate in any Federal penal institution shall be discriminated against on the grounds of race, color, creed or national origin, in any phase of institutional activities. There shall be no segregation on these grounds in housing, work assignments, eating accommodations, religious, recreational, educational or medical services." See James Bennett to Wardens, memorandum, September 9, 1943, quoted in Keve, *Prisons*, 206; and Acting Director Wilkinson, memorandum to all institutions, August 7, 1964, quoted in King, *Separate and Unequal*, 166.

6. Because the history of prison minstrelsy remains to be written, this account relies on reviews of the performances and reprinted programs published in the prison newspaper. It is possible that more shows were produced at Leavenworth. Minstrelsy was inside prisons by 1899, when prisoners who had "walked the boards of the variety stage before they came

to grief and a cell in prison" performed at Sing Sing prison in New York, and as late as 1920, when a minstrel show was performed at the Massachusetts State Prison. See "Minstrel Show at Sing Sing," *New York Times*, December 26, 1899, and "Pomeroy, Jesse," *New York Times Index* 8, no. 1 (January–March 1920). For an account of prison performances that mimic the structure of minstrelsy, see Daniel Bergner, *God of the Rodeo: The Quest for Redemption in Louisiana's Angola Prison* (New York: Ballantine Books, 1998). See also Childs's analysis of prison minstrel shows in *Slaves of the State*, 105.

7. *Leavenworth New Era*, March 9, 1917.

8. *Leavenworth New Era*, October 22, 1915; *Leavenworth New Era*, October 9, 1914.

9. *Leavenworth New Era*, October 9, 1914.

10. The shows, written by military prisoner Harold Craft, who "possesses more than ordinary ability as a 'puller' of black-face comedy," derided Black culture with racist content that celebrated the South in songs like "Mrs. Sippi You're a Gran' Ol' Girl," "Alabama Jubilee," "Caroline Can't You Hear Me Callin'," "My Old Kentucky Home Jubilee," "For Dixie and Uncle Sam," and "Come Back to Alabama."

11. Alexander Saxton, "Blackface Minstrelsy and Jacksonian Ideology," *American Quarterly* 27, no. 1 (March 1975): 3–25. Robert C. Toll's *Blacking Up* (New York: Oxford University Press, 1974) argues that minstrelsy represented the exploitation and manipulation of "Afro-Americans and their culture to please and benefit whites" (51). For accounts of the conventions of minstrelsy, its roles and three-part structure, and its shifts in form, see Annemarie Bean, James V. Hatch, and Brooks McNamara, eds., *Inside the Minstrel Mask* (Middletown, CT: Wesleyan University Press, 1996); Eric Lott, *Love and Theft: Blackface Minstrelsy and the American Working Class* (New York: Oxford University Press, 1993); David R. Roediger, *Wages of Whiteness* (New York: Verso, 1991); and Cedric J. Robinson, "Blackface Minstrelsy and Black Resistance," in *Forgeries of Memory and Meaning: Black and the Regimes of Race in American Theatre and Film before World War II* (Chapel Hill: University of North Carolina Press, 2007).

12. *Leavenworth New Era*, March 9, 1917.

13. "What 55 Liberated Prisoners Did," *American Red Cross Magazine*, January 1915, 157.

14. John B. Riley, "Prisons and the Various Changes in the System," in New York State Senate, *Forty-Ninth Annual Report of the State Board of Charities* (Albany, March 1916), 1139.

15. E. F. Doree to his wife, May 29, 1921, in Ellen Doree Rosen, *A Wobbly Life: IWW Organizer E. F. Doree* (Detroit, MI: Wayne State University Press, 2004), 45–46.

16. Wharton, *House of Whispering Hate*, 161, 226.

17. Philip S. Foner, *The Industrial Workers of the World, 1905–1917* (New York: International Publishers, 1972).

18. Emma F. Langdon, *Labor's Greatest Conflicts* (Denver, CO: Emma Langdon, 1908), 13.

19. Franklin Rosemont, *Joe Hill: The IWW and the Making of a Revolutionary Working-class Counterculture* (Oakland, CA: PM Press, 2015).

20. *The Wobblies*, dir. Deborah Schaffer and Stewart Bird, Docurama Films, New Video, 2006. In the film's opening scene, an interrogator's voice asks various Wobblies a series of questions: "What's your nationality?" "None." "What country are you a citizen of?" "I am a citizen of industry . . . I'm an Industrial Worker of the World."

21. W. E. McDermut, ed., *Proceedings of the First Convention of the Industrial Workers of the World* (New York: New York Labor News, 1905), www.iww.org/en/history/founding.

See also the graphic account of the founding convention in Paul Buhle and Nicole Shulman, *Wobblies! A Graphic History of the Industrial Workers of the World* (New York: Verso, 2005).

22. *Leavenworth New Era,* September 1918.

23. See IWW, "An Open Letter to President Harding from 52 Members of the IWW in Leavenworth Penitentiary Who Refuse to Apply for Individual Clemency," General Defense Committee, Chicago, August 1922, I.W.W. Digital Collection, Michigan State University Libraries, http://archive.lib.msu.edu/DMC/AmRad/openletterpresident.pdf.

24. See Ralph Chaplin's discussion of the trial in the chapter of his memoir entitled "We Face Judge Landis." Ralph Chaplin, *Wobbly: The Rough-and-Tumble Story of an American Radical* (Chicago: University of Chicago Press, 1948), 239–49.

25. "IWW Leaders Get 20-Year Terms," *New York Times,* August 31, 1918. For the only book-length source on Ben Fletcher, see Peter Cole, *Ben Fletcher: The Life and Times of a Black Wobbly* (Chicago: Charles Kerr, 2007).

26. E. F. Doree to his wife, November 18, 1921, in E. Rosen, *Wobbly Life,* 156.

27. James Rowan, "The Imprisoned IWW at Leavenworth," *Nation,* August, 3, 1921.

28. Earl Browder, unpublished, untitled, undated memoir in my possession, 110.

29. E. F. Doree to his wife, November 24, 1921, published in E. Rosen, *Wobbly Life,* 158.

30. Chaplin's drawing was published in *One Big Union Monthly,* July 1920, 38. In addition to his writings in the prison's newspaper under the heading "News and Views of the Labor World," he published a collection of poetry written at Leavenworth, *Bars and Shadows: The Prison Poems of Ralph Chaplin* (New York: Leonard Press, 1922). In addition to his memoir, *Wobbly,* Chaplin's postprison writings include "Confessions of a Radical," *Empire Magazine,* February 17, 1957, 12 and February 24, 1957; and "Why I Wrote Solidarity Forever," *American West* 5, no. 1 (January 1968): 18.

31. "Fire Destroyed Large Building at Federal Pen," *Leavenworth Times,* March 13, 1919.

32. IWW, *Open Letter to President Harding* (Chicago: General Defense Committee, [1922]), pamphlet, I.W.W. Digital Collection, Michigan State University Libraries, http://archive.lib.msu.edu/DMC/AmRad/openletterpresident.pdf.

33. Caesar Tabil and Edward Quigley had contracted tuberculosis, while Frederick Esmond had been transferred to a mental hospital in Washington, D.C.

34. Bill Haywood's *The Autobiography of Big Bill Haywood* (New York: International Publishers, 1929) is an interesting story, but it was apparently ghost-written by the Communist Party in Russia as Haywood was dying and should be read in this context. Other materials about Haywood include Peter Carlson's *Roughneck: The Life and Times of Big Bill Haywood* (New York: Norton, 1983).

35. Chaplin, *Wobbly,* 106.

36. The term *barbarous* was intended to refer to the colonial form of the Mexican state as antidemocratic and dictatorial rather than to the Mexican people. John Kenneth Turner, *Barbarous Mexico* (1910; repr., Austin: University of Texas Press, 1969). For a bilingual compilation of *Regeneración,* see Armando Bartra, *Regeneración, 1900–1918* (Mexico City: Hadise, 1972). Chaplin notes in his memoir that he drew "a series of small posters for use by the agrarian revolutionary forces in Mexico," which featured the slogan "Viva Tierra y Libertad!" Chaplin, *Wobbly,* 117.

37. The United States would not extradite the PLM to Mexico on the basis that their crimes were political in nature. Instead, the United States proceeded to punish the PLM within US law, which replicated the relationship between the United States and Mexico

established by the Treaty of Guadalupe-Hidalgo in 1848. The treaty positioned the United States as Mexico's legal superior. For an account of the trial, see Colin M. MacLachlan, *Anarchism and the Mexican Revolution: The Political Trials of Ricardo Flores Magón in the United States* (Berkeley: University of California Press, 1991); W. Dirk Raat, *Revoltosos: Mexico's Rebels in the United States, 1903–1923* (College Station: Texas A&M University Press, 1981); Poole, *Land and Liberty*; Juan Gomez-Quiñones, *Sembradores: Ricardo Flores Magon y el Partido Liberal Mexicano: A Eulogy and Critique* (Los Angeles: Aztlán Publications, Chicano Studies Center, UCLA, 1973); Diego Abad de Santillan, *Ricardo Flores Magon: El apostol de la revolucion social mexicana* (Mexico City: Grupo Cultural "Ricardo Flores Magon," 1925).

38. Memorandum for Mr. Bettman, January 29, 1919, Case Files on Enrique Flores Magón, Records of the Department of Justice, RG 60, NA KC.

39. Warden Biddle to Heber H. Votaw, Superintendent of Prisons, Department of Justice, November 14, 1922, Prison File of Ricardo Flores Magón, RG 129, NA KC.

40. US Attorney to Attorney General, February 28, 1919, Case Files on Enrique Flores Magón, Records of the Department of Justice, RG 60, NA KC.

41. Memorandum from Alfred Bettman, February 7, 1919, Case Files on Enrique Flores Magón, Records of the Department of Justice, RG 60, NA KC.

42. Harry Weinberger, "Two Political Prisoners at Leavenworth," *New Republic*, July 5, 1922.

43. Memo from Langworthy and Langworthy, October 16, 1922, Ricardo Flores Magón Prison File, RG 129, NA KC.

44. The telegram is signed by Librado Rivera and is located in his prison file, which is not housed with the rest of the files at the National Archives but remains in the custody of the Bureau of Prisons. The report from the prison physician, A. F. Yohe, to Warden Biddle, November 21, 1922, is contained in both the prison file of Ricardo Flores Magón as part of RG 129, NA KC, and in the Case Files on Enrique Flores Magón, Records of the Department of Justice, RG 60, NA KC.

45. File No. 15416, Librado Rivera, Records of the Bureau of Prisons, Office of Communications and Archives, Federal Bureau of Prisons, Washington, DC.

46. Claudio Lomnitz, *The Return of Comrade Ricardo Flores Magón* (New York: Zone Books, 2014), 500.

47. Ricardo Flores Magón to Lilly Sarnoff (Ellen White), December 28, 1920, in Paul Avrich, "Prison Letters of Ricardo Flores Magon to Lilly Sarnoff," *International Review of Social History* 22, no. 3 (December 1977): 392.

48. Ricardo Flores Magón, "The Intervention and the Prisoners of Texas," May 31, 1914, in *Dreams of Freedom: A Ricardo Flores Magón Reader*, ed. Chaz Bufe and Mitchell Cowen Verter (Oakland, CA: AK Press, 2005), 215.

49. Ricardo Flores Magón, "Francisco Ferrer," speech presented October 13, 1911, in Bufe and Verter, *Dreams of Freedom*, 263.

50. Ibid., 264.

51. Warden Biddle to Pardon Attorney Finch, telegram, January 20, 1923, File No. 15416, Librado Rivera, Records of the Bureau of Prisons, Office of Communications and Archives, Federal Bureau of Prisons, Washington, DC.

52. Robert V. Haynes, *A Night of Violence: The Houston Riot of 1917* (Baton Rouge: Louisiana State University Press, 1976), 84.

53. Ibid., 58.

54. Ibid., 119.

55. *Crisis,* April 1918.

56. Haynes, *Night of Violence,* 149.

57. Ibid., 149.

58. Chicago Defender, October 28, 1922, Section 9: Series C, Reel 4, Frame 171, Records of the NAACP. The Twenty-Fourth Infantry was dissolved in the early 1950s and was reconstituted in the 1990s.

59. Walter Johnson to Walter White, January 9, 1924, Section 9: Series C, Reel 5, Slide 155, Records of the NAACP.

60. W. E. B. Du Bois to James Weldon Johnson, November 17, 1920, Section 9: Series C, Reel 4, Frame 290, Records of the NAACP.

61. Address of James Weldon Johnson at Leavenworth Prison, September 1, 1925, Section 9: Series C, Reel 4, Frame 405, Records of the NAACP.

62. *Crisis,* November 1923 and December 1923.

63. Leroy Pinkett to Walter White, January 21, 1929, Section 9: Series C, Reel 5, Frame 187, Records of the NAACP.

64. H. F. Kane to Secretary of the NAACP, December 24, 1923, Section 9: Series C, Reel 5, Frame 139, Records of the NAACP.

65. IWW, "Open Letter to President Harding," 9.

66. Connor to Senator Henry Cabot Lodge, December 22, 1922, in Kohn, *American Political Prisoners,* 66.

67. Letter from the Warden, Section 9: Series C, Section 9: Series C, Reel 1, Frame 871, Records of the NAACP.

68. Letter from the Warden, Section 9: Series C, Reel 1, Frame 871, Records of the NAACP.

69. The actual legal language of the Mann Act prohibits interstate "prostitution or debauchery or any other immoral purpose," but any man traveling with a woman not his wife could be prosecuted. See Al-Tony Gilmore's *Bad N—* (Port Washington, NY: Kennikat Press, 1975). Johnson was sentenced in 1913, but in consultation with his mother, who said she would rather see him dead than in prison, Johnson left the United States. From 1913 to 1920 he avoided his prison sentence, and while he was traveling the world his first autobiography was published in French as *Mes combats* in 1914. It was a collection of a series of articles Johnson wrote as serials in a French sports magazine in 1911 entitled *Ma vie et mes combats.* This work has been edited, translated, and published in English as Jack Johnson's *My Life and Battles* (Westport, CT: Praeger, 2007). Johnson published another autobiographical account in 1927 entitled *Jack Johnson: In the Ring and Out* (Chicago: National Sports Publishing, 1927).

70. Chaplin, *Wobbly,* 267.

71. While photos of his return to the ring were published in the *New Era* and circulated as postcard images, film footage of Johnson's return to the ring at Leavenworth was lost after the Kansas governor objected to its circulation. "The footage seems to have disappeared." *New York Times,* December 16, 1920.

72. Geoffrey C. Ward, *Unforgivable Blackness: The Rise and Fall of Jack Johnson* (New York: Alfred K. Knopf, 2004). See also Randy Roberts, *Papa Jack: Jack Johnson and the Era of White Hopes* (New York: Free Press, 1983).

73. James J. Fisher, "Boxer's Words Go Free after Years in Prison," *Kansas City Star*, June 22, 1997. Johnson appointed another prisoner named Melville C. Butler (File No. 15509) as his editor, so part of the manuscript was found in Butler's file as well.

74. H. F. Kane to Secretary of the NAACP, December 24, 1923, Section 9: Series C, Reel 5, Frame 139, Records of the NAACP.

75. Ibid.

76. Cristina Heatherton, "University of Radicalism: Ricardo Flores Magón and Leavenworth Penitentiary," *American Quarterly* 66, no. 3 (September 2014): 557–81.

77. See Mulford Sibley and Ada Wardlaw, *Conscientious Objectors in Prison, 1940–1945* (Philadelphia: Pacifist Research Bureau, 1945). They were eventually transferred to Fort Leavenworth's prison, where they engaged in a general strike. See Carl Haessler, "The Fort Leavenworth General Strike of Prisoners," *Labor Defender*, January 1947. See also Winthrop Lane, "The Strike at Fort Leavenworth," *Survey* 41, February 15, 1919, 687, and Winthrop Lane, "Military Prisons and the Conscientious Objector," *Survey*, May 17, 1919. For an important archive of material on the prosecution and punishment of conscientious objectors and the strike at Fort Leavenworth, see the Swarthmore College Peace Collection at www.swarthmore.edu/Library/peace/peacewebsite/scpcWebsite/Documents/COsources.htm. See also Stephen M. Kohn, "The Fort Leavenworth General Strike," in *Nonviolence in America: A Documentary History*, ed. Staughton Lynd (Maryknoll, NY: Orbis Books, 1995), 123–28.

78. As part of strategy of division, Puerto Rican political prisoners were separated after trial and sent to different prisons, but they later reconvened at Leavenworth after incarcerations in Marion, Alcatraz, and other federal prisons. See Gabriel Torres-Rivera, "'Estoy como cuero de jicotea que ni las balas me pasan': An Interview with Rafael Cancel Miranda," in *Behind Bars: Latino/as and Prison in the United States*, ed. Suzanne Oboler (New York: Palgrave-Macmillan, 2008), 227–35.

79. Morgan v. Willingham, 424 F.2d 200 (1970).

80. Ibid.

81. In this case, judge Arthur Stanley ruled on eight cases at once. Long v. Harris, 332 F. Supp. 262 (D. Kan. 1971); Shimabuku v. Britton, 357 F. Supp. 825 (D. Kan. 1973).

82. Gonzales et al. v. Kleindienst et al., Complaint for Declaratory Judgment, Mandamus and Injunctive Relief (1972). While the case was dismissed and is therefore not documented within state legal archives, a copy is preserved in the Salinas Archives.

83. Daughtery v. Harris, 476 F.2d 292 (1973).

84. For the original "El Plan de Aztlán," see *AZTLÁN: Chicano Journal of Social Science and Arts*, 1, no. 1 (1970). For CORA's incorporation of its principles, see *Aztlán de Leavenworth*, May 5, 1970, Salinas Archives. See also the work of Alan Eladio Gómez in "'Nuestras vidas corren casi paralelas': Chicanos, Puerto Rican Independentistas, and the Prison Rebellion Years at Leavenworth, 1969–1972," in Oboler, *Behind Bars*, 67–96.

85. The handwritten vote count remains in Series 3, Box 6, Folder 20 of the Salinas Files, Special Collections, Stanford University.

86. Raúl Salinas, "Resisting Mindfuck, from *Sunfighter*," in *raúlsalinas and the Jail Machine*, ed. Louis G. Mondoza (Austin: University of Texas Press, 2006), 297. For an important history of prison litigation at Marion, see Alan Eladio Gómez, "Resisting Living Death at Marion Federal Penitentiary, 1972," *Radical History Review* 96 (Fall 2006): 58–86; see also

Malcolm M. Feeley and Edward L. Rubin, *Judicial Policy Making and the Modern State: How the Courts Reformed America's Prisons* (Cambridge: Cambridge University Press, 2000).

87. Salinas, "Resisting Mindfuck," 297.

88. Salinas, letter to Mario G. Obledo, reprinted in Salinas, *raúlrsalinas*. On the legal legacy of resisting Marion, see Adams v. Carlson 488 F.2d 619 (1973).

89. Raúl Salinas, quoted by Gómez in "'Nuestras vidas corren casi paralelas,'" 68.

90. Alan Eladio Gómez, "Troubadour of Justice: An Interview with raúlsalinas," in Oboler, *Behind Bars*, 213–22.

91. Harry Jones, "Riot Planned by a Few Inmates," *Kansas City Star*, August 3, 1973, clipping in Subject Files of the Warden, USP Leavenworth, 1963–1984, RG 129, NA KC; Harry Jones, "Prison Theory Rejected," *Kansas City Star*, July 29, 1973, clipping in Subject Files of the Warden, USP Leavenworth, 1963–1984, RG 129, NA KC.

92. Jones, "Riot Planned."

93. *Afro-American*, August 20–24, 1974.

94. Leavenworth Brothers Offense/Defense Committee, *The Leavenworth Rebellion and the Case of the Leavenworth Brothers* (Wichita, KS: Leavenworth Brothers Offense/Defense Committee, 1974), 32.

95. Bennett was charged with rioting, Jasper with assault, resisting a federal officer and rioting, and Evans and Hill with assault and rioting.

96. *Afro-American*, August 20–24, 1974.

97. An anonymous prisoner sent this message to a congressional subcommittee. Quoted in Leavenworth Brothers Offense/Defense Committee, *Leavenworth Rebellion*, 48. On the idea of Leavenworth as the next Attica, see William Claiborne, "Leavenworth: New Attica?," *Washington Post*, March 13, 1974, clipping in Subject Files of the Warden, USP Leavenworth, 1963–1984, RG 129, NA KC. The Attica Liberation Faction's Manifesto of Demands and Anti-Depression Platform is Appendix 1 in J. James, *New Abolitionists*, 303–10. See also *The Last Graduation*, dir. Barbara Zahm (Zahm Productions and Deep Dish TV, 1997); John K. Simon, "Michel Foucault on Attica"; and Heather Thompson, *Blood in the Water: The Attica Prison Uprising of 1971 and Its Legacy* (New York: Vintage, 2017).

98. Harry Jones and J. J. Maloney, "An Eye for an Eye? The 70-Year-Old US Penitentiary at Leavenworth, Kansas," *Kansas City Star*, n.d., clipping in Kansas Vertical Files—US Penitentiary, Leavenworth Public Library.

99. See Leavenworth Brothers Offense/Defense Committee, *Leavenworth Rebellion*.

100. "USP to Close 'within 10 Years,'" *Leavenworth Times*, September 12, 1974.

## POSTSCRIPT

1. "Editorial: New Prison Feasible?" *Leavenworth Times*, July 29, 1975.

2. Harry Jones, "Warden Counting on Inmate Initiative," *Kansas City Star*, January 28, 1975, clipping in Subject Files of the Warden, USP Leavenworth, 1963–1984, RG129, NA KC.

3. Earley, *Hot House*, 103.

4. Ibid., 114.

5. Ibid., 163.

6. "Prison Disclosure Brings Mixed Reaction: No Shock to Those Active in Penal Work," *Leavenworth Times*, September 12, 1974.

7. Peter Wagner and Brenda Wright, "One Last Chance to Avoid Prison Gerrymandering in Kansas," Prison Policy Initiative, May 28, 2012, https://www.prisonersofthecensus.org/kansas/one_last_chance.pdf.

8. Jean Casella, "Federal Appeals Court Considers Tommy Silverstein's Thirty Years in Extreme Solitary Confinement," *Solitary Watch,* September 25, 2013. Silverstein remains in federal custody in Florence, Colorado, and has spent more years in total solitary confinement than any other federal prisoner. Before him, that distinction went to Robert Stroud, the Birdman of Alcatraz.

9. Earley, *Hot House,* 107.

10. James Bennett, "If Not Prisons—What?," paper presented at the Institute of Illinois Academy of Criminology, April 2, 1955, and partially reprinted in John W. Roberts, "View from the Top," *Federal Prisons Journal* 1, no. 4 (Summer 1990): 32.

11. Rosalind S. Helderman, "In Surprise Move, Maryland Closes Jessup Prison," *Washington Post,* March 19, 2007; Yvonne Wegener, "Maryland House of Corrections," *Baltimore Sun,* July 14, 2012.

# BIBLIOGRAPHY

**Archival Sources**
*California*
*Stanford*
   Raúl Salinas Files, Department of Special Collections, Green Library, Stanford University

*Kansas*
   *Leavenworth*
   Leavenworth Public Library, Subject Files
   *Topeka*
   Kansas State Historical Society

*Maryland*
   *College Park*
   National Archives II
   Record Group 60: Records of the Department of Justice
   Record Group 129: Records of the Federal Bureau of Prisons

*Missouri*
   *Kansas City*
   Kansas City National Archives, Central Plains Region Branch, Kansas City, MO
   Record Group 129: Records of the Federal Bureau of Prisons

*Oklahoma*
   *Oklahoma City*
   Oklahoma State Archives
   Oklahoma State Historical Society

*Washington, DC*
Records of the Bureau of Prisons, Office of Communications and Archives, Federal Bureau of Prisons

*Digital Archives*
I.W.W. Digital Collection, Michigan State University Libraries
Papers of the National Association for the Advancement of Colored People (NAACP), microfilm
Territorial Kansas Online/Kansas Memory

**Periodicals**
*Appeal to Reason*
*Boston Evening Transcript*
*Congressional Globe*
*Congressional Record*
*The Crisis*
*Fort Leavenworth Lamp*
*Kansas City Star*
*Kansas Tribune*
*Labor Defender*
*Lawrence Journal World*
*Leavenworth Daily Conservative*
*Leavenworth Daily Times*
*Leavenworth Evening Bulletin*
*Leavenworth New Era*
*Leavenworth Standard*
*Leavenworth Times*
*Missouri Gazette*
*Nation*
*Native American*
*New Republic*
*New York Age*
*North American Review*
*Omaha World-Herald*
*One Big Union Monthly*
*Red Man*
*Seattle Star*
*Solitary Watch*
*Squatter Sovereign*
*Survey*

**Legal Cases**
Adams v. Carlson, 488 F.2d 619 (1973).
Anthony v. Halderman, 7 Kan. 50, 1871 WL 696 (Kan.) (1871).
Daughtery v. Harris, 476 F.2d 292 (1973).
Draper v. United States, 164 U.S. 240 (1896).

Dred Scott v. Sandford, 60 U.S. 393 (1857).

Elk v. Wilkins, 112 U.S. 94 (1884).

Ex Parte Crow Dog, 109 U.S. 556 (1883).

Gonzales et al. v. Kleindienst et al. (1972).

Hunt v. Kansas, 4 Kan. 60 (1866).

Kansas Indians, 72 U.S. 737 (1867).

Long v. Harris, 332 F. Supp. 262 (D. Kan. 1971).

Morgan v. Willingham, 424 F.2d 200 (1970).

North Carolina v. Mann, 13 N.C. 263 (N.C. 1830).

Rachel v. Walker (1836).

Rubideaux v. Vallie, 12 Kan. 28 (1873).

Ruffin v. Commonwealth, 62 Va. 790 (1871).

Shimabuku v. Britton, 357 F. Supp. 825 (D. Kan. 1973).

State of Missouri v. Celia, a Slave (1855).

State v. Tackett, 8 N.C. 210 (1820).

United States v. Amy, 24 Fed. 792 (C.C. Va. 1859).

United States v. Clapox, 33 F. 575 (1888).

United States v. Coppersmith, 4 Fed. 199 (C.C. Tenn., 1880).

United States v. John Ward, 1 Kan. 601 (1863).

United States v. McBratney, 104 U.S. 621 (1881).

United States v. Rogers, 45 U.S. 567 (1846).

## Laws and Statutes

### Federal

An Act to Establish a Site for the Erection of a Penitentiary on the Military Reservation at Fort Leavenworth, Kansas, June 10, 1896, Chapter 400, 29 Stat. 380 (1896).

An Act to Reorganize the Administration of Federal Prisons, Pub. L. No. 71–218, 46 Stat. 325 (1930).

Major Crimes Act, 48th Cong., 2nd Sess., Chapter 341, 23 Stat. 385 (1885).

Trade and Intercourse Act, June 30, 1834, 23rd Cong., 1st Sess., Chapter 161.

Espionage Act, June 15, 1917, 40 Stat. 217 (1917).

Sedition Act, May 16, 1918, 40 Stat. 553 (1918).

### State

#### Kansas

Enrolled Kansas Territorial Laws (1855).

An Act Concerning Attorneys at Law.

An Act Concerning Crimes and the Punishment of Offenses.

An Act Providing a System of Confinement and Hard Labor.

An Act Regulating Crimes and Punishments . . .

An Act Regulating Proceedings on Writs of Habeas Corpus.

An Act Relating to Crimes Punishable by Death.

An Act to Punish Offenses against Slave Property.

An Act to Regulate Elections.

An Act to Regulate the Infliction of the Death Penalty.

*Missouri*
  Revised Statutes of Missouri (1835), Crimes and Punishments, Article 1, Section 7, and Article 3, Section 31.

*Maryland*
  Laws of Maryland, Chapter 138, Section 21, November 1809.
  *Virginia*
  Code of Virginia (1860).

**Indian Nations**
  Act of the Chickasaw Nation, October 12, 1876.
  Act of the Choctaw Nation, November 20, 1867.
  Muskogee Laws, Chapter 4, Article 1, Sections 1–3.

**Constitutions**
**Kansas**
  Topeka Constitution, 1855
  Lecompton Constitution, 1857
  Leavenworth Constitution, 1858
  Wyandotte Constitution, 1859

**Treaties**
  Fort Laramie Treaty, 1851
  Fort Wise Treaty, 1861
  Ioway Treaty, 1805
  Prairie du Chien Treaty, 1825
  Treaty with the Cherokee, 1866
  Treaty with the Choctaw and Chickasaw, 1866
  Treaty with the Creeks, 1866

**Primary Sources**
Abad de Santillan, Diego. *Ricardo Flores Magón: El apostol de la revolucion social mexicana.* Mexico City: Grupo Cultural "Ricardo Flores Magón," 1925.
Abbott, Edith, and Alida C. Bowler. *Report on Crime and the Foreign Born.* National Commission on Law Observance and Enforcement [Wickersham Commission]. Washington, DC: Government Printing Office, 1931.
Abbott, James B. "The Rescue of Dr. John W. Doy." In Sheridan, *Freedom's Crucible*, 21–36.
Anderson, Gary Clayton, and Alan R. Woolworth, eds. *Through Dakota Eyes: Narrative Accounts of the Minnesota Indian War of 1862.* St. Paul: Minnesota Historical Society Press, 1988.
Andrews, William L., and Henry Louis Gates Jr., eds. *Slave Narratives.* New York: Library of America, 2000.
Attica Liberation Faction. "Attica Liberation Faction Manifesto of Demands and Anti-Depression Platform." Appendix 1 in J. James, *New Abolitionists*, 303–10.
Avrich, Paul. "Prison Letters of Ricardo Flores Magon to Lilly Sarnoff." *International Review of Social History* 22, no. 3 (December 1977): 379–422.

Beaumont, Gustave de. "Note on the Social and Political Condition of the Negro Slave and of Free People of Color." In *Marie Or, Slavery in the United States: A Novel of Jacksonian America*, translated by Barbara Chapman, 189–215. Baltimore: Johns Hopkins University Press, 1958.

Beaumont, Gustave de, and Alexis de Tocqueville. *On the Penitentiary System in the United States and Its Application in France*. New York: Augustus Kelley, 1970.

Bennett, James V. *I Chose Prison*. New York: Alfred A. Knopf, 1970.

———. "If Not Prisons—What?" Paper presented at the Institute of Illinois Academy of Criminology, April 2, 1955, and partially reprinted in John W. Roberts, "View from the Top," *Federal Prisons Journal*, 1, no. 4 (Summer 1990): 31–33.

———. Introduction to *Handbook of Correctional Institution Design and Construction*, by US Bureau of Prisons. Washington, DC: US Bureau of Prisons, 1949.

Bentham, Jeremy. *The Panopticon Writings*. London: Verso, 1995.

———. "Rationale of Punishment." Part II of "Principles of Penal Law." In *The Works of Jeremy Bentham*, edited by John Bowring, 1:388–524. London: Simpkin, Marshal, 1838.

Bibb, Henry. *Narrative of the Life and Adventures of Henry Bibb*. In William Andrews and Gates, *Slave Narratives*, 425–566.

Bond, Fred. *Flatboating on the Yellowstone, 1877*. New York: New York Public Library, 1925.

Brown, William Wells. *Narrative of William W. Brown*. In William Andrews and Gates, *Slave Narratives*, 369–424.

Bruce, H. C. *The New Man: Twenty-Nine Years a Slave, Twenty-Nine Years a Free Man*. York, PA: Anstadt and Sons, 1895.

Bufe, Chaz, and Mitchell Cowen Verter, eds. *Dreams of Freedom: A Ricardo Flores Magón Reader*. Oakland, CA: AK Press, 2005.

Calahan, Margaret Werner. *Historical Correction Statistics in the United States, 1850–1984*. Rockville, MD: US Department of Justice, Bureau of Justice Statistics, 1986.

Canku, Clifford, and Michael Simon. *The Dakota Prisoner of War Letters*. St. Paul: Minnesota Historical Society Press, 2013.

Carter, Clarence E., ed. *Territorial Papers of the United States*. Vol. 13. *The Territory of Louisiana-Missouri, 1803–1806*. Washington, DC: US Government Printing Office, 1948

Casella, Jean. "Federal Appeals Court Considers Tommy Silverstein's Thirty Years in Extreme Solitary Confinement." *Solitary Watch*, September 25, 2013.

Chaplin, Ralph. *Bars and Shadows: The Prison Poems of Ralph Chaplin*. New York: Leonard Press, 1922.

———. "Confessions of a Radical." *Empire Magazine*, February 17, 1957, 12, and February 24, 1957.

———. "Why I Wrote Solidarity Forever." *American West* 5, no. 1 (January 1968): 18.

———. *Wobbly: The Rough-and-Tumble Story of an American Radical*. Chicago: University of Chicago Press, 1948.

Chief Joseph. *That All People May Be One People*. Kooskia, ID: Mountain Meadow Press, 1995.

Claiborne, William. "Leavenworth: New Attica?" *Washington Post*, March 13, 1974.

Cory, C. E. "Slavery in Kansas." *Kansas Historical Collections* 7 (1902): 229–42.

Crawford, William. *Report of William Crawford on the Penitentiaries of the United States*. London: House of Commons, 1834.

Day, Douglas, ed. *The Prison Notebooks of Ricardo Flores Magón*. New York: Houghton Mifflin Harcourt, 1991.

Dickens, Charles. *American Notes*. New York: Fromm, 1985.

Douglass, Frederick. *Narrative of the Life*. In William Andrews and Gates, *Slave Narratives*, 267–368.

Doy, John. *The Narrative of John Doy*. New York: Thomas Holman, 1860.

Eames, William, and Thomas Young. "Federal Prison, Atlanta Georgia." *American Architect*, June 2, 1920. American Periodicals Series Online.

———. *Specifications for the United States Penitentiary, Leavenworth, Kansas*. St. Louis, MO: William Eames and Thomas Young, 1910.

Earley, Pete. *The Hot House: Life inside Leavenworth Penitentiary*. New York: Bantam, 1992.

Elmes, James. *Hints for the Improvement of Prisons*. London: W. Bulmer, 1817.

Federal Writers' Project. Work Projects Administration. *Slave Narratives: A Folk History of Slavery in the United States from Interviews with Former Slaves*. Vol. 6. *Kansas Narratives*. Washington, DC, 1941.

Fisher, James J. "Boxer's Words Go Free after Years in Prison." *Kansas City Star*, June 22, 1997.

———. "Prison Files Show Its Earliest Inmates." *Kansas City Star*, August 15, 1995.

———. "Records Tell." *Kansas City Star*, January 11, 1998.

Flores Magón, Ricardo. "Farewell!" In *Land and Liberty: Anarchist Influences in the Mexican Revolution*, edited by David Poole, frontispiece. Orkney: Cienfuegos Press, 1977.

———. "Francisco Ferrer." Speech presented October 13, 1911. In Bufe and Verter, *Dreams of Freedom*, 263–66.

———. "The Intervention and the Prisoners of Texas." In Bufe and Verter, *Dreams of Freedom*, 214–19.

Gilmore, Al-Tony. *Bad N—*. Port Washington, NY: Kennikat Press, 1975.

Gómez, Alan Eladio. "Troubadour of Justice: An Interview with Raúlsalinas." In Oboler, *Behind Bars*, 213–22.

Haywood, Bill. *The Autobiography of Big Bill Haywood*. New York: International Publishers, 1929.

Helderman, Rosalind S. "In Surprise Move, Maryland Closes Jessup Prison." *Washington Post*, March 19, 2007.

Hinton, Richard J., and George B. Gill. "John Brown and the Rescue of Missouri Slaves." In Sheridan, *Freedom's Crucible*, 77–88.

Howard, John. *An Account of the Principal Lazarettos in Europe*. London, 1789.

Jackson, Joe. *Leavenworth Train: A Fugitive's Search for Justice in the Vanishing West*. New York: Carroll and Graf, 2001.

James, Joy, ed. *The New Abolitionists: (Neo)Slave Narratives and Contemporary Prison Writings*. Albany: SUNY Press, 2005.

James, Louise Boyd. "Burying the Hatchet: The German Family Makes Peace with the Cheyenne." *Persimmon Hill*, Autumn 1991.

Jefferson, Thomas. *The Writings of Thomas Jefferson*. Edited by H. A. Washington. Vol. 5. New York: Derby and Jackson, 1859.

Johnson, Jack. *Jack Johnson: In the Ring and Out*. Chicago: National Sports Publishing, 1927.

———. *My Life and Battles*. Westport, CT: Praeger, 2007.

Johnson, James Weldon. "Lynching—American's Disgrace." In *The Selected Writings of James Weldon Johnson*, edited by Sondra Kathryn Wilson, vol. 2, *Social, Political, and Literary Essays*, 71–78. New York: Oxford University Press, 1995.

Jones, Harry. "Prison Theory Rejected." *Kansas City Star*, July 29, 1973.

———. "Riot Planned by a Few Inmates." *Kansas City Star*, August 3, 1973.

———. "Warden Counting on Inmate Initiative." *Kansas City Star*, January 28, 1975.

*The Kansas Inferno: A Study of the Criminal Problem by a Life Prisoner*. Wichita, KS: Wonderland, 1906.

Kappler, Charles J., ed. *Indian Affairs: Laws and Treaties*. Washington, DC: Government Printing Office, 1904.

Kelley, Nicole. "Group Decries Boyda's Earmark for Prison Museum." *Lawrence Journal World*, July 11, 2007.

Lane, Winthrop. "Military Prisons and the Conscientious Objector." *Survey*, May 17, 1919.

———. "The Strike at Fort Leavenworth." *Survey* 41, February 15, 1919, 687.

Langdon, Emma F. *Labor's Greatest Conflicts*. Denver, CO: Emma Langdon, 1908.

Larimer, Harry G. *Kansas Constitution Convention, A Reprint of the Proceedings and Debates . . . at Wyandotte in July 1859*. Topeka: Kansas State Printing Plant, 1920.

*The Last Graduation*. Dir. Barbara Zahm. Zahm Productions and Deep Dish TV, 1997.

Leavenworth Brothers Offense/Defense Committee. *The Leavenworth Rebellion and the Case of the Leavenworth Brothers*. Wichita, KS: Leavenworth Brothers Offense/Defense Committee, 1974.

Lieber, Francis. *A Popular Essay on Subjects of Penal Law*. Philadelphia: Philadelphia Society for Alleviating the Miseries of Public Prisons, 1838.

Littell, William, and Jacob Swigert. *A Digest of the Statute Law of Kentucky*. Frankfort, KY: Kendall and Russell, 1922.

*Lost Nation: The Ioway*. Dir. Kelly Rundle. Fourth Wall Films, 2008.

Low, Denise. *The Turtle's Beating Heart: One Family's Story of Lenape Survival*. Lincoln: University of Nebraska Press, 2017.

Martin, Baird. "There Are Many Roads Enroute to Present." *McAlester News-Capital and Democrat*, April 1988.

Maryland—Penitentiary. *Report of the Committee on Prison Manufactures, Maryland Penitentiary, Sept. 1842*. Baltimore: Lucas and Deaver, 1842.

McDermut, W. E., ed. *Proceedings of the First Convention of the Industrial Workers of the World*. New York: New York Labor News, 1905. www.iww.org/en/history/founding.

McWhorter, Lucullus V. *Yellow Wolf: His Own Story*. 1940. Reprint, Caldwell, ID: Caxton Press, 1991.

Miller, Nyle H., Edgar Langsdorf, and Robert W. Richmond, eds. *Kansas in Newspapers*. Topeka: Kansas State Historical Society, 1963.

Oklahoma Department of Charities and Corrections. *First Annual Report of the Commissioner of Charities and Corrections of the State of Oklahoma*. Guthrie, OK: Leader Printing, 1908. Oklahoma State Archives.

———. *Second Report of the Commissioner of Charities and Corrections*. Oklahoma City: Warden Printing, 1910. Oklahoma State Archives.

Peltier, Leonard. *Prison Writings: My Life Is My Sun Dance*. New York: St. Martin's Griffin, 1999.

Perryman, L.C., comp. *Constitution and Laws of the Muskogee Nation.* Muskogee Indian Territory: Phoenix Printing, 1890. https://www.loc.gov/law/help/american-indian-consts/PDF/28014185.pdf.

Poe, Allison. *Poe Brothers or the Sequel to a Conspiracy.* Wynnewood, OK, 1910.

Ponce, Pearl T. *Kansas's War: The Civil War in Documents.* Athens: Ohio University Press, 2011.

Prucha, Francis Paul, ed. *Documents of United States Indian Policy.* Lincoln: University of Nebraska Press, 2000.

Redpath, James. "Dedication." *The Roving Editor, Or, Talks with Slaves in the Southern States.* 1859. Reprint, University Park: Pennsylvania State University Press, 1996.

Reed, Little Rock. "The American Indian in the White Man's Prisons: A Story of Genocide." In J. James, *New Abolitionists*, 133–50.

Reed, Little Rock, Lenny Foster, and Art Solomon. *The American Indian in the White Man's Prisons.* Taos, NM: UnCompromising Books, 1993.

Reynolds, John N. *A Kansas Hell: Or, Life in the Kansas Penitentiary.* Atchison, KS: Bee, 1889.

———. *The Twin Hells: A Thrilling Narrative of Life in the Kansas and Missouri Penitentiaries.* Chicago: M.A. Donahue, 1890.

Riley, John B. "Prisons and the Various Changes in the System." In New York State Senate, *Forty-Ninth Annual Report of the State Board of Charities*, 1132–40. Albany, March 1916.

Rowan, James. "The Imprisoned IWW at Leavenworth." *Nation,* August, 3, 1921.

Salinas, Raúl. "Resisting Mindfuck, from *Sunfighter.*" In *raúlrsalinas and the Jail Machine*, edited by Louis G. Mondoza, 297–304. Austin: University of Texas Press, 2006.

Select Committee on Negro Exodus, US Senate. *Report and Testimony of the Select Committee to Investigate the Causes of the Removal of the Negroes from the Southern to the Northern States.* Washington, DC, 1880. https://www.kansasmemory.org/item/210634.

Siddali, Silvana R. *Missouri's War: The Civil War in Documents.* Athens: Ohio University Press, 2009.

Smith, George W. *A Defence of the System of Solitary Confinement of Prisoners Adopted by the State of Pennsylvania.* Philadelphia: Philadelphia Society for Alleviating the Miseries of Prisoners, 1833.

"Status of Indians before State and Federal Courts." *Columbia Law Review* 14, no. 7 (1914): 587–90.

Thompson, George. *The Prison Bard: Or, Poems on Various Subjects.* Hartford, CT: William H. Burleigh, 1848.

———. *Prison Life and Reflections: Or, A Narrative of the Arrest, Trial of Work, Burr, and Thompson.* Hartford, CT: Alanson Work, 1855.

Tocqueville, Alexis de, and Gustave de Beaumont. *Alexis de Tocqueville and Gustave de Beaumont in America.* Edited by Olivier Zunz. Translated by Arthur Goldhammer. Charlottesville: University of Virginia Press, 2010.

Torres-Rivera, Gabriel. "'*Estoy como cuero de jicotea que ni las balas me pasan*': An Interview with Rafael Cancel Miranda." In Oboler, *Behind Bars*, 227–35.

US Bureau of Indian Affairs. *Annual Report of the Commissioner of Indian Affairs to the Secretary of the Interior for the Year 1872.* Washington, DC, 1872.

———. *Annual Report of the Commissioner of Indian Affairs to the Secretary of the Interior for the Year 1875.* Washington, DC, 1875.

———. *Annual Report of the Commissioner of Indian Affairs to the Secretary of the Interior for the Year 1884.* Washington, DC, 1884.

———. *Report of the Commissioner of Indian Affairs for the Year 1862.* Washington, DC, 1863.

US Bureau of Prisons. *Handbook of Correctional Institution Design and Construction.* Washington, DC: US Bureau of Prisons, 1949.

US Department of Justice. *Annual Report of the Attorney General of the United States for the Year [1896–1910].* Washington, DC, 1896–1910.

———. "Letter from the Attorney General in Response to Senate Resolution of January 13, 1896, Relative to Jails in the Indian Territory." 54th Cong., 1st Sess., Senate Document No. 202, in *Congressional Serial Set: Reports, Documents, and Journals of the U.S. Senate and House of Representatives,* 1–4. Washington, DC, 1896.

US Department of the Interior. Office of Indian Affairs. "Rules Governing the Court of Indian Offenses." March 30, 1883. https://rclinton.files.wordpress.com/2007/11/code-of-indian-offenses.pdf.

US Penitentiary, Leavenworth, Kansas. *Annual Report for Fiscal Year Ending June 30, 1910.* Leavenworth: Press of US Penitentiary, Leavenworth, Kansas.

US War Department. *Annual Report, Secretary of War, 1828.* In appendix to *Register of the Debates in Congress, Comprising the Leading Debates and Incidents of the Second Session of the Twentieth Congress,* 7–10. Washington, DC: Gales and Seaton, 1830.

———. *Report of the Secretary of War.* Washington, DC, 1877.

Wagner, Peter, and Brenda Wright. "One Last Chance to Avoid Prison Gerrymandering in Kansas." Prison Policy Initiative, May 28, 2012. https://www.prisonersofthecensus.org/kansas/one_last_chance.pdf.

Walsh, Joel. "Leavenworth Touted as Site for New Federal Prison." *Lawrence Journal World,* July 4, 2007.

Wegener, Yvonne. "Maryland House of Corrections." *Baltimore Sun,* July 14, 2012.

Weinberger, Harry. "Two Political Prisoners at Leavenworth." *New Republic,* July 5, 1922.

Weld, Theodore. *American Slavery as It Is.* New York: American Anti-Slavery Society, 1839.

Wells, Ida B. *Mob Rule in New Orleans: Robert Charles and His Fight to the Death.* Chicago, 1900.

———. *A Red Record: Tabulated Statistics and Alleged Causes of Lynchings in the United States, 1892–1893–1894.* Chicago: Donohue and Henneberry, 1895.

———. *Southern Horrors: Lynch Law in All Its Phases.* New York: New Age, 1892.

Wharton, Charles S. *The House of Whispering Hate, by Charles S. Wharton, Ex-Congressman, Ex-Lawyer, Ex-Convict.* Chicago: Madelaine Mendelsohn, 1932.

Wines, Frederick Howard. "A Republic of Criminals." *New York Times,* February 6, 1898.

Yost, Genevieve. "History of Lynchings in Kansas." *Kansas Historical Quarterly* 2 (1933): 182–219.

## Secondary Sources

Agonito, Rosemary, and Joseph Agonito. "Resurrecting History's Forgotten Women: A Case Study from the Cheyenne Indians." *Frontiers: A Journal of Women Studies* 6, no. 3 (Autumn 1981): 8–16.

Alexander, M. Jacqui. *Pedagogies of Crossing: Meditations on Feminism, Sexual Politics, Memory, and the Sacred.* Durham, NC: Duke University Press, 2005.

Alexander, Michelle. *The New Jim Crow.* New York: New Press, 2010.

Anderson, Hattie Mabel. *A Study in Frontier Democracy: The Social and Economic Bases of the Rise of the Jackson Group in Missouri, 1815–1828.* Columbia: Missouri Historical Review, 1940.

Andrews, Wayne. *American Gothic: Its Origins, Its Trials, Its Triumphs.* New York: Vintage, 1975.

———. *Pride of the South: A Social History of Southern Architecture.* New York: Atheneum, 1979.

Anzaldúa, Gloria. *Borderlands/La Frontera.* San Francisco: Aunt Lute Books, 1999.

Aptheker, Herbert. *American Negro Slave Revolts.* New York: International Publishing, 1963.

Ayers, Edward L. *Vengeance and Justice: Crime and Punishment in the 19th-Century American South.* Oxford: Oxford University Press, 1984.

Baigell, Matthew. "John Haviland." PhD diss., University of Pennsylvania, 1965.

———. "John Haviland in Philadelphia." *Journal of the Society of Architectural Historians* 25, no. 3 (October 1966): 197–208.

Baker, David V. "American Indian Executions in Historical Context." *Criminal Justice Studies* 20, no. 4 (December 2007): 315–73.

Ballagh, James Curtis. *A History of Slavery in Virginia.* 1902. Reprint, New York: Johnson Reprint, 1968.

Barker, Joann. *Native Acts: Law, Recognition, and Cultural Authenticity.* Durham, NC: Duke University Press, 2011.

Barnard, Lewis. "Old Arkansas State Penitentiary." *Arkansas Historical Quarterly* 13, no. 3 (Autumn 1954): 321–23.

Barry, Louise. "Legal Hangings in Kansas." *Kansas Historical Quarterly* 18 (1950): 279–301.

Bartra, Armando. *Regeneración, 1900–1918.* Mexico City: Hadise, 1972.

Bayer-Berenbaum, Linda. *The Gothic Imagination: Expansion in Gothic Literature and Art.* London: Associated University Presses, 1982.

Bean, Annemarie, James V. Hatch, and Brooks McNamara. *Inside the Minstrel Mask.* Middletown, CT: Wesleyan University Press, 1996.

Beccaria, Cesare. *On Crimes and Punishments.* Indianapolis: Hackett, 1986.

Beck, E. M., and Stewart E. Tolnay. "When Race Didn't Matter: Black and White Mob Violence against Their Own Color." In *Under Sentence of Death: Lynching in the South,* edited by W. Fitzhugh Brundage, 132–54. Chapel Hill: University of North Carolina Press, 1997.

Beckett, Katherine, and Naomi Murakawa. "Mapping the Shadow Carceral State: Toward an Institutionally Capacious Approach to Punishment." *Theoretical Criminology* 16, no. 2 (Spring 2012): 221–44.

Bender, John. *Imagining the Penitentiary: Fiction and the Architecture of the Mind in Eighteenth-Century England.* Chicago: University of Chicago Press, 1987.

Benton-Short, Lisa, and John Rennie Short. *Cities and Nature.* New York: Routledge, 2013.

Berg, Scott W. *Grand Avenues: The Story of the French Visionary Who Designed Washington, DC.* New York: Pantheon Books, 2007.

Bergner, Daniel. *God of the Rodeo: The Quest for Redemption in Louisiana's Angola Prison.* New York: Ballantine Books, 1998.

Berlin, Ira. *Slaves without Masters: The Free Negro in the Antebellum South.* New York: Vintage, 1976.

Best, Stephen, and Saidiya Hartman. "Fugitive Justice." *Representations* 92 (2005): 1–15.

Blaine, Martha Royce. *The Ioway Indians.* Norman: University of Oklahoma Press, 1995.

*The Border War: The Rivalry between Kansas and Missouri.* Dir. Erik Ashel, Metro Sports, 2008.

Bosworth, Mary. *The U.S. Federal Prison System.* Thousand Oaks, CA: Sage Publications, 2002.

Botting, Fred. *Gothic: The New Critical Idiom.* London: Routledge, 2014.

Bowker, Lee. *Prisoner Subcultures.* Lexington, MA: Lexington Books, 1977.

Boye, Alan. *Holding Stone Hands: On the Trail of the Cheyenne Exodus.* Lincoln: University of Nebraska Press, 1999.

Brackett, Jeffrey R. *The Negro in Maryland: A Study of the Institution of Slavery.* Baltimore: Johns Hopkins University, 1889.

Brodhead, Michael J. *Isaac Parker: Federal Justice on the Frontier.* Norman: University of Oklahoma Press, 2003.

Broome, Jeff. *Dog Soldier Justice: The Ordeal of Susanna Alderdice in the Kansas Indian War.* Lincoln: University of Nebraska Press, 2003.

Brown, Michelle. *The Culture of Punishment.* New York: New York University Press, 2009.

Brundage, W. Fitzhugh. *Lynching in the New South: Georgia and Virginia, 1880–1930.* Cambridge, MA: Harvard University Press, 1988.

Buhle, Paul, and Nicole Shulman. *Wobblies! A Graphic History of the Industrial Workers of the World.* New York: Verso, 2005.

Burton, Jeffrey. *Indian Territory and the United States: Courts, Government, and the Movement for Oklahoma Statehood, 1866–1906.* Norman: University of Oklahoma Press, 1995.

Butler, James Davie. "British Convicts Shipped to American Colonies." *American Historical Review* 2, no. 1 (October 1896): 12–33.

Byrd, Jodi. *Transit of Empire: Indigenous Critiques of Colonialism.* Minneapolis: University of Minnesota Press, 2011.

Calavita, Kitty. *Immigrants at the Margins: Law, Race and Exclusion in Southern Europe.* Cambridge: Cambridge University Press, 2005.

Caldwell, Martha. "Introduction: Records of the Squatter Association, Whitehead District, Doniphan County." *Kansas Historical Quarterly* 13, no. 4 (1944): 16–35.

Campbell, Stanley W. *The Slave Catchers: Enforcement of the Fugitive Slave Law, 1850–1860.* Chapel Hill: University of North Carolina Press, 1970.

Carleton, Mark T. *Politics and Punishment: A History of the Louisiana State Penal System.* Baton Rouge: Louisiana State University Press, 1971.

Carlson, Peter. *Roughneck: The Life and Times of Big Bill Haywood.* New York: Norton, 1983.

Carrott, Richard G. *The Egyptian Revival: Its Sources, Monuments, and Meaning, 1808–1858.* Berkeley: University of California Press, 1978.

Castel, Albert. "Civil War Kansas and the Negro." *Journal of Negro History* 51, no. 2 (1966): 125–38.

Chadbourn, James Harmon. *Lynching and the Law.* Chapel Hill: University of North Carolina Press, 1933.

Chang, David. "From Indian Territory to White Man's Country: Race, Nation, and the Politics of Land Ownership in Eastern Oklahoma." PhD diss., University of Wisconsin-Madison, 2002.

Chapman, Berlin N., and Berlin B. Chapman. "Nimiipuus in Indian Territory: An Archival Study." *Oregon Historical Quarterly* 50, no. 2 (June 1949): 102–10.

Chavez, Ernest Kikuta. "My Brother's Keeper: Mass Death in the Carceral State." *Social Justice* 43, no. 2 (Spring 2016): 21–36.

Chesson, Michael B. *Richmond after the War, 1865–1890.* Richmond: Virginia State Library, 1981.

Childs, Dennis. *Slaves of the State: Black Incarceration from the Chain Gang to the Penitentiary.* Minneapolis: University of Minnesota Press, 2015.

Chomsky, Carol. "The United States-Dakota War Trials: A Study in Military Justice." *Stanford Law Review* 43, no. 13 (1990): 13–98.

Clark, Charles. "Benjamin F. Stringfellow." *Kansas Bogus Legislature,* n.d. Accessed October 31, 2018. http://kansasboguslegislature.org/mo/stringfellow_b_f.html.

———. "Law & Order Party." *Kansas Bogus Legislature,* n.d. Accessed October 31, 2018. http://kansasboguslegislature.org/laworder/.

Clark, Tom. Foreword to *Handbook of Correctional Institution Design and Construction,* by US Bureau of Prisons. Washington, DC: US Bureau of Prisons, 1949.

Clemins, Jonathan C. *West Virginia Penitentiary.* Images of America. Charleston, SC: Arcadia, 2010.

Cloyd, Benjamin G. *Haunted by Atrocity: Civil War Prisons in American Memory.* Making the Modern South. Baton Rouge: Louisiana State University Press, 2010.

Cole, Peter. *Ben Fletcher: The Life and Times of a Black Wobbly.* Chicago: Charles Kerr, 2007.

Cooper, William J. *The South and the Politics of Slavery.* Baton Rouge: Louisiana State University Press, 1980.

Cope, Jack. Under the supervision of G. Cuthbertson. *1300 Metropolitan Avenue: A History of the United States Penitentiary at Leavenworth.* Leavenworth, KS: US Printing Office, 1963.

Cordley, Richard. "The Convention Epoch in Kansas History." *Kansas Historical Collections* 5 (1882): 42–47.

———. *A History of Lawrence, Kansas.* Lawrence, KS: Lawrence Journal Press, 1895.

Coulthard, Glen Sean. *Red Skin, White Masks: Rejecting the Colonial Politics of Recognition.* Minneapolis: University of Minnesota Press, 2014.

Cox, Thomas C. *Blacks in Topeka, Kansas, 1865–1915.* Baton Rouge: Louisiana State University, 1982.

Crow, Charles L. *American Gothic.* Cardiff: University of Wales Press, 2009.

Crow Dog, Leonard. *Crow Dog: Four Generations of Sioux Medicine Men.* New York: Harper, 1995.

Crowe, F. Hilton. "Indian Prisoner-Students at Fort Marion: The Founding of Carlisle was Dreamed in St. Augustine." *Regional Review* 5, no. 6 (December 1940): 5–8, 30.

Cunningham, Bill. *Castle: The Story of a Kentucky Prison.* Kuttawa, KY: McClanahan, 1995.

Curtin, Mary Ellen. *Black Prisoners and Their World, Alabama, 1865–1900.* Charlottesville: University Press of Virginia, 2000.

Cutler, William G. *History of the State of Kansas.* Chicago: A. T. Andreas, 1883.

Davis, Angela Y. *Are Prisons Obsolete?* New York: Seven Stories, 2003.

———. "From the Prison of Slavery to the Slavery of Prison: Frederick Douglass and the Convict Lease System." In *The Angela Y. Davis Reader,* edited by Joy James, 74–95. Malden, MA: Blackwell, 1998.

———. "Masked Racism: Reflections on the Prison Industrial Complex." *Colorlines Magazine,* September 10, 1998.

———. "The Prison: A Sign of Democracy?" Lecture presented at the Center for Cultural Studies, University of California, Santa Cruz, November 28, 2007.

———. "Racialized Punishment and Prison Abolition." In *The Angela Y. Davis Reader,* edited by Joy James, 96–110. Malden, MA: Blackwell, 1998.

———. "Surveillance, Imprisonment and the Quotidian Work of Race." Lecture presented at the University of Virginia, April 16, 2009.

Davis, Angela Y., and Gina Dent. "Prison as a Border: A Conversation on Gender, Globalization, and Punishment." *Signs* 26, no. 4 (Summer 2001): 1235–41.

Davis, Mike. "Hell Factories in the Field: A Prison Industrial Complex." *Nation,* February 20, 1995.

Davison, Carol Margaret. *Gothic Literature, 1764–1824.* Cardiff: University of Wales Press, 2009.

Dayan, Colin. *The Law Is a White Dog: How Legal Rituals Make and Unmake Persons.* Princeton, NJ: Princeton University Press, 2011.

———. "Legal Slaves and Civil Bodies." In *Materializing Democracy toward a Revitalized Cultural Politics,* edited by Dana Nelson and Russ Castronovo, 53–93. Durham, NC: Duke University Press, 2002.

de Bourbon, Soma. "Indigenous Genocidal Tracings: Slavery, Transracial Adoption, and the Indian Child Welfare Act." PhD diss., University of California Santa Cruz, 2013.

Deer, Sarah. "Federal Indian Law and Violent Crime." In *Color of Violence: The INCITE! Anthology,* edited by INCITE! Women of Color Against Violence, 32–41. Cambridge, MA: South End Press, 2006.

De Genova, Nicholas, and Nathalie Peutz. *The Deportation Regime: Sovereignty, Space and the Freedom of Movement.* Durham, NC: Duke University Press, 2010.

De Giorgi, Alessandro. "Back to Nothing: Prisoner Reentry and Neoliberal Neglect." *Social Justice* 44, no. 1 (Winter 2017): 83–120.

———. "Immigration Control, Post-Fordism, and Less Eligibility: A Materialist Critique of the Criminalization of Immigration across Europe." *Punishment and Society* 12, no. 2 (April 2010): 147–67.

Derbes, Brett Josef. "Secret Horrors: Enslaved Women and Children at the Louisiana State Penitentiary, 1833–1862." *Journal of African American History* 98, no. 2 (Spring 2013): 277–90.

Dickens, Charles. *Tale of Two Cities.* New York: Allyn and Bacon, 1945.

Dillon, Merton Lynn. "The Anti-slavery Movement in Illinois: 1824–1835." *Journal of Illinois State Historical Society* 47, no. 2 (1954): 149–66.

Dillon, Richard H. *Burnt-Out Fires*. Englewood Cliffs, NJ: Prentice-Hall, 1973.

Dilts, Andrew. *Punishment and Inclusion: Race, Membership, and the Limits of American Liberalism*. New York: Fordham University Press, 2014.

Du Bois, W. E. B. *Black Reconstruction in America, 1860–1880*. 1935. Reprint, New York: Free Press, 1998.

——. "Jesus Christ in Texas." In *Darkwater: Voices from within the Veil*, 70–77. New York: Oxford University Press, 2007.

——. *John Brown*. 1909. Reprint, New York: International Publishers, 1962.

——. "The Spawn of Slavery: The Convict-Lease System in the South." In *African American Classics in Criminology and Criminal Justice*, edited by Shaun L. Gabbidon, Helen Taylor Greene, and Vernetta D. Young, 81–88. Thousand Oaks, CA: Sage Publications, 2002.

Dudziak, Mary, and Leti Volpp. Introduction to Dudziak and Volpp, *Legal Borderlands*

——, eds. *Legal Borderlands: Law and the Construction of American Borders*. Baltimore: Johns Hopkins University Press, 2006.

Dumm, Thomas. *Democracy and Punishment: Disciplinary Origins of the United States*. Madison: University of Wisconsin Press, 1987.

Du Val, Kathleen. *The Native Ground: Indians and Colonists in the Heart of the Continent*. Philadelphia: University of Pennsylvania Press, 2006.

Dzur, Albert W. *Punishment, Participatory Democracy, and the Jury*. Oxford: Oxford University Press, 2012.

Earle, Jonathan, and Diane Mutti Burke, eds. *Bleeding Kansas, Bleeding Missouri: The Long Civil War on the Border*. Lawrence: University of Kansas Press, 2013.

Early, Frances H. *A World without War: How US Feminists and Pacifists Resisted World War I*. Syracuse, NY: Syracuse University Press, 1997.

Eason, John M. *Big House on the Prairie: Rise of the Rural Ghetto and Prison Proliferation*. Chicago: University of Chicago Press, 2017.

Ekirch, A. Roger. *Bound for America: The Transportation of British Convicts to the Colonies, 1718–1775*. Oxford: Clarendon Press, 1987.

Epp, Todd D. "The State of Kansas versus Wild Hog et al." *Kansas History* 5, no. 2 (Summer 1982): 139–46.

Etcheson, Nicole. *Bleeding Kansas: Contested Liberty in the Civil War Era*. Lawrence: University of Kansas Press, 2004.

Evans, Robin. *The Fabrication of Virtue: English Prison Architecture, 1750–1840*. New York: Cambridge University Press, 1982.

Feeley, Malcolm M., and Edward L. Rubin. *Judicial Policy Making and the Modern State: How the Courts Reformed America's Prisons*. Cambridge: Cambridge University Press, 2000.

Fellman, Michael. *Inside War: The Guerrilla Conflict in Missouri during the American Civil War*. New York: Oxford University Press, 1990.

Fields, Barbara Jeanne. *Slavery and Freedom on the Middle Ground: Maryland during the Nineteenth Century*. New Haven, CT: Yale University Press, 1985.

Finkelman, Paul. "Slavery, the 'More Perfect Union,' and the Prairie State." *Illinois Historical Journal* 80 (1987): 248–69.

Foley, William E. "Different Notions of Justice: The Case of the 1808 St. Louis Murder Trials." *Gateway Heritage*, Winter 1988–89, 2–13.

Foner, Philip S. *The Industrial Workers of the World, 1905–1917.* New York: International Publishers, 1972.

Fordham, Monique. "Within the Iron Houses: The Struggle for Native American Religious Freedom in American Prisons." *Social Justice* 20, nos. 1/2 (Spring/Summer 1993): 165–71.

Foreman, James, Jr. "Racial Critiques of Mass Incarceration: Beyond the New Jim Crow." *New York University Law Review* 87, no. 1 (2012): 21–69.

Forret, Jeff. "Before Angola: Enslaved Prisoners in the Louisiana State Penitentiary." *Louisiana History* 54, no. 2 (Spring 2013): 133–71.

Forster, Colin. *France and Botany Bay: The Lure of a Penal Colony.* Melbourne: Melbourne University Press, 1996.

Fortier, Alcee. *History of Louisiana.* Vol. 1. *Early Explorers and the Domination of the French.* New York: Manzi, Joyant, 1904.

Foster, Doug. "Imperfect Justice: The Modoc War Crimes Trial of 1873." *Oregon Historical Quarterly* 100, no. 3 (Fall 1999): 246–87.

Foster, Lance M. *The Indians of Iowa.* Iowa City: University of Iowa Press, 2009.

Foucault, Michel. *Discipline and Punish.* Translated by Alan Sheridan. New York: Random House, 1977.

Francis, Megan Ming. *Civil Rights and the Making of the Modern American State.* Cambridge: Cambridge University Press, 2014.

Fraser, Joelle. "An American Seduction: Portrait of a Prison Town." In *Prison Nation,* edited by Tara Herivel and Paul Wright, 73–84. New York: Routledge, 2003.

Frazier, Harriet C. *Runaway and Freed Missouri Slaves and Those Who Helped Them, 1763–1865.* Jefferson, NC: McFarland Press, 2010.

———. *Slavery and Crime in Missouri, 1773–1865.* Jefferson, NC: McFarland Press, 2009.

Frymer, Paul. *Building an American Empire: The Era of Territorial and Political Expansion.* Princeton, NJ: Princeton University Press, 2017.

Gable, Frank M. "The Kansas Penitentiary." *Kansas Historical Collections* 14 (1915–18): 379–437.

Gardner, Albert Ten Eyck. "A Philadelphia Masterpiece: Haviland's Prison." *Metropolitan Museum of Art Bulletin,* 14, no. 4 (December 1955): 103–8.

Garland, David. *The Culture of Control: Crime and Social Order in Contemporary Society.* Chicago: University of Chicago Press, 2001.

———. "Introduction: The Meaning of Mass Imprisonment." In *Mass Imprisonment: Social Causes and Consequences,* edited by David Garland, 1–3. Thousand Oaks, CA: Sage Publications, 2001.

Garman, James C. *Detention Castles of Stone and Steel: Landscape, Labor, and the Urban Penitentiary.* Knoxville: University of Tennessee Press, 2005.

Gates, Paul. *Fifty Million Acres: Conflicts over Kansas Land Policy.* Norman: University of Oklahoma Press, 1997.

Gettleman, Marvin E. "The Maryland Penitentiary in the Age of Tocqueville." *Maryland Historical Magazine* 56 (1961): 269–90.

Gilchrist, Agnes Addison. "John Haviland before 1816." *Journal of the Society of Architectural Historians,* 20, no. 3 (October 1961): 136–37.

Gilmore, Kim. "Slavery and Prison: Understanding the Connections." *Social Justice* 27, no. 3 (Fall 2000): 195–205.

Gilmore, Ruth Wilson. *Golden Gulag*. Berkeley: University of California Press, 2007.

Gilpin, R. Blakeslee. *John Brown Still Lives! America's Long Reckoning with Violence, Equality, and Change*. Chapel Hill: University of North Carolina Press, 2011.

Goeman, Mishuana. "From Place to Territories and Back Again: Centering Storied Land in the Discussion of Indigenous Nation-Building." *International Journal of Critical Indigenous Studies* 1, no. 1 (2008): 23–34.

Goldberg, David Theo. *The Racial State*. Oxford: Blackwell, 2002.

Goldsby, Jacqueline. *A Spectacular Secret: Lynching in American Life and Literature*. Chicago: University of Chicago Press, 2006.

Gómez, Alan Eladio. "'Nuestras vidas corren casi paralelas': Chicanos, Puerto Rican Independentistas, and the Prison Rebellion Years at Leavenworth, 1969–1972." In Oboler, *Behind Bars*, 67–96.

———. "Resisting Living Death at Marion Federal Penitentiary, 1972." *Radical History Review* 96 (Fall 2006): 58–86.

Gomez-Quiñones, Juan. *Sembradores: Ricardo Flores Magon y el Partido Liberal Mexicano: A Eulogy and Critique*. Los Angeles: Aztlán Publications, Chicano Studies Center, UCLA, 1973.

Goodrich, Thomas. *Bloody Dawn: The Story of the Lawrence Massacre*. Kent, OH: Kent State University Press, 1991.

———. *War to the Knife: Bleeding Kansas, 1854–1861*. Lincoln: University of Nebraska Press, 1988.

Gottschalk, Marie. *Caught: The Prison State and the Lockdown of American Politics*. Princeton, NJ: Princeton University Press, 2015.

———. "Democracy and the Carceral State in America." *Annals of the American Academy of Political and Social Science* 651 (January 2014): 288–95.

Greene, Jerome. *Washita: The U.S. Army and the Southern Cheyenne, 1867–1869*. Norman: University of Oklahoma Press, 2004.

Gregory, Jack, and Rennard Strickland. *Hell on the Border: He Hanged Eighty-Eight Men*. Muskogee, OK: Indian Heritage Association, 1971.

Grinnell, G. B. *The Fighting Cheyenne*. New York: Scribner, 1915.

Grobsmith, Elizabeth S. *Indians in Prison: Incarcerated Native Americans in Nebraska*. Lincoln: University of Nebraska Press, 1994.

Guild, June Purcell. *Black Laws of Virginia: A Summary of the Legislative Acts of Virginia Concerning Negroes*. New York: Negro Universities Press, 1969.

Gutheim, Frederick, and Antoinette J. Lee. *Worthy of the Nation: Washington, DC, from L'Enfant to the National Capital Planning Commission*. Baltimore: Johns Hopkins University Press, 2006.

Hadden, Sally E. *Slave Patrols: Law and Violence in Virginia and the Carolinas*. Cambridge, MA: Harvard University Press, 2001.

Haessler, Carl. "The Fort Leavenworth General Strike of Prisoners." *Labor Defender*, January 1947.

Hahn, Nicole Fischer. "Female State Prisoners in Tennessee: 1831–1979." *Tennessee Historical Quarterly*, 39, no. 4 (Winter 1980): 485–97.

Hale, Grace. *Making Whiteness: The Culture of Segregation in the South, 1890–1940*. New York: Vintage, 1999.

Haley, Sarah. *No Mercy Here: Gender, Punishment, and the Making of Jim Crow Modernity.* Chapel Hill: University of North Carolina Press, 2016.

Hamlin, Talbot. *Benjamin Henry Latrobe.* New York: Oxford University Press, 1955.

Harring, Sidney L. *Crow Dog's Case: American Indian Sovereignty, Tribal Law, and United States Law in the Nineteenth Century.* Cambridge: Cambridge University Press, 1994.

Harris, Cheryl. "Whiteness as Property." *Harvard Law Review* 106, no. 8 (June 1993): 1707–91.

Harrison, George. *The IWW Trial: The Story of the Greatest Trial in Labor's History.* New York: Arno Press, 1969.

Harrold, Stanley. *Border War: Fighting over Slavery before the Civil War.* Chapel Hill: University of North Carolina Press, 2010.

Hartman, Saidiya V. *Scenes of Subjection: Terror, Slavery, and Self-Making in Nineteenth-Century America.* New York: Oxford University Press, 2010.

Haynes, Robert V. *A Night of Violence: The Houston Riot of 1917.* Baton Rouge: Louisiana State University Press, 1976.

Heatherton, Cristina. "University of Radicalism: Ricardo Flores Magón and Leavenworth Penitentiary." *American Quarterly* 66, no. 3 (September 2014): 557–81.

Henry, Howell Meadoes. *The Police Control of the Slave in South Carolina.* Emory, VA, 1914.

Hernandez, Kelly Lytle. *City of Inmates: Conquest, Rebellion, and the Rise of Human Caging in Los Angeles, 1771–1965.* Chapel Hill: University of North Carolina Press, 2017.

———. "'Persecuted Like Criminals': The Politics of Labor Emigration and Mexican Migration Controls in the 1920s and 1930s." *Aztlán: A Journal of Chicano Studies* 34, no. 1 (Spring 2009): 219–39.

Herring, Joseph. *The Enduring Indians of Kansas: A Century and a Half of Acculturation.* Lawrence: University Press of Kansas, 1990.

Higginbotham, A. Leon, Jr. *In the Matter of Color: Race and the American Legal Process.* New York: Oxford University Press, 1978.

Hill, Mozell C. "The All-Negro Communities of Oklahoma: The Natural History of a Social Movement: Part I." *Journal of Negro History* 31, no. 3 (1946): 254–68.

Hill, Rebecca N. *Men, Mobs, and Law: Anti-lynching and Labor Defense in U.S. Radical History.* Durham, NC: Duke University Press, 2008.

Hindus, Michael Stephen. *Prison and Plantation: Crime, Justice, and Authority in Massachusetts and South Carolina, 1767–1878.* Chapel Hill: University of North Carolina Press, 1980.

Hinton, Elizabeth. *From the War on Poverty to the War on Crime: The Making of Mass Incarceration in America.* Cambridge, MA: Harvard University Press, 2016.

Hobbes, Thomas. *Leviathan.* Edited by C. B. Macpherson. Penguin Classics. Harmondsworth: Penguin, 1986.

Hoffer, Peter C. Introduction to *Criminal Proceedings in Colonial Virginia,* edited by Peter Hoffer and William B. Scott. Athens, GA: American Historical Association, 1984.

Holloway, Pippa. *Living in Infamy: Felon Disenfranchisement and the History of American Citizenship.* Oxford: Oxford University Press, 2013.

Hopkins, Ruth. "Fighting with Spirit: How Greasy Grass Was Won." *Last Real Indians* (blog), January 20, 2016. https://lastrealindians.com/fighting-with-spirit-how-greasy-grass-was-won-by-ruth-hopkins/lastrealindians/.

Horwitz, Tony. *Midnight Rising: John Brown and the Raid That Sparked the Civil War.* New York: Henry Holt, 2011.

Hougen, Harvey. "The Strange Career of the Kansas Hangman: A History of Capital Punishment in the Sunflower State to 1944." PhD diss., Kansas State University, 1979.

Hughes, Robert. *The Fatal Shore.* New York: Alfred A. Knopf, 1987.

Hulbert, Matthew Christopher. *The Ghosts of Guerrilla Memory: How Civil War Bushwhackers Became Gunslingers in the American West.* Athens: University of Georgia Press, 2016.

Hunt, Elvid. *History of Fort Leavenworth, 1827–1937.* Fort Leavenworth, KS: Command and General Staff School Press, 1937.

Hurtado, Albert L. "The Modocs and the Jones Family Indian Ring: Quaker Administration of the Quapaw Agency, 1873–1879." In *Oklahoma's Forgotten Indians,* edited by Robert E. Smith, 86–107. Oklahoma City: Oklahoma Historical Society, 1981.

Hyde, George E. *Spotted Tail's Folk: A History of the Brulé Sioux.* 1961. Reprint, Norman: University of Oklahoma Press, 1987.

Jackson, Donald. Introduction to *Black Hawk: An Autobiography,* edited by Donald Jackson, 1–40. Chicago: University of Illinois Press, 1987.

Jackson, Joseph. *Early Philadelphia Architects and Engineers.* Philadelphia, 1923.

Jacobs, James B. "Race Relations and the Prisoner Subculture." *Crime and Justice* 1 (1979): 1–27.

James, Cheewa. *Modoc: The Tribe That Wouldn't Die.* Happy Camp, CA: Naturegraph, 2008.

Jessee, Sharon. "The Contrapuntal Historiography of Toni Morrison's *Paradise*: Unpacking the Legacies of the Kansas and Oklahoma All-Black Towns." *American Studies* 47, no. 1 (Spring 2006): 81–112.

Johnston, J. H. *Leavenworth Penitentiary: A History of America's Oldest Federal Prison.* Leavenworth, KS: J. H. Johnston, 2005.

Johnston, Norman. "The Development of Radial Prisons: A Study in Cultural Diffusion." PhD diss., University of Pennsylvania, 1958.

———. *The Human Cage: A Brief History of Prison Architecture.* New York: Walker, 1973.

———. "John Haviland." In *Pioneers in Criminology,* edited by Hermann Mannheim, 91–112. Montclair, NJ: Patterson Smith, 1971.

———. "John Haviland, Jailor to the World." *Journal of the Society of Architectural Historians,* 23, no. 2 (May 1964): 101–5.

Junker, Patricia A. *John Steuart Curry: Inventing the Middle West.* Manchester, VT: Hudson Hills, 1998.

Kadlecek, Edward, and Mabell Kadlecek. *To Kill an Eagle: Indian Views on the Death of Crazy Horse.* Boulder, CO: Johnson, 1983.

Kann, Mark. *Punishment, Prisons, and Patriarchy: Liberty and Power in the Early American Republic.* New York: New York University Press, 2005.

Kaplan, Amy. "Where Is Guantanamo?" In Dudziak and Volpp, *Legal Borderlands,* 239–66. Baltimore: Johns Hopkins University Press, 2006.

Kato, Daniel. *Liberalizing Lynching: Building a New Racialized State.* Oxford: Oxford University Press, 2016.

Kay, Marvin L., and Lorin L. Cary. "The Planters Suffer Little or Nothing: North Carolina Compensations for Executed Slaves, 1748–1772." *Science and Society* 40 (1976): 288–306.

Kendall, M. Sue. *Rethinking Regionalism: John Steuart Curry and the Kansas Mural Controversy*. Washington, DC: Smithsonian, 1985.

Keve, Paul W. *History of Corrections in Virginia*. Charlottesville: University of Virginia Press, 1987.

———. *The McNeil Century: The Life and Times of an Island Prison*. Chicago: Nelson-Hall, 1984.

———. *Prisons and the American Conscience: A History of U.S. Federal Corrections*. Carbondale: Southern Illinois University Press, 1991.

Kilby, Clyde S. "Three Anti-slavery Prisoners." *Journal of Illinois State Historical Society* 52, no. 3 (1959): 419–30.

King, Desmond. *Separate and Unequal: Black Americans and the US Federal Government* Oxford: Clarendon Press, 1995.

King, Desmond, and Robert Lieberman. "Ironies of State Building: A Comparative Perspective on the American State." *World Politics* 61, no. 3 (July 2009): 547–88.

Kirkpatrick, Jennet. *Uncivil Disobedience*. Princeton, NJ: Princeton University Press, 2008.

Kleuskens Shanisse, Justin Piche, Kevin Walby, and Ashley Chen. "Reconsidering the Boundaries of the Shadow Carceral State." *Theoretical Criminology* 20, no. 4 (Winter 2016): 566–91.

Knepper, Paul. "Thomas Jefferson, Criminal Code Reform, and the Founding of the Kentucky Penitentiary at Frankfort." *Register of the Kentucky Historical Society* 91, no. 2 (1993): 129–49.

Kohn, Stephen M. *American Political Prisoners: Prosecutions under the Espionage and Sedition Acts*. Westport, CT: Praeger, 1994.

———. "The Fort Leavenworth General Strike." In *Nonviolence in America: A Documentary History*, edited by Staughton Lynd, 123–28. Maryknoll, NY: Orbis Books, 1995.

LaMaster, Kenneth. *U.S. Penitentiary Leavenworth*. Chicago: Arcadia, 2008.

Landrum, Francis. *Guardhouse, Gallows, and Graves: The Trial and Execution of Indian Prisoners of the Modoc Indian War by the U.S. Army*. Klamath Falls, OR: Klamath County Museum, 1988.

Leiker, James N., and Ramon Powers. *The Northern Cheyenne Exodus in History and Memory*. Norman: University of Oklahoma Press, 2011.

Lewis, W. David. *From Newgate to Dannemora: The Rise of the Penitentiary in New York, 1796–1848*. Ithaca, NY: Cornell University Press, 1965.

Lichtenstein, Alexander C. *Twice the Work of Free Labor: The Political Economy of Convict Labor in the New South*. New York: Verso, 1996.

Littlefield, Daniel F. *Seminole Burning: A Story of Racial Vengeance*. Jackson: University of Mississippi Press, 1996.

Littlefield, Daniel F., and Lonnie E. Underhill. "Black Dreams and 'Free' Homes: The Oklahoma Territory." *Phylon* 34 (December 1973): 342–57.

———. "Negro Marshals in the Indian Territory." *Journal of Negro History* 56, no. 2 (April 1971): 77–87.

Locke, John. *Second Treatise*. 1690. Reprint, Indianapolis: Hackett, 1980.

Lomnitz, Claudio. *The Return of Comrade Ricardo Flores Magón*. New York: Zone Books, 2014.

Lott, Eric. *Love and Theft: Blackface Minstrelsy and the American Working Class*. New York: Oxford University Press, 1993.

Lowe, Lisa. *The Intimacies of Four Continents.* Durham, NC: Duke University Press, 2015.

Loyd, Jenna M., Matt Mitchelson, and Andrew Burridge. *Beyond Walls and Cages: Prisons, Borders, and Global Crisis.* Athens: University of Georgia Press, 2012.

Lubiano, Wahneema. *The House That Race Built.* New York: Vintage, 1998.

Lujan, Carol Chiago, and Gordon Adams. "U.S. Colonization of Indian Justice Systems: A Brief History." *Wicazo Sa Review* 19, no. 2 (Autumn 2004): 9–23.

Lusebrink, Hans-Jurgen, and Rolf Reichardt. *The Bastille: A History of a Symbol of Despotism and Freedom.* Durham, NC: Duke University Press, 1997.

Lynch, Mona. *Sunbelt Justice: Arizona and the Transformation of American Punishment.* Stanford, CA: Stanford University Press, 2010.

Lynn, Elizabeth Cook. *A Separate Country: Postcoloniality and American Indian Nations.* Lubbock: Texas Tech University Press, 2011.

MacLachlan, Colin M. *Anarchism and the Mexican Revolution: The Political Trials of Ricardo Flores Magón in the United States.* Berkeley: University of California Press, 1991.

Mancini, Matthew J. *One Dies, Get Another: Convict Leasing in the American South, 1866–1928.* Columbia: University of South Carolina Press, 1996.

Markovitz, Jonathan. *Legacies of Lynching.* Minneapolis: University of Minnesota Press, 2004.

Matthews, John Joseph. *The Osages: Children of the Muddy Waters.* Norman: University of Oklahoma Press, 1981.

McBride, Keally. *Punishment and Political Order.* Ann Arbor: University of Michigan Press, 2007.

McCarty, Ronald R. "Eames and Young." In *The Grove Encyclopedia of American Art*, edited by Joan Marter, 124. Oxford: Oxford University Press, 2011.

McEntire, Melissa. "Post Part of Nez Perce Historic Trail." *Fort Leavenworth Lamp*, November 24, 2004.

McGaa, Ed/Eagle Man. *Crazy Horse and Chief Red Cloud.* Minneapolis, MN: Four Directions, 2005.

McKelvey, Blake. *American Prisons: A History of Good Intentions.* Montclair, NJ: Patterson Smith, 1977.

McLaurin, Melton A. *Celia, a Slave.* New York: Avon, 1991.

McMurtry, Larry. *Crazy Horse: A Life.* New York: Penguin, 1999.

McNamara, John. *In Perils by Mine Own Countrymen: Three Years on the Kansas Border by a Clergyman of the Episcopal Church.* 1856. Reprint, Ann Arbor: University of Michigan Library, 2005.

McWhorter, Lucullus V. *Hear Me, My Chiefs! Nez Perce Legend and History.* 1952. Reprint, Caldwell, ID: Caxton Press, 2001.

Meiners, Erica R. *For the Children? Protecting Innocence in a Carceral State.* Minneapolis: University of Minnesota Press, 2016.

Meranze, Michael. *Laboratories of Virtue: Punishment, Revolution, and Authority in Philadelphia, 1760–1835.* Chapel Hill: University of North Carolina Press, 1996.

Meredith, Grace E. *Girl Captives of the Cheyenne.* 1927. Reprint, Mechanicsville, PA: Stackpole Books, 2004.

Merrill, Boynton. *Jefferson's Nephews: A Frontier Tragedy.* New York: Avalon, 1978.

Miller, Vivien M. L. *Hard Labor and Hard Time: Florida's "Sunshine Prison" and Chain Gangs.* Gainesville: University Press of Florida, 2012.

Million, Dian. "Policing the Rez: Keeping No Peace in Indian Country." *Social Justice* 27, no. 3 (Fall 2000): 101–19.

Miner, H. Craig., and William E. Unrau. *The End of Indian Kansas: A Study of Cultural Revolution, 1854–1871.* Lawrence: Regents Press of Kansas, 1978.

Monjeau-Marz, Corrine L. *The Dakota Indian Internment at Fort Snelling, 1862–1864.* St. Paul, MN: Prairie Smoke Press, 2005.

Monnett, John H. *Tell Them We Are Going Home: The Odyssey of the Northern Cheyenne.* Norman: University of Oklahoma Press, 2001.

Moore, John H. "Cheyenne Political History, 1820–1894." *Ethnohistory* 21, no. 4 (Fall 1974): 329–59.

Moran, Dominique. *Carceral Geography: Spaces and Practices of Punishment.* Burlington, VT: Ashgate, 2015.

Moran, Leslie J. "Law and the Gothic Imagination." In *The Gothic,* edited by Fred Botting, 87–108. Cambridge: English Association, 2001.

Moreton-Robinson, Aileen. "Virtuous Racial States." *Griffith Law Review* 20, no. 3 (Winter 2011): 641–58.

———. *The White Possessive: Property, Power, and Indigenous Sovereignty.* Minneapolis: University of Minnesota Press, 2015.

Morrison, Toni. *Paradise.* 1997. Reprint, New York: Vintage, 2014.

Muhammad, Khalil Gibran. *The Condemnation of Blackness: Race, Crime, and the Making of Modern Urban America.* Cambridge, MA: Harvard University Press, 2010.

Mullis, Tony R. *Peacekeeping on the Plains: Army Operations in Bleeding Kansas.* Columbia: University of Missouri Press, 2004.

Muñiz, Ana. *Police, Power, and the Production of Racial Boundaries.* New Brunswick, NJ: Rutgers University Press, 2015.

Murakawa, Naomi. *The First Civil Right: How Liberals Built Prison America.* New York: Oxford University Press, 2014.

Murphy, Paul. *World War I and the Origin of Civil Liberties in the United States.* New York: Norton, 1979.

Murray, Keith. *The Modocs and Their War.* Norman: University of Oklahoma Press, 1959.

Mutti-Burke, Diane. *On Slavery's Border: Missouri's Small-Slaveholding Households, 1815–1865.* Athens: University of Georgia Press, 2010.

Napier, Rita. "Economic Democracy in Kansas: Speculation and Townsite Preemption in Kickapoo." *Kansas Historical Quarterly* 40, no. 3 (Fall 1974): 349–69.

Neal, David. *The Rule of Law in a Penal Colony: Law and Power in Early New South Wales.* New York: Cambridge University Press, 1991.

Neely, Jeremy. *The Border between Them: Violence and Reconstruction on the Kansas-Missouri Line.* Columbia: University of Missouri Press, 2007.

Nelson, Scott Reynolds. *Steel Drivin' Man: John Henry, the Untold Story of an American Legend.* New York: Oxford University Press, 2006.

Nichols, David A. *Lincoln and the Indians: Civil War Policy and Politics.* St. Paul: Minnesota Historical Society Press, 2012.

Novak, William J. "The Myth of the 'Weak' American State." *American Historical Review* 113, no. 3 (June 2008): 752–72.

Obermeyer, Brice. *Delaware Tribe in a Cherokee Nation.* Lincoln: University of Nebraska Press, 2009.

Oboler, Suzanne, ed. *Behind Bars: Latino/as and Prison in the United States*. New York: Palgrave-Macmillan, 2008.

Oertal, Kristen Tegtmeier. *Bleeding Borders: Race, Gender, and Violence in Pre-Civil War Kansas*. Baton Rouge: Louisiana State University Press, 2009.

Oliphant, Albert D. *The Evolution of the Penal System in South Carolina from 1866 to 1916*. Columbia, SC: State Company, 1916.

Olson, Greg. *The Ioway in Missouri*. Columbia: University of Missouri Press, 2008.

——. "Navigating the White Road: White Cloud's Struggle to Lead the Ioway along the Path of Acculturation." *Missouri Historical Review* 99, no. 2 (January 2005): 93–114.

Orren, Karen, and Stephen Skowronek. *The Search for American Political Development*. Cambridge: Cambridge University Press, 2004.

Osborne, Alan. "The Exile of the Nez Perce in Indian Territory, 1878–1885." *Chronicles of Oklahoma* 56 (Winter 1978–79): 450–71.

Oshinsky, David. *"Worse Than Slavery": Parchman Farm and the Ordeal of Jim Crow Justice*. New York: Simon and Schuster, 1996.

Painter, Nell Irvin. *Exodusters: Black Migration to Kansas after Reconstruction*. New York: Alfred A. Knopf, 1977.

Pearson, J. Diane. *The Nez Perce in the Indian Territory: Nimiipuu Survival*. Norman: University of Oklahoma Press, 2008.

Perkinson, Robert. *Texas Tough: The Rise of America's Prison Empire*. New York: Metropolitan Books, 2010.

Peterson, H.C., and Gilbert C. Fite. *Opponents of War, 1917–1918*. Madison: University of Wisconsin Press, 1957.

Phillips, Christopher. "'The Crime against Missouri': Slavery, Kansas, and the Cant of Southerners in the Border West." *Civil War History* 48, no. 1 (2002): 60–81.

Phillips, Ulrich B. "Slave Crime in Virginia." *American Historical Review* 20 (1915): 798–816.

Poole, David. *Land and Liberty: Anarchist Influences in the Mexican Revolution*. Orkney: Cienfuegos Press, 1977.

Poupart, Lisa M. "Crime and Justice in American Indian Communities." *Social Justice* 29, nos. 1/2 (Spring/Summer 2002): 144–59.

Preston, William. *Aliens and Dissenters: Federal Suppression of Radicals, 1903–1933*. Urbana: University of Illinois Press, 1994.

Prestritto, Ronald J. *Founding the Criminal Law: Punishment and Political Thought in the Origins of America*. DeKalb: Northern Illinois University Press, 2000.

Preyer, Kathryn. "Crime, the Criminal Law, and Reform in Post-Revolutionary Virginia." *Law and History Review* 1 (1983): 53–85.

——. "Penal Measures in the American Colonies: An Overview." *American Journal of Legal History* 26 (1982): 326–53.

Price, Catherine. "Communities in Peril: Native Americans of Nineteenth-Century Kansas and Nebraska." *Reviews in American History* 20, no. 4 (December 1992): 459–63.

Punter, David. *Gothic Pathologies: The Text, the Body, and the Law*. New York: St. Martin's Press, 1998.

Pybus, Cassandra, and Hamish Maxwell-Stewart. *American Citizens, British Slaves: Yankee Political Prisoners in an Australian Penal Colony, 1839–1850*. East Lansing: Michigan State University Press, 2002.

Raat, W. Dirk. *Revoltosos: Mexico's Rebels in the United States, 1903–1923*. College Station: Texas A&M University Press, 1981.

Rawley, James A. *Race and Politics: "Bleeding Kansas" and the Coming of the Civil War*. Lincoln: University of Nebraska Press, 1969.

Reinhart, Christopher. "Castle Doctrine and Self-Defense." Office of Legal Research Report 2007-R-0052, January 17, 2007. www.cga.ct.gov/2007/rpt/2007-r-0052.htm.

Reynolds, David S. *John Brown, Abolitionist*. New York: Vintage, 2005.

Rice, Jim. "'This Province, So Meanly and Thinly Inhabited': Punishing Maryland's Criminals, 1681–1850," *Journal of the Early Republic* 19, no. 1 (Spring 1999): 15–42.

Richardson, William A. "Dr. David Nelson and His Times." *Journal of Illinois State Historical Society* 13 (1920): 433–63.

Riney, Scott. "Power and Powerlessness: The People of the Canton Asylum for Insane Indians." In *The Sioux in South Dakota History*, edited by Richmond L. Clow, 41–64. Pierre: South Dakota State Historical Society Press, 2007.

Ringel, Faye. "Building the Gothic Image in America: Changing Icons, Changing Times." *Gothic Studies* 4, no. 2 (November 2002): 145–54.

Rios, Victor. *Punished: Policing the Lives of Black and Latino Boys*. New York: New York University Press, 2011.

Roberts, John W. "Grand Designs, Small Details: The Management Style of James V. Bennett." *Federal Prisons Journal* 3, no. 3 (Winter 1994): 29–40.

Roberts, Randy. *Papa Jack: Jack Johnson and the Era of White Hopes*. New York: Free Press, 1983.

Robinson, Cedric J. "Blackface Minstrelsy and Black Resistance." In *Forgeries of Memory and Meaning: Black and the Regimes of Race in American Theatre and Film before World War II*. Chapel Hill: University of North Carolina Press, 2007.

Roediger, David R. *Wages of Whiteness*. New York: Verso, 1991.

Ronda, James P. "'We Have a Country:' Race, Geography, and the Invention of Indian Territory." *Journal of the Early Republic* 19, no. 4 (Winter 1999): 739–55.

Rose, Christina. "Native History: Chief Little Wolf Surrenders, Establishes Reservation." *Indian Country Today*, March 25, 2017.

Rosen, Deborah A. *American Indians and State Law: Sovereignty, Race, and Citizenship, 1790–1880*. Lincoln: University of Nebraska Press, 2007.

———. "Colonization through Law: The Judicial Defense of State Indian Legislation, 1790–1880." *American Journal of Legal History* 46, no. 1 (January 2004): 26–54.

Rosen, Ellen Doree. *A Wobbly Life: IWW Organizer E. F. Doree*. Detroit, MI: Wayne State University Press, 2004.

Rosemont, Franklin. *Joe Hill: The IWW and the Making of a Revolutionary Workingclass Counterculture*. Oakland, CA: PM Press, 2015.

Ross, Luana. *Inventing the Savage: The Social Construction of Native American Criminality*. Austin: University of Texas Press, 1998.

Rothman, David J. *The Discovery of the Asylum: Social Order and Disorder in the New Republic*. London: Little, Brown, 1990.

Rusche, Georg, and Otto Kirchheimer. *Punishment and Social Structure*. New York: Columbia University Press, 1939.

Russell, John Henderson. *The Free Negro in Virginia, 1619–1865*. Baltimore: Johns Hopkins University Press, 1913.

Sandoz, Mari. *Crazy Horse: The Strange Man of the Oglalas*. 1942. Reprint, Lincoln: University of Nebraska Press, 1992.

Savage, W. Sherman. "The Contest over Slavery between Illinois and Missouri." *Journal of Negro History* 28, no. 3 (1943): 311–25.

Savoy, Eric. "The Rise of American Gothic." In *Cambridge Companion to Gothic Fiction*, edited by Jerrold E. Hogle. Cambridge: Cambridge University Press, 2002.

Saxton, Alexander. "Blackface Minstrelsy and Jacksonian Ideology." *American Quarterly* 27, no. 1 (March 1975): 3–25.

Schoenfeld, Heather. *Building the Prison State: Race and the Politics of Mass Incarceration*. Chicago: University of Chicago Press, 2018.

Schultz, Duane. *Quantrill's War: The Life and Times of William Clarke Quantrill*. New York: St. Martin's, 1996.

Schultz, Marvin E. "Running the Risks of Experiments: The Politics of Penal Reform in Tennessee, 1807–1829." *Tennessee Historical Quarterly*, 52, no. 2 (Summer 1993): 86–97.

Schwarz, Philip J. "The Transportation of Slaves from Virginia, 1801–1865," *Slavery and Abolition: A Journal of Comparative Studies* 7, no. 3 (Summer 1986): 215–40.

———. *Twice Condemned: Slaves and the Criminal Laws, 1705–1865*. Baton Rouge: Louisiana State University Press, 1988.

Schwendemann, Glen. "Wyandotte and the First 'Exodusters' of 1879." *Kansas Historical Quarterly* 26, no. 3 (Autumn 1960): 233–49.

Scott, James C. *Seeing Like a State*. New Haven, CT: Yale University Press, 1999.

Sellin, Thorsten. *Slavery and Penal System*. New York: Elsevier, 1976.

Shaw, A. G. L. *Convicts and the Colonies: A Study of Penal Transportation from Great Britain and Ireland to Australia and Other Parts of the British Empire*. London: Faber and Faber, 1966.

Shaw, Rosalind. *Memories of the Slave Trade*. Chicago: University of Chicago Press, 2002.

Shelden, Randall G. *Controlling the Dangerous Classes: A Critical Introduction to the History of Criminal Justice*. Boston: Allyn and Bacon, 2001.

Sheridan, Richard B. "Editor's Commentary." In Sheridan, *Freedom's Crucible*, 123–67.

———, ed. *Freedom's Crucible: The Underground Railroad in Lawrence and Douglas County, 1854–1865*. Lawrence: University of Kansas Press, 1998.

———. "From Slavery in Missouri to Freedom in Kansas: The Influx of Black Fugitives and Contrabands into Kansas, 1854–1865." *Kansas History* 12, no. 1 (1989): 28–47.

———. Introduction to Sheridan, *Freedom's Crucible*, xiii–xxxviii.

Shirley, Glenn. *Law West of Fort Smith: A History of Frontier Justice in the Indian Territory, 1834–1896*. Lincoln: University of Nebraska Press, 1957.

Shugg, Wallace. *A Monument of Good Intentions: The Story of the Maryland Penitentiary, 1804–1995*. Baltimore: Maryland Historical Society, 2000.

Sibley, Mulford, and Ada Wardlaw. *Conscientious Objectors in Prison, 1940–1945*. Philadelphia: Pacifist Research Bureau, 1945.

Simon, John K. "Michel Foucault on Attica: An Interview." *Social Justice* 18, no. 3 (1991): 26–34.

Simon, Jonathan. *Governing through Crime*. Oxford: Oxford University Press, 2007.

Simpson, Audra. *Mohawk Interruptus: Political Life across the Borders of Settler States*. Durham, NC: Duke University Press, 2014.

———. "Settlement's Secrets." *Cultural Anthropology* 26, no. 2 (May 2011): 205–17.

———. "Subjects of Sovereignty: Indigeneity, the Revenue Rule, and Juridics of Failed Consent." *Law and Contemporary Problems* 71, no. 3 (Summer 2008): 191–216.

Slickpoo, Allen P., and Deward E. Walker. *Noon Nee-Me-Poo (We, the Nez Perces): Culture and History of the Nez Perces.* [Lapwai, ID]: Nez Perce Tribe of Idaho, 1973.

Smith, Caleb. *The Prison and the American Imagination.* New Haven, CT: Yale University Press, 2009.

Smith, Linda Tuhiwai. *Decolonizing Methodologies: Research and Indigenous Peoples.* London: Zed Books, 2002.

Smith, Nancy. "The 'Liberty Line' in Lawrence, Kansas Territory." In Sheridan, *Freedom's Crucible*, 1–10.

Sneed, William C. *A Report on the History and Mode of Management of the Kentucky Penitentiary from Its Origin, in 1798 to March 1, 1860.* Frankfurt: J. B. Major, 1860.

Spivak, Gayatri Chakravorty. "Can the Subaltern Speak?" In *Marxism and the Interpretation of Culture,* edited by C. Nelson and L. Grossberg. Macmillan: Basingstroke, 1988.

Stanley, Amy Dru. *From Bondage to Contract: Wage Labor, Marriage, and the Market in the Age of Slave Emancipation.* Cambridge: Cambridge University Press, 1998.

Stratton, Jon. "Two Rescues, One History: Everyday Racism in Australia." *Social Identities* 12, no. 6 (November 2006): 657–81.

Strickland, Rennard. *Fire and the Spirit: Cherokee Law from Clan to Court.* Norman: University of Oklahoma Press, 1975.

Sudbury, Julia. *Global Lockdown: Race, Gender, and the Prison-Industrial Complex.* New York: Routledge, 2006.

Sutton, Imre. "Preface to Indian Country: Geography and Law." *American Indian Culture and Research Journal* 15, no. 2 (1991): 3–35.

Sutton, Robert K. *Stark Mad Abolitionists: Lawrence, Kansas, and the Battle over Slavery in the Civil War Era.* New York: Skyhorse, 2017.

Szabo, Joyce M. *Imprisoned Art, Complex Patronage: Plains Drawings by Howling Wolf and Zotom at the Autry National Center.* Santa Fe, NM: School for Advanced Research Press, 2011.

Tate, Thad W. *The Negro in Eighteenth-Century Williamsburg.* Charlottesville: Colonial Williamsburg Foundation, 1972.

Taylor, Quintard. *In Search of the Racial Frontier: African-Americans in the American West, 1528–1990.* New York: Norton, 1998.

Thomas, John Charles. "The Development of 'an Institution': The Establishment and First Years of the South Carolina Penitentiary, 1795–1881." MA thesis, University of South Carolina, 1983.

Thomas, John Rochester. *History of Prison Architecture.* New York: J. J. Little, 1892.

Thomas, William H. *Unsafe for Democracy: World War I and the US Justice Department's Covert Campaign to Suppress Dissent.* Madison: University of Wisconsin Press, 2008.

Thompson, E. Bruce. "Penal Reform in Tennessee, 1820–1850." *Tennessee Historical Quarterly* 1 (1942): 291–308.

Thompson, Heather. *Blood in the Water: The Attica Prison Uprising of 1971 and Its Legacy.* New York: Vintage, 2017.

———. "Why Mass Incarceration Matters: Rethinking Crisis, Decline, and Transformation in Postwar American History." *Journal of American History* 97, no. 3 (December 2010): 703–34.

Thompson, Scott M. *I Will Tell of My War Story: A Pictorial Account of the Nez Perce War.* Seattle: University of Washington Press, 2000.

Toll, Robert C. *Blacking Up.* New York: Oxford University Press, 1974.

Tolnay, Stewart E., and E. M. Beck. *A Festival of Violence: An Analysis of Southern Lynchings, 1882–1930.* Champaign: University of Illinois Press, 1995.

Toth, Stephen A. *Beyond Papillon: The French Overseas Penal Colonies, 1854–1952.* Lincoln: University of Nebraska Press, 2006.

Trafzer, Clifford E. "The Palouse in Eekish Pah." *American Indian Quarterly* 9, no. 2 (Spring 1985): 169–82.

Trennert, Robert A. "The Business of Indian Removal: Deporting the Potawatomi from Wisconsin, 1851." *Wisconsin Magazine of History* 63, no. 1 (Fall 1979): 36–50.

Trexler, Harrison Anthony. *Slavery in Missouri, 1804–1865.* Baltimore: Johns Hopkins University Press, 1914.

Trinkley, Michael, and Debi Hacker. *The Penitentiary Cemetery, Columbia, South Carolina.* Columbia, SC: Chicora Foundation, 2009.

Tropp, Martin. *Images of Fear: How Horror Stories Helped Shape Modern Culture, 1818–1918.* Jefferson, NC: McFarland, 1999.

Turner, John Kenneth. *Barbarous Mexico.* 1910. Reprint, Austin: University of Texas Press, 1969.

Tushnet, Mark. *The American Law and Slavery, 1810–1860.* Princeton, NJ: Princeton University Press, 1981.

Twain, Mark. *Life on the Mississippi.* New York: Dover, 2000.

———. *Pudd'nhead Wilson.* 1894. Reprint, New York: Norton, 1980.

Unrau, William E. *The Kansa Indians: A History of the Wind People, 1673–1873.* Norman: University of Oklahoma Press, 1971.

———. *The Rise and Fall of Indian Country, 1825–1855.* Lawrence: University of Kansas Press, 2007.

Utley, Robert M. *Frontiersman in Blue: The United States Army and the Indian, 1848–1865.* New York: Macmillan, 1967.

Valelly, Richard M., Suzanne Mettler, and Robert C. Lieberman. *The Oxford Handbook of American Political Development.* Oxford: Oxford University Press, 2016.

Vandal, Gilles. "Regulating Louisiana's Rural Areas: The Functions of Parish Jails, 1840–1885." *Louisiana History* 42, no. 1 (Winter 2001): 59–92.

Van Deusen, John G. "The Exodus of 1879." *Journal of Negro History* 20, no. 2 (April 1936): 111–29.

Violette, Eugene. "The Black Code in Missouri." *Proceedings of the Mississippi Valley Historical Association* 6 (1912–13): 287–316.

Volpp, Leti. "The Indigenous as Alien." *UC Irvine Law Review* 5 (2015): 289–326.

Wade, Edwin L. "The Artistic Legacy of Fort Marion: Beyond the Prison Gate." *Southwest Art,* July 1993.

Wade, Richard C. *Slavery in the Cities: The South, 1820–1860.* New York: Oxford University Press, 1964.

Wakefield, W. H. T. "Squatter Courts in Kansas." *Kansas Historical Collection* 5 (1896): 71–74.

Waldrep, Christopher. *The Many Faces of Judge Lynch: Extralegal Violence and Punishment in America.* New York: Palgrave, 2002.

Wallace, Anthony F. C. *Jefferson and the Indians: The Tragic Fate of the First Americans.* Cambridge, MA: Harvard University Press, 1999.

Walton, George. *Sentinel of the Plains: Fort Leavenworth and the American West.* Englewood Cliffs, NJ: Prentice-Hall, 1973.

Ward, Geoffrey C. *Unforgivable Blackness: The Rise and Fall of Jack Johnson.* New York: Alfred K. Knopf, 2004.

Waters, Joseph G. "Fifty Years of the Wyandotte Constitution." *Kansas Historical Collections* 11 (1910): 47–52.

Watson, Alan D. "North Carolina Slave Courts, 1715–1785." *North Carolina Historical Review* 60 (1983): 24–36.

Watts, Dale E. "How Bloody Was Bleeding Kansas? Political Killings in Kansas Territory, 1854–1861." *Kansas History: A Journal of the Central Plains* 18, no. 2 (Summer 1995): 116–29.

Waziyatawin. *In the Footsteps of Our Ancestors.* St. Paul, MN: Living Justice Press, 2006

———. *What Does Justice Look Like: The Struggle for Liberation in Dakota Homeland.* St. Paul, MN: Living Justice Press, 2008.

Weaver, Vesla. "Frontlash: Race and the Development of Punitive Crime Policy." *Studies in American Political Development* 21, no. 2 (Fall 2007): 230–65.

Weaver, Vesla, and Amy Lerman. "Political Consequences of the Carceral State." *American Political Science Review* 104, no. 4 (November 2010): 817–33.

Welch, Michael. *Escape to Prison: Penal Tourism and the Pull of Punishment.* Oakland: University of California Press, 2015.

West, Elliot. *The Contested Plains: Indians, Goldseekers, and the Rush to Colorado.* Lawrence: University Press of Kansas, 1998.

White, Crystal. "Honoring Nez Perce History in the Heartland." Lecture presented at Lewis-Clark State College, Lewiston, ID, September 28, 2005.

White, Jonathan W. "When Emancipation Finally Came, Slave Markets Took on a Redemptive Purpose." *Smithsonian Magazine,* February 26, 2018. https://www.smithsonianmag.com/history/when-emancipation-finally-came-slave-markets-took-redemptive-purpose-180968260/.

White, Walter. "Lynching and Laws: Is There a Way Out?" In *Rope and Faggot: A Biography of Judge Lynch,* 196–226. New York: Arno Press, 1969.

Willoughby, Robert J. "'I'll Wade in Missouri Blood': Daggs v. Frazier: A Case of Missouri Runaway Slaves." *Missouri Historical Review* 99 (January 2005): 115–38.

Wilson, Shawn. *Research Is Ceremony: Indigenous Research Methods.* Black Point, Nova Scotia: Fernwood, 2009.

Wilson, Waziyatawin Angela. *Remember This! Dakota Decolonization and the Eli Taylor Narratives.* Lincoln: University of Nebraska Press, 2005.

*The Wobblies.* Dir. Deborah Schaffer and Stewart Bird. Docurama Films, New Video, 2006.

Wolfe, Patrick. "Settler Colonialism and the Elimination of the Native." *Journal of Genocide Studies* 8, no. 4 (Winter 2006): 387–409.

Wood, Amy Louise. *Lynching and Spectacle: Witnessing Racial Violence in America.* Chapel Hill: University of North Carolina Press, 2009.

Wood, Peter. *Black Majority: Negroes in Colonial South Carolina from 1670 through the Stono Rebellion.* New York: Alfred Knopf, 1974.

Woods, Randall B. "Integration, Exclusion, or Segregation? The 'Color Line' in Kansas: 1878–1900." *Western Historical Quarterly* 14 (1983): 181–98.

# INDEX

www.ingramcontent.com/pod-product-compliance
Lightning Source LLC
Chambersburg PA
CBHW070329270326
41926CB00017B/3824